TIME®
LIFE
BOOKS

For information on and a full description of
any of the Time-Life Books series listed above,
please call 1-800-621-7026 or write:

Reader Information
Time-Life Customer Service
P.O. Box C-32068
Richmond, Virginia 23261-2068

This volume is one of a series that chronicles
in full the events of the Second World War.

Scanning the surface through a periscope, an American submarine commander searches for enemy ships in Japanese waters. The enormous toll of Japanese shipping taken by the U.S. submarine service played a crucial role in the war in the Pacific.

WAR UNDER THE PACIFIC

WORLD WAR II · TIME-LIFE BOOKS · ALEXANDRIA, VIRGINIA

BY KEITH WHEELER
AND THE EDITORS OF TIME-LIFE BOOKS

WAR UNDER THE PACIFIC

Time-Life Books is a division of Time Life Inc.

TIME LIFE INC.
PRESIDENT and CEO: George Artandi

TIME-LIFE BOOKS
PRESIDENT: Stephen R. Frary
PUBLISHER/MANAGING EDITOR: Neil Kagan
VICE PRESIDENT, MARKETING: Joseph A. Kuna

WORLD WAR II

DIRECTOR, NEW PRODUCT DEVELOPMENT:
Elizabeth D. Ward
DIRECTOR OF MARKETING: Pamela R. Farrell

Dust Jacket Design: Barbara M. Sheppard

Editorial Staff for *War under the Pacific*
Editor: Gerald Simons
Designer/Picture Editor: Raymond Ripper
Chief Researcher: Charles S. Clark
Text Editors: Bobbie Conlan, Brian McGinn, Mark M. Steele
Staff Writers: Peter Kaufman, Glenn Martin McNatt, John Newton, Peter Pocock
Researchers: Betty Ajemian, Kristin Baker, Mary G. Burns, Patricia A. Cassidy, Jane Freundel, Lucinda Moore, Cronin Buck Sleeper, Paula York
Copy Coordinators: Victoria Lee, Barbara F. Quarmby
Art Assistant: Mary L. Orr
Picture Coordinator: Alvin L. Ferrell
Editorial Assistant: Connie Strawbridge

Special Contributors: Robin Richman (pictures), Champ Clark (text)
Correspondents: Christine Hinze (London), Christina Lieberman (New York)

Director of Finance: Christopher Hearing
Directors of Book Production: Marjann Caldwell, Patricia Pascale
Director of Publishing Technology: Betsi McGrath
Director of Photography and Research: John Conrad Weiser
Director of Editorial Administration: Barbara Levitt
Production Manager: Carolyn Bounds
Quality Assurance Manager: James King
Chief Librarian: Louise D. Forstall

The Author: KEITH WHEELER has been a reporter for a South Dakota newspaper, a war correspondent for the Chicago *Daily Times,* and a writer for *Life* magazine. While covering the war in the Pacific for the *Daily Times,* he was critically wounded at Iwo Jima. He has published a number of novels and nonfiction volumes, among them *The Pacific Is My Beat* and *We Are the Wounded.* He is the author of five books in Time-Life Books' Old West series: *The Railroaders, The Townsmen, The Chroniclers, The Alaskans* and *The Scouts.*

The Consultants: COL. JOHN R. ELTING, USA (Ret.), is a military historian and author of *The Battle of Bunker's Hill, The Battles of Saratoga* and *Military History and Atlas of the Napoleonic Wars.* He edited *Military Uniforms in America: The Era of the American Revolution, 1775-1795* and *Military Uniforms in America: Years of Growth, 1796-1851,* and was associate editor of *The West Point Atlas of American Wars.*

HENRY H. ADAMS is a retired Navy captain who served aboard the destroyer U.S.S. *Owen* in the major campaigns of the central Pacific. A native of Ann Arbor, Michigan, he graduated from the University of Michigan and received his M.A. and Ph.D. degrees from Columbia University. After his service in World War II he was a professor at the U.S. Naval Academy in Annapolis, Maryland, and was later head of the English Department at Illinois State University. His books include *1942: The Year That Doomed the Axis, Years of Deadly Peril, Years of Expectation, Years to Victory* and *Harry Hopkins: A Biography.*

GEORGE W. GRIDER served in World War II on the U.S. submarines *Wahoo, Pollack* and *Hawkbill* before assuming command in 1944 of the U.S.S. *Flasher,* which set the record for enemy tonnage sunk. During his service he was awarded the Navy Cross, the Silver Star and the Bronze Star for extraordinary heroism in action. A graduate of the U.S. Naval Acadamy and the University of Virginia Law School, he went on to become a U.S. Congressman. He co-authored *War Fish,* which recounts his wartime experiences.

R 10 9 8 7 6 5 4 3 2 1

Library of Congress Cataloging-in-Publication Data
Wheeler, Keith
  War under the Pacific

  (World War II)
  Bibliography.
  Includes index.
  1. World War, 1939-1945—Pacific Ocean
2. World War, 1939-1945—Naval operations—Submarine
3. Submarine boats.
I. Time-Life Books. II. Title. III Series.
D767.W47   940.54′51   80-13222
ISBN 0-7835-5708-6

CONTENTS

EVOLUTION OF A WEAPON

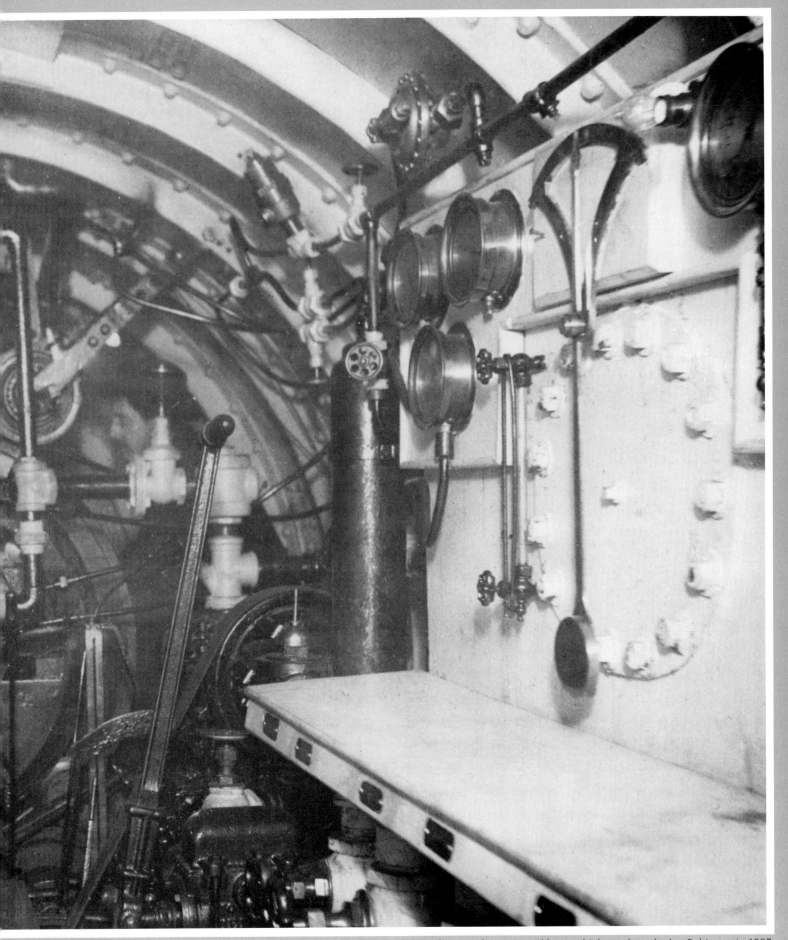

Submarine pioneer Simon Lake (left) examines the engine room of his Argonaut, a 36-foot gasoline-powered boat, which was launched at Baltimore in 1897.

THE SUBMARINE'S UNLIKELY ANCESTORS

The U.S. submarines that fought in the Pacific during World War II were descended from an unlikely cockleshell craft that had made the first undersea attack on record more than 160 years before. On the night of September 6, 1776, the *Turtle,* a tiny, egg-shaped submarine built out of barrel staves by a Connecticut doctor named David Bushnell, bobbed across New York Harbor and submerged beside a British frigate.

The volunteer pilot, a sergeant in the American Revolutionary Army, hoped to sink His Majesty's frigate with a 150-pound charge of gunpowder mounted outside the craft and designed to explode underwater. Also protruding from the *Turtle* was a gimlet that was intended to attach the gunpowder charge to the ship's wooden flank. As things worked out, instead of piercing the hull the gimlet glanced off a piece of metal; the charge floated away, to explode harmlessly. By then the *Turtle* had made good her escape.

This abortive effort marked the start of a long, frustrating endeavor for a handful of Americans who were fascinated by the possibilities of undersea craft in time of war. They labored for more than a century without support or even encouragement from the Navy, whose tradition-bound officers scoffed at their contention that the submarine could play a key role in naval warfare. The officers had cause for skepticism. The submersibles were riddled with flaws, and the designers themselves hardly inspired confidence. Most of them were unbusiness-like tinkerers with a crankish sense of independence and no formal training as engineers.

Still, at least one of the inventors was no mere dreamer. In 1806 the U.S. Navy turned down a copper-hulled submarine developed by the man who later built the first practical steamboat. Robert Fulton's design incorporated several promising features, such as the use of compressed air to extend a crew's stay underwater. And he managed, in a primitive way, to provide what was a vital necessity—separate modes of propulsion for traveling on the surface and submerged. Eighty years would pass before this principle was mechanically realized in a true submarine.

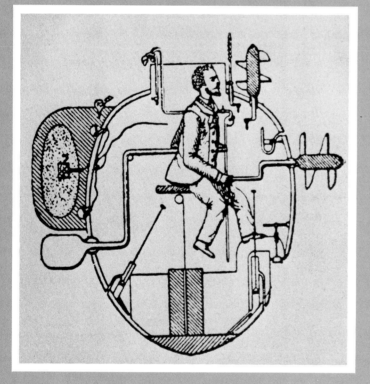

The submarine Turtle severely tested its pilot's dexterity. While sighting through portholes in the conning tower, the pilot had to operate the horizontal and vertical propellers, hold the rudder, run the ballast pumps, screw a gimlet into the enemy ship's hull and release the gunpowder charge—all in 30 minutes, before the Turtle's air supply was exhausted.

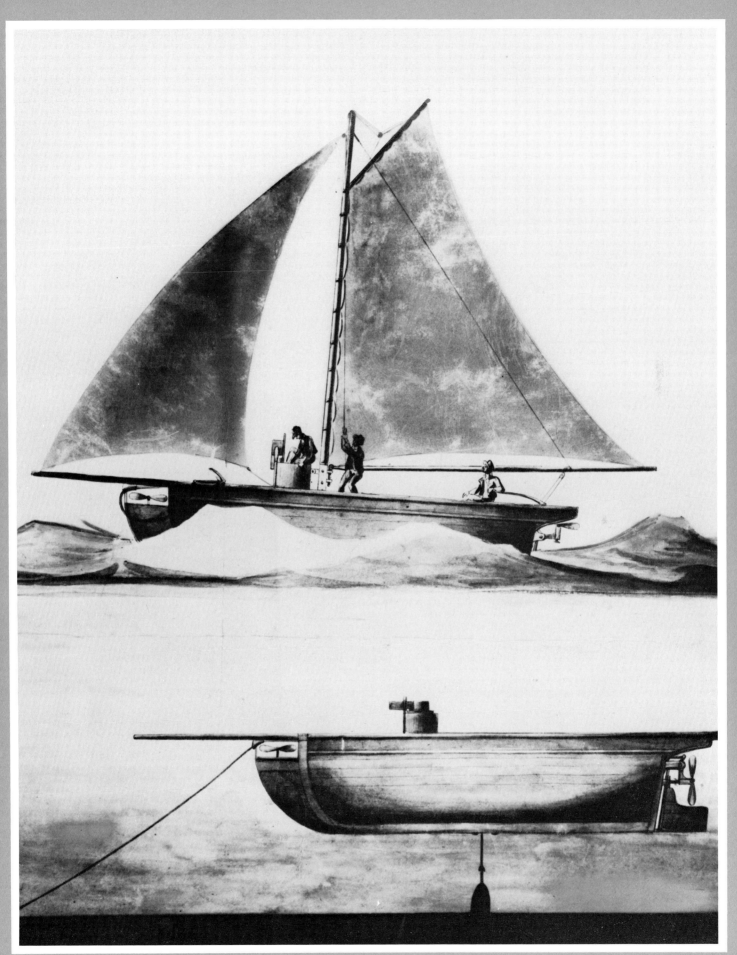

Sketches by Robert Fulton illustrate his submarine's main feature: hand-cranked propellers for underwater travel and sails for running on the surface.

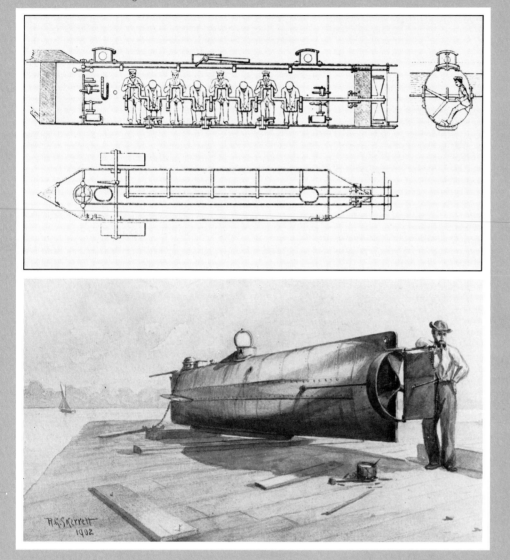

THE FIRST SINKING BY A SUBMARINE

During the American Civil War, the Confederacy built more than a dozen submersibles in its efforts to break the Union's blockade of Southern seaports. The boats were called Davids, after the Biblical giant-killer, but only a few of them saw significant action.

The original David, a steam-driven boat, made an encouraging sally on the night of October 5, 1863. Carrying an explosive charge at the end of a long spar, she rammed into the hull of the *New Ironsides,* an armored warship that was blockading Charleston, South Carolina. The explosion did little damage to the Union vessel, but the Confederate submariners were eager to try again.

A new David, named after donor Horace L. Hunley, was launched in Mobile, Alabama, toward the end of 1863. This submarine, propelled by hand cranks, was jinxed from the start. During her diving trials the *Hunley* sank several times, drowning her volunteer crews (as well as Hunley himself). She was raised each time, but the Confederates soon gave the submarine a grim nickname, The Peripatetic Coffin.

The *Hunley* finally made her first attack on the night of February 17, 1864. Swimming across Charleston Bay, the Confederate boat rammed a 90-pound charge of gunpowder against the hull of the *Housatonic,* a 1,200-ton Federal sloop. The explosion blew off the *Housatonic's* stern. The sloop went to the bottom in five minutes—becoming the first ship ever sunk by a submarine in battle.

But the victory was fatal to the victor. The *Hunley* was dragged down to the bottom by her victim, and all nine crewmen were killed.

One of nine Confederate submersibles captured by the Union at the close of the Civil War lies aground on the beach at Charleston, South Carolina, in 1865. The steam-powered craft were more like torpedo boats than true submarines; they ran only partially submerged in order to keep the boiler's fresh-air intake and smokestack above water.

The submarine Intelligent Whale, the North's answer to the South's submersibles, rests abandoned at the New York Navy Yard long after the Civil War. The Whale never saw action; she was not launched until 1872, and was discarded by the Navy the same day.

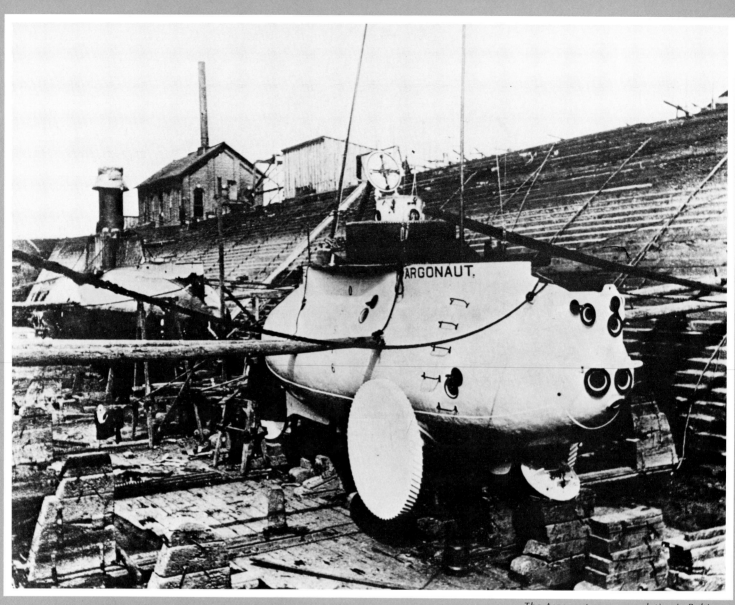

The Argonaut nears completion in Baltimore in 1897. Lake built the submarine with $2,500 he raised by selling shares to friends.

A DREAMER WHO BUILT BOATS FOR WAR

At the age of 17, Simon Lake quit school and, inspired by the undersea adventures in Jules Verne's novel *Twenty Thousand Leagues under the Sea*, began working on designs for a submarine of his own. After nine years, the young inventor developed a wood and canvas submersible, which he launched in New Jersey in 1894. Three years later, Lake improved on his design with the steel-hulled *Argonaut*, a cigar-shaped submarine that achieved local notoriety by terrifying fishermen.

Unlike his contemporary John Holland, Lake built submarines for peacetime pursuits, such as salvage and exploration. His boats had wheels for excursions on the bottom, portholes for use by naturalists and photographers, and air locks to permit divers to enter and exit. His submarine the *Protector* incorporated a rotating omniscope, a forerunner of the periscope.

The U.S. Navy ridiculed Lake's ungainly creations. What would happen, Naval officers inquired sarcastically, when one of his wheeled submarines came to the edge of an underwater precipice?

Nettled by such rebuffs, Lake in 1898, during the Spanish-American War, maneuvered his *Argonaut* into the waters by the naval base at Hampton Roads, Virginia. Wheeling cautiously along the harbor bottom, he charted the mines guarding the base. Lake triumphantly presented a map of the defenses to Naval authorities and then the Army. Instead of buying his boat, officials threatened to jail him for spying.

To keep his fledgling torpedo-boat company solvent, Lake sold his submarines to a number of European navies. He failed to sell a boat to Germany because he had neglected to register his patents there, and the Krupp industrial empire appropriated his designs without paying him a cent.

Finally in 1912, one of Lake's submarines—this one without wheels—won acceptance by his own navy and went into service as the *Seal*. To Lake, Navy recognition was pleasant indeed, but hardly the apogee of his career. The high point had come in November 1898, after he and the *Argonaut* had weathered a fierce Atlantic gale that sank dozens of surface ships. This much-heralded feat brought him a cable of congratulations from the man Lake called "the director general of my life"—Jules Verne himself.

The Protector, Lake's third submarine, plows ahead on a trial run near Newport, Rhode Island, in 1902. She was purchased by the Russian Navy in 1904.

Views of the Protector show her with her wheels retracted into the hull (left) and (right) her forward torpedo tubes and relatively comfortable crew quarters.

The 161-foot Seal, seen at her commissioning in 1912, was the U.S. Navy's largest and fastest submarine, with an unheard-of submerged speed of 10 knots.

13

The Holland slides down the ways at Elizabethport, New Jersey, during her May 1897 launching. The Holland was 54 feet long, displaced 74 tons, carried three torpedoes and cruised on a 50-horsepower gasoline engine similar to the one the Model T Ford used.

Nearsighted and frail, John P. Holland peers out from the conning tower of his submarine, the Holland. The inventor admitted to being such a poor sailor that "no one would trust me even to row a two-oared boat."

Five submarines built by the Holland Torpedo Boat Company ride at anchor at a New York dock in 1902. The Plunger (center), an improved version of the Holland, displaced 120 tons, carried five torpedoes and was driven by a 160-horsepower gasoline engine.

A FLEDGLING FLEET OF DANGEROUS CRAFT

John P. Holland, an Irish immigrant and onetime schoolteacher turned submarine designer, sold plans for a submersible to the U.S. Navy in 1895, but became furious when the Navy kept altering his design. The resulting boat, Holland said, was "a monster," far too big to be practical. He reluctantly let his company finish building the boat, but when the submarine was sent on her first sea trial her enormous 1,500-horsepower steam engine put out so much heat that the crew nearly suffocated.

In the meantime, Holland scraped up the funds to build a submarine that was more to his liking, the Holland. Expanding on Robert Fulton's idea, Holland equipped the little boat with separate propulsion systems for her two very different types of operation. Traveling on the surface the submarine was driven by a gasoline engine, but underwater she was powered by great banks of electric storage batteries, which were periodically recharged by the gasoline motor.

The Navy bought the Holland and, with six similar boats, formed the U.S. Submarine Force in 1903. But the Holland was a dangerous boat. Salt water leaking from the hatch into the open-celled batteries formed poisonous chlorine gas, and the charging of the batteries generated explosive hydrogen gas, which could be ignited by a random spark. The gasoline engine also exuded explosive vapors.

These hazards were noticed by President Theodore Roosevelt during a test dive aboard the Plunger (above) in 1905, and he ordered a pay increase for submarine crews. The raise inspired the submariners' sardonic slogan: A dollar a dive, and six months' pay if I don't come up.

15

Veteran skipper Chester Nimitz (center) visits the New London, Connecticut, submarine base in 1917.

MAKING THE SWITCH TO DIESEL ENGINES

The submarines' vital change-over from dangerous gasoline engines to safer and more reliable diesel engines was largely the work of a skipper who was destined to command the U.S. Pacific Fleet in World War II. Lieutenant Chester W. Nimitz studied diesels in the German workshops of inventor Rudolf Diesel, and his tireless campaign for the conversion finally paid off in 1912 with the launching of the first American diesel boat.

The next year, the U.S. Navy began ordering numbers of diesel submarines and had sent 25 down the ways by January 1917. Nimitz prepared a dozen of the new diesel submarines for service in World War I. But the boats performed so poorly that the Navy planners were forced to face up to an unpleasant fact: The Germans and British, both late starters who had borrowed Holland and Lake designs, had outdistanced them in submarine technology.

While on patrol duty, the U.S. submarine L-10 passes an American battleship in Ireland's Bantry Bay during the First World War. Seven diesel-powered L-class submarines were based in Ireland during that war.

Workmen put the finishing touches on the 172-foot hull of an O-class submarine at New Hampshire's Portsmouth Navy Yard in September of 1918. Eight boats of this new class were on their way to Europe when World War I ended in November of 1918.

The 993-ton S-51, shown undergoing sea trials in 1922, was one of 51 S-class boats commissioned between 1919 and 1925.

In dry dock at the Portsmouth Navy Yard in March of 1928, the 2,660-ton mine-laying Argonaut dwarfs the 520-ton O-2.

The 2,025-ton Bonita,

REDOUBLED EFFORTS AND COSTLY FLOPS

Exasperated by the poor performance of U.S. submarines in World War I, Navy designers began drafting plans for a fleet boat—a big oceangoing submarine fast enough to keep pace with the 17-knot cruising speed of the surface fleet. In the interim, shipyards built dozens of S-boats, which were larger, improved versions of the wartime K, L and O classes, but which still had inadequate range and speed.

In 1919 the Navy received some help when the United States took over six German submarines as war reparations. After a transatlantic test run on one of the big U-boats, a veteran U.S. submarine skipper said: "The bridge, hull, periscope, guns, torpedo tubes, machinery and compartment design were far superior to ours."

Using the war prizes as models, the U.S. Navy in 1921 began building nine enormous fleet submarines of the V class. The boats took 12 years to complete—at the unprecedented cost of $6.5 million each. The behemoth of the class was the 381-foot V-4, or the *Argonaut*, the largest diesel submarine ever built in the United States.

The mammoth boats failed to live up to the Navy's expectations. Their flaws were many. Said the skipper of one V-class submarine: "They were too large for easy handling, too slow in submerging, and too easily seen as targets."

launched in 1925, exhibits the dolphin-shaped bow that marked the first three V-class submarines. She carried 16 torpedoes and had a 12,000-mile range.

THE TIMELY DEBUT OF A GENUINE FLEET BOAT

The year 1933 was a watershed for the U.S. submarine service. Navy designers, who had exhausted the alphabet in naming new classes of disappointing submarines, finally produced plans for a practical (and unalphabetized) fleet submarine.

Though they scaled down the 2,000-ton V-boats to a more maneuverable 1,500 tons, they managed to keep a hull length of 300 feet to give crews elbowroom for long war patrols. The key to the design was a new, reliable, lightweight diesel engine. Equipped with four such engines, the new boats could reach a top speed of more than 20 knots and make 10,000-mile cruises without the breakdowns that plagued earlier submarines.

Between 1934 and 1941, forty of the new fleet boats—called *Pike-, Salmon-* and *Tambor*-class boats after the first submarine of each type—were constructed with funds appropriated by the administration of President Franklin D. Roosevelt, himself a submarine booster since his days as assistant secretary of the Navy during World War I. These boats formed the backbone of the 56-boat U.S. submarine fleet that was assigned to the Pacific at the outbreak of war in December 1941.

President Franklin D. Roosevelt (right rear in the touring car) arrives to inspect the 1,475-ton fleet boat Tautog during a visit he made to the New London submarine base in August of 1940. The Tautog was faster and better armed as well as more maneuverable and more habitable than any of her precursors.

1

In the first three days of the war in the Pacific, the U.S. submarine force was abruptly thrust into a role of unexpected and frightening importance. According to plan, the submarines were to serve as scouts and combat auxiliaries to the surface fleet in case of war with Japan. But no one had imagined Japan's devastating strategy, designed to knock out every American attack force and expand the Empire before the United States could respond.

At Pearl Harbor on December 7, 1941, torpedo planes and bombers from Japanese aircraft carriers sank or crippled eight battleships, leaving the U.S. Pacific Fleet too weak to launch any major offensive for months. Two days later—on December 10, local time—Japanese bombers paid a series of ruinous visits to the Philippines. They flattened the Cavite Naval Station in Manila Bay, home base of the U.S. Asiatic Fleet—a fleet so feeble in any case that its largest warship was a cruiser. Meanwhile, other flights of bombers destroyed the U.S. planes at Philippine airfields; there would be no air attacks on Japan and no air cover for General Douglas MacArthur's American-Filipino army. The assaults doomed the Philippines and opened the door for Japanese conquests in the southwest Pacific and Southeast Asia.

For all practical purposes, the American submarines were now the only U.S. weapons capable of carrying the war to Japan. Three aircraft carriers had survived the debacle at Pearl Harbor, but they were the last line of defense—all that stood between the United States and Japanese domination of the Pacific. So it was that Commander Stuart S. Murray, a senior officer at Cavite, passed on a grim warning to his submarine skippers on December 8, as he sent them out on their first war patrol. "Listen, dammit," Murray said, "don't try to go out there and win the Congressional Medal of Honor in one day. The submarines are all we have left."

And those submarines were few, far between and woefully unprepared.

In the entire Pacific there were just 55 boats assigned to the two uncoordinated submarine commands: 28 at Cavite and the other 27 at Pearl Harbor. A dozen of the 55 were obsolete S-class boats, relics of the 1920s, and they lacked adequate range, firepower and underwater endurance. Eleven more of the submarines were unavailable for combat duty, because they were undergoing major overhauls in stateside ports or patrolling coastal waters in the

A FORCE UNREADY FOR WAR

Western Hemisphere. And one boat, the *Sealion,* had already become the first U.S. submarine casualty of the War. She had been sunk—and five submariners had been killed—during the Japanese attack on Cavite.

Furthermore, this meager force was plagued by large and small problems of every sort. Its strategy and tactics were as obsolete as its overage boats. Much of the submarines' equipment was either old and crude or new and ill-tested. The submarine service had no combat tradition whatsoever. In its 38 years of organized existence, including Atlantic picket duty in the First World War, it had sunk not a single enemy ship. Yet this tiny, poorly equipped undersea force would carry the offensive to the enemy from the very start. And before they finished waging their deadly campaign, the U.S. submarines would write one of the greatest chapters in the history of naval warfare.

No American—and certainly no Japanese Naval officer—could have imagined the extent of the retribution that the U.S. submarines would eventually exact from Japan's Imperial Navy. In the course of the War the American boats would sink no fewer than 201 Japanese warships, for a total of 540,192 tons, including one battleship, four large carriers, four small carriers, three heavy cruisers, eight light cruisers, 43 destroyers and 23 large submarines. And that was the least of it.

Of vastly greater importance to the War's outcome, the submarines would send to the ocean's floor 1,113 Japanese merchant ships of more than 500 tons each, for a staggering tonnage of 4,779,902, only a million tons less than the entire prewar Japanese merchant fleet. At their peak of efficiency, the submarines destroyed merchant ships at a rate three times faster than Japanese yards could turn them out—a state of affairs that was fatal for an island nation poor in raw materials of its own. Altogether, the submarines would sink 55 per cent of all Japanese ships lost in the War, more than the U.S. surface navy, its carrier planes and the Army's air forces combined.

While so doing, the submarines would run innumerable special missions: hauling ammunition, transporting troops for lightning attacks, rescuing refugees from behind enemy lines and depositing there secret agents and guerrilla leaders. In their most satisfying special assignment the submariners would serve as lifeguards, plucking from the sea hundreds of fliers who had been shot down or otherwise forced to ditch in the watery wilderness.

For its many vital achievements the submarine service would pay a terrible price. In the course of the War, 52 boats and 3,505 submariners would fail to return; officially, they were listed as missing in action, which meant, in their lonely, violent trade, that they were dead on the bottom. This casualty rate amounted to 16 per cent of the officers and 13 per cent of the enlisted men who fought in U.S. submarines. And yet other submarine forces suffered much higher casualties. By war's end, Germany's U-boat fleet had sunk 14.5 million tons of merchant shipping—almost three times the American total—but at a cost of 784 boats and 28,000 crewmen.

But the greatest successes of the U.S. submarine force would be a long time in coming. First, in the Pacific war's early months, the undersea service entered a protracted period of alarming discoveries, painful reappraisals, furious controversy and slow, slow change. While all this went on, the submarines struggled at sea under the tremendous burden of command mistakes and oversights that dated back to the founding of the service in 1903.

Strategically, the U.S. Navy and its submarine service had been wed to a stand-by war plan, code-named *Orange,* that had been devised around the turn of the century. Over the decades the plan had undergone several face-lifts, and by 1941 it had been renamed *Rainbow Five.* Yet basically it remained unchanged, and by many of those privy to its existence it was still called Plan *Orange.*

The plan had accurately envisioned Japan as the Pacific enemy and the Philippines as the target of a Japanese thrust at the outbreak of war. With considerably less foresight, the planners had underestimated the capacity of the Japanese to mount more than one major operation at a time; they assumed that Japan's Imperial Navy would throw everything it had into the Philippines assault.

As originally conceived, Plan *Orange* called for the U.S. Army garrison in the Philippines to fight a holding action while American warships steamed across the Pacific; those from the East Coast were to transit the Panama Canal, which President Theodore Roosevelt had built with Plan *Orange* in mind. The assembled fleet was to lay over in Hawaii and Guam to refuel and take on other supplies, then sail in stately array to the Philippines, where it would meet and defeat the Japanese fleet in a single battle, thus winning the war in a trice.

In 1940, President Franklin Roosevelt had ordered the U.S. Pacific Fleet to shift its base from mainland ports to Pearl Harbor. This move, however, was less in fundamental amendment to Plan *Orange* than in hope of deterring Japanese aggression by the American presence.

Attempting to fit themselves into the grand scheme, the American submariners had a bitter time of it. Their aim and ambition had long been to operate as an integral part of the nation's battle fleet. The submariners saw themselves as scouting outriders in the early stages of combat and then, in the hurly-burly of the decisive surface battle, as underwater attack vessels dealing death and dismay to the enemy. But such hopes were repeatedly dashed; despite a succession of improved submarine models, American designers were unable to bring into existence a boat that could travel with the surface fleet for great distances at the necessary average speed of 17 knots.

As a result, submarines were relegated chiefly to the coastal defense of the U.S. mainland, Hawaii, the Philippines and Panama. Later, after still further attempts to develop a true fleet boat had proved futile, a new mission evolved: American submarines from Pearl Harbor, Manila and Dutch Harbor, Alaska, would do sentry duty in Japan's home waters and off its mandated islands, keeping headquarters posted by radio about potentially hostile fleet movements. And in case of war, the patrolling submarines would be called upon to attack enemy capital ships as they sallied forth from their bases.

Yet the submarine force could not fulfill even these limited functions—as its failure to detect the Pearl Harbor attack fleet so dismally demonstrated. The reason for this failure has never been satisfactorily explained; it was probably due to a combination of overconfidence, distaste for a boring and seemingly trivial task, and a reluctance to provoke the Japanese by sending numbers of submarines to lurk in or near their coastal waters.

Ironically, in the late 1930s, the United States did develop genuine fleet boats, capable of operating under the conditions imposed by Plan *Orange*. And numbers of them were in service by 1941. But by then the surface fleet with which the boats could operate had been reduced to little more than a handful of aircraft carriers and their escorts. The debacle at Pearl Harbor required—said a submarine commander—"a quick adjustment in thinking. Plan *Orange* was a dead issue."

Ravaged though it was by the Japanese attack, the U.S. Pacific Fleet at least retained its home base at Pearl Harbor. At Manila the wrecked Cavite Naval Station was rendered untenable by a Japanese invasion of Luzon on December 11. The Asiatic Fleet and its submarine command immediately began a series of base changes that would, under relentless Japanese pressure, take them farther and farther from Japan: first to Surabaya in the Dutch East Indies, thence to Tjilatjap on the south coast of Java and finally to Fremantle, near Perth on the southwest coast of Australia.

Even as the boats retreated, the search for a viable new Pacific strategy got under way. With the fall of the Philippines in the spring of 1942, the Americans joined with the British and Dutch in a desperate and futile attempt to stop the Japanese surge short of the Malay barrier—an effort that Admiral Ernest J. King, an old submariner who took on double duty as Chief of Naval Operations and Commander in Chief United States Fleet, later called "a magnificent display of very bad strategy." As part of that wishful plan, submarines were sent to lurk about probable Japanese staging areas, to provide early warning (of little consequence, since Allied surface and air forces were still too weak to use the alert to advantage) and to attack the enemy invasion fleets as they headed southward (which failed to deter the Japanese one iota).

Not until late in 1943, after nearly two years of trial and error, did American submarines begin to take fullest advantage of the Japanese maritime traffic patterns dictated by Pacific and Asian geography. Only then did the submarines convert into wholesale killing grounds such relatively narrow seas as Luzon Strait, between the northernmost of the Philippine Islands and Formosa, through which Japanese warships and merchantmen necessarily traveled in great numbers between the home islands and the Empire's newly conquered possessions to collect essential raw materials from Borneo, the Dutch East Indies, Malaya and Indochina.

Through all the years in which Plan *Orange* was the strategic bible, the idea of waging a slow, strangling war of attrition against Japanese merchant shipping played no part whatever in U.S. planning. The very thought of it was odious to Americans. The United States had entered World War I in specific outrage against the "unrestricted warfare" waged by German U-boats against all commerce, neutral or otherwise, that helped Great Britain.

In the interim between the World Wars, a strong body of idealistic opinion held that submarines should be banned by international law, along with such weapons as poison gas, dumdum bullets and saw-toothed bayonets. Although the United States declined to go that far, it was an enthusiastic signatory to the London Naval Arms Limitation Treaty of 1930, which declared that submarines "may not sink or render incapable of navigation a merchant vessel without having first placed passengers, crew and ship's papers in a place of safety." Since a submarine observing such amenities stood an excellent chance of being sunk by an armed merchantman, the requirement amounted to prohibition.

All through the remainder of the decade, the United States honored its treaty obligations. Every plan and preparation was based on the idealistic notion of a war to be fought exclusively against enemy warships. Submarine captains were warned again and again that combat vessels were to be their only target and that if they attacked enemy merchant ships they would be subject to war-crimes trial "as pirates."

All this was swept aside by the Japanese attack on Pearl Harbor. Six hours after the first planes struck, orders arrived from the Navy Department in Washington: EXECUTE UNRESTRICTED SUBMARINE WARFARE AGAINST JAPAN.

The submariners, enraged by the sneak attack on Pearl Harbor, had no compunctions about carrying out the order for unrestricted warfare. Besides, as a submarine officer said of the Japanese, "every ship they had, combat or merchant, was engaged in the war effort one way or another." But old notions die hard. Captain John Wilkes, commander of the Cavite submarine force, sent his first war patrols forth from Manila with orders placing enemy supply ships at the lowest level of target priorities; he and Rear Admiral Thomas Withers Jr. at Pearl Harbor ordered that no more than one or two torpedoes be expended on a merchant ship.

Although U.S. submarines did attack merchantmen from the outset, they were too often and for too long diverted from that vital job by the temptations of enemy warships. Strangely enough, much of the distraction was caused by a top-secret American asset.

In September 1940, American cryptanalysts had broken the Imperial Navy code known as JN-25. The resulting in-

Wrecked installations litter the dockside at Cavite Naval Station's submarine base in the Philippines after a Japanese air attack on December 10, 1941. With all shore facilities destroyed, the camouflaged tender Canopus kept the Asiatic submarine fleet supplied and serviced for three weeks, until the fleet moved to Surabaya in the Dutch East Indies.

formation on the movements of Japanese warships was priceless—if wisely used. But the shore commanders sometimes forgot that battleships and carriers were faster than submarines and difficult to sink even if they were successfully intercepted, while cargo ships were slow and extremely vulnerable. All too frequently the U.S. boat commanders would be ordered to break off lucrative hunts for merchant vessels so as to chase some distant warship—in vain.

In tactics as in strategy, U.S. submarines began the War burdened by peacetime misconceptions. As senior Naval officers grew increasingly apprehensive of air power, caution became the watchword throughout the fleets. Some of the boats started the War with SD radar, a primitive air-search device that gave early warning of the presence of aircraft. Even so, to avoid being detected from the air, submarine skippers were instructed to attack from a depth of 100

Submariners race to man deck guns on the Narwhal (center) during the Japanese attack on Pearl Harbor, December 7, 1941. The Narwhal, which survived the bombing unscathed, shared the credit for downing an enemy plane with the submarine Tautog and a nearby destroyer.

feet or more, locating their targets with the boats' sonar equipment, whose ultrasonic waves registered the presence of steel-hulled ships with a series of metallic pings.

In fact, the risk of aerial detection seemed considerably greater than it was, and for an obvious but disregarded reason: Under controlled exercise conditions, a U.S. observation plane had little trouble finding a U.S. submarine. In clear, calm seas, the telltale shape of a submarine traveling at a depth of 60 feet could be seen from the air. But it was quite a different matter in everyday conditions of wind and wave—even assuming that Japanese patrol pilots knew where to look in eight million square miles of the Pacific.

Nevertheless, the U.S. tactical book decreed deep submergence and sonar tracking, which presented insuperable problems. Since the sonar's loud range-finding pings would alert enemy ships to the submarines' underwater presence, the shore commanders urged skippers to use only their sound gear's listening components, which furnished much less precise information on the target's bearing. This data was so vague that the boats were virtually launching torpedoes by guess. In the course of the War not a single enemy vessel was sunk by a U.S. submarine relying exclusively on its listening equipment at deep submergence.

A few aggressive skippers experimented with maneuvering at periscope depth with their targets in plain view. But this tactic had a major drawback; the periscopes in older boats had nothing like an adequate range-finding feature. So the skippers shaped their tactics in an effort to compensate. Most skippers tried to minimize the factors of range and firing angle by shooting their torpedoes to run perpendicular to the track of the target. But of course the target was moving all the while, and misses were more frequent than hits. Even if the torpedoes did strike the target, their peculiarities were such that a right-angle hit was the worst of all angles from which to sink an enemy ship—though the submariners did not realize this for many months.

A number of skippers tried night attacks on the surface—a tactic that was officially frowned on as being too dangerous. In fact, night surface attacks were, and would remain, hazardous until the sophisticated SJ surface-search radar was introduced in August 1942. But even before then, the tactic was more dangerous than it should have been. For the sake of underwater concealment, American submarines were painted black. But except on the most Stygian of moonless nights, that color presented the submarine as a conspicuous dark mass upon the surface of the ocean. It was later found, after tests that might easily have been conducted in peacetime, that a splotchy pale gray was the most effective all-purpose camouflage color for boats both on and beneath the surface. Eventually, nearly all of the submarines were painted gray.

Prewar tactical practice of every kind was backward at best. At Cavite, Captain Wilkes held occasional exercises, presiding aboard a tender and using signal flags to put his surfaced boats through wildly inappropriate maneuvers. These maneuvers, recalled an officer on the submarine *Seawolf,* amounted to little more than "the old 'squads-right and squads-left' type of drill. It was just one big bloody mess, which never contributed a thing toward improving our readiness."

The submarine fleet commander at Pearl Harbor, Admiral Withers, had a considerably better conception of the nature and function of undersea boats. On his arrival at Pearl in January 1941, he recognized a dismal situation when he saw it and did his best to prepare his boats for war. He discovered, for example, that the submarines had rarely dived even to their 100-foot attack depth, and he immediately ordered them to do so. He also instructed the skippers to dive to test depth, the lowest depth certified as safe for each of the several types of submarines. (The test depth for the fleet boats then at Pearl was 250 feet, although when necessary they could—and later did—go much deeper.)

Withers was dumfounded to discover that the Navy had very little information on how submarines and their crews might endure the prolonged patrols required in wartime. To find out, he dispatched four boats on extended missions across the Pacific. The results were encouraging: Crews, Withers decided, could probably sustain up to 60 days on patrol without suffering undue psychological harm. He also found out that returning boats and their crews would require no more than three weeks of refit and rest before they could venture forth again.

But even Withers' measures were only a beginning. As a general rule, the theme of caution was pursued with excessive zeal in 1941. The result was inevitable: At the outbreak

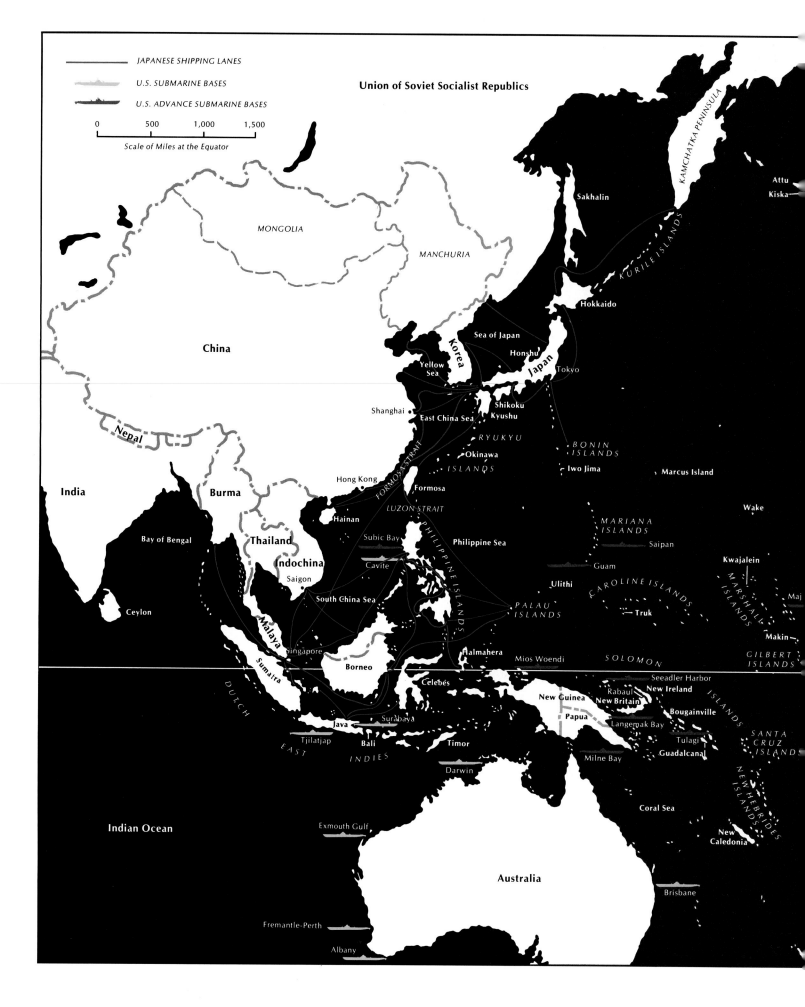

JAPANESE SHIPPING LANES
U.S. SUBMARINE BASES
U.S. ADVANCE SUBMARINE BASES

0   500   1,000   1,500
Scale of Miles at the Equator

Union of Soviet Socialist Republics

KAMCHATKA PENINSULA

Attu
Kiska

Sakhalin

KURILE ISLANDS

Hokkaido

MONGOLIA

MANCHURIA

Sea of Japan

Honshu

Korea

China

Yellow Sea

Japan

Tokyo

Shanghai

Shikoku
Kyushu

East China Sea

RYUKYU

BONIN ISLANDS

Marcus Island

Okinawa

ISLANDS

Iwo Jima

Nepal

Hong Kong

Formosa

FORMOSA STRAIT

Wake

India

Burma

Hainan

LUZON STRAIT

MARIANA ISLANDS

Bay of Bengal

Thailand

Subic Bay

Philippine Sea

Saipan

Kwajalein

MARSHALL ISLANDS

Indochina

Cavite

PHILIPPINE ISLANDS

Guam

Maj

Saigon

Ulithi

CAROLINE ISLANDS

Ceylon

South China Sea

Truk

PALAU ISLANDS

Makin

Malaya

GILBERT ISLANDS

Singapore

Sumatra

Halmahera

Mios Woendi

SOLOMON

Borneo

DUTCH

Celebes

Seeadler Harbor

New Ireland

EAST

Java

Surabaya

New Guinea

Rabaul
New Britain

Bougainville

ISLANDS

Tjilatjap

Bali

Papua

Langemak Bay

SANTA CRUZ ISLANDS

INDIES

Timor

Tulagi

Milne Bay

Guadalcanal

Darwin

NEW HEBRIDES ISLANDS

Exmouth Gulf

Indian Ocean

Coral Sea

New Caledonia

Australia

Brisbane

Fremantle-Perth

Albany

28

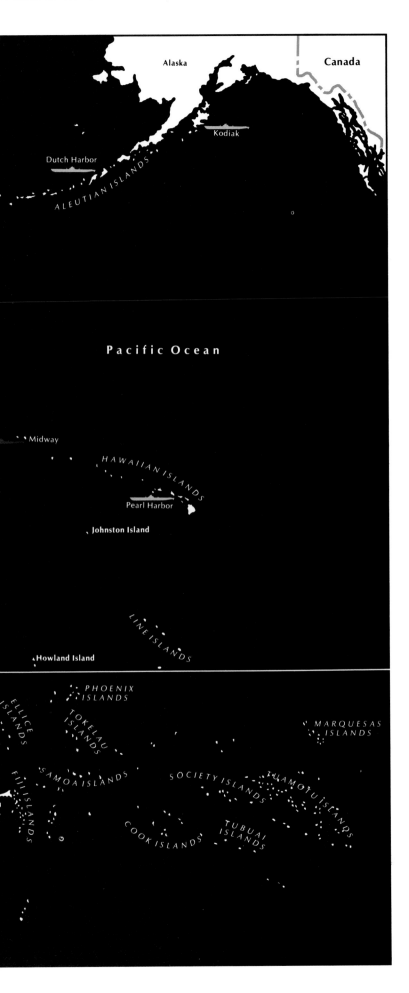

Alaska

Canada

Kodiak

Dutch Harbor

ALEUTIAN ISLANDS

Pacific Ocean

Midway

HAWAIIAN ISLANDS

Pearl Harbor

Johnston Island

LINE ISLANDS

Howland Island

PHOENIX ISLANDS

ELLICE ISLANDS

TOKELAU ISLANDS

MARQUESAS ISLANDS

SAMOA ISLANDS

FIJI ISLANDS

SOCIETY ISLANDS

TUAMOTU ISLANDS

COOK ISLANDS

TUBUAI ISLANDS

of war, many U.S. submarines were commanded by skippers who dutifully enforced spit-and-polish discipline, paid careful attention to their paper work and adhered strictly to the letter of the Navy's conservative tactical book.

To such men, war in the raw would come as a shocking, indeed debilitating, experience. Before too long, stories of timorous captains were told throughout the submarine fleets, and a derisive ditty—composed by a junior officer—made the rounds:

> The Captain is a rugged guy
> With hair upon his chest.
> O'er a glass of beer in peacetime
> He's at his fighting best.
>
> His nerves are surely made of steel,
> His voice has a confident sound,
> And he never gets excited
> When danger's not around.

By the time the war in the Pacific was a year old, 40 skippers—nearly 30 per cent of the total in the growing submarine force—would be relieved of command, mostly for unproductive patrols. Time and again, squadron commanders removed skippers for the same shortcoming: for example, "This patrol of the *Grampus* was not conducted in a sufficiently aggressive manner," and "The past two cruises of the *Snapper* have been devoid of aggressive hunting for the enemy." However, one senior officer made it clear that "opportunities were lost to inflict damage on the enemy" not because the skipper lacked courage, but because of "a lack of basic training."

Yet for all its manifold shortcomings, the U.S. submarine service had one great strength: its junior officers and enlisted men. The men who served in the boats were the pick of the fleet, so far as a battery of physicians, psychologists and senior submariners could determine. Every man and officer was a volunteer. The doctors had pronounced them healthy, emotionally stable and temperamentally capable of getting along well with other men in long periods of close confinement during which nobody but the skipper, the officer of the deck and the lookouts saw sun or stars or smelled air untainted with the fumes of diesel oil.

Once chosen for the service, a man set out on a long,

The geography of the western Pacific shaped the strategy of the U.S. submarine service in its war against Japan. At first the submarines made unproductive efforts to patrol the perimeter of the Japanese Empire. Later they concentrated on the major shipping lanes connecting Japan with its southern sources of raw material (red lines). Ultimately, the boats took their greatest toll in narrow, heavily traveled waters such as the Luzon and Formosa Straits. As this winning strategy developed, American reconquest of key island groups permitted the undersea force to move up from rear-area bases (pink submarines) and to establish advance bases (red submarines) within easy reach of the prime hunting grounds.

29

hard road toward becoming a qualified submariner. All officers and most men—cooks and mess stewards were exceptions—took a rigorous course of training at the Submarine School near New London, Connecticut. But graduation did not complete their education—far from it.

They were assigned to a submarine, and their main course of study became the boat itself. They had to be familiar with every valve, gear, pipe, switch or hatch from bow to stern; they had to be able to draw accurate diagrams of the more than 30 principal systems in a submarine's complex entrails. Every man had to know his own specialty by heart and learn that of another man as well; for example, a torpedoman could, if called upon, double as a motor machinist's mate, an electrician as a radar operator.

A vital lesson learned by the crewmen on their assigned boat was to place unquestioning faith in the judgment, skill and valor of the skipper, whom they called captain but whose actual rank was almost always lieutenant commander. With rare exceptions, his was the only eye at the periscope, giving him alone knowledge of what was happening outside the hull. Upon him rested the fateful decisions—to attack, to wait, to run. As in no other type of warship, the commander of a submarine held in his hand the lives of all those aboard.

Only when a man could convince both his section chief and the skipper that he had done his job well was a submariner qualified and entitled to wear the silver dolphins insignia of the service. Whatever his rating, he received 50 per cent more than standard pay for doing hazardous duty. He considered himself a member of an elite force and was so considered by Navy men who only sailed on the surface.

And he needed all of his *esprit de corps* and well-honed skills to survive the War's hectic early patrols. This was a time when approved tactics failed miserably, when skippers broke the rules and failed just as miserably—when nearly everything that could go wrong did go wrong.

In the aftermath of the Pearl Harbor disaster, the boats at both Pearl and Cavite put out to sea as quickly as possible. Supplies and fuel were crammed aboard each submarine. Torpedoes were stored with care; most of them were the top-secret, new Mark 14 torpedoes, and since they were in short supply, the old Mark 10 torpedoes were added to make up a full load. The Mark 14s were sophisticated devices that had been under development for more than 15 years. The Navy's top commanders had the utmost confidence in them. But that confidence was utterly misplaced. Though no one suspected it at the time, the Mark 14s would soon prove to be the submarine force's most serious and persistent problem of the entire War.

Four of the submarines based at Pearl Harbor were off on simulated patrols when the Japanese attacked; they received war orders by radio. The *Argonaut*, originally built as a minelayer and even as such well past her prime, and the *Trout* were off Midway at the time and commenced operations there.

After sunset on December 7, the boats surfaced on opposite sides of the atoll—and were welcomed by the roar of naval gunfire from two Japanese destroyers staging a nuisance raid. The submarines had almost no chance of doing business. The *Trout* happened to be on the island's far side and thus out of the action. The skipper of the *Argonaut*, Stephen G. Barchet, prudently followed the tactical book and took his boat deep for a sonar attack. He went even deeper when one of the destroyers passed overhead, and by the time he was ready to try another approach, the enemy ships had departed. The *Argonaut* and the *Trout* returned to Pearl without firing a torpedo.

Two other Pearl boats on practice patrol, the *Triton* and the *Tambor*, were at Wake Island, and at least they fired some torpedoes. On the night of December 10, skipper Willis A. Lent and the *Triton* were making way on the surface south of the island when lookouts sighted an enemy destroyer. The ship suddenly turned and came boiling toward the submarine. Lent went deep and, after the Japanese warship had passed overhead without dropping depth charges, fired all four torpedoes from his stern tubes. Lent later reported hearing dull explosions. But postwar Japanese records disclosed no damage sustained by a warship near Wake on that date.

To the north of Wake in the *Tambor*, John W. Murphy Jr. saw three enemy warships on the night of December 11, but failed in his efforts to maneuver his boat into attack position. The next day, the *Tambor* fired her first torpedo—by accident and into an empty sea. Then Murphy turned his submarine toward base, to be followed shortly by the *Triton*.

Before these boats arrived empty-handed at Pearl Harbor, Admiral Withers had sent four of his seven available submarines to the Marshall Islands, where he expected the Japanese carrier force would rendezvous for a second attack on Pearl. For all four boats the result was fiasco.

One boat was the *Dolphin,* an aged submarine now clearly unfit for service. Skipper Gordon B. Rainer counted no fewer than 35 mechanical breakdowns during his first —and only—wartime patrol. Rainer collapsed under the strain and was relieved of command by his executive officer, who brought the *Dolphin* limping back to Pearl.

Near Kwajalein, Joseph Willingham Jr. in the *Tautog* fired three torpedoes at a small minelayer and missed with them all. Then, plagued by a fogging periscope, he went home.

The *Thresher,* under William L. Anderson, found little game in the Marshalls and continued on to Guam, which had fallen almost immediately to the Japanese. There, Anderson fired six torpedoes at a Japanese freighter—four more than the official quota for a merchant ship. Anderson heard one "fish" hit and claimed a sinking. He was later proved wrong; the ship did not sink. Even if the ship had gone down, five misses out of six torpedoes was not a very good score.

In the *Pompano,* Lewis S. Parks had an eventful patrol. While steering westward toward the Marshall Islands, the *Pompano* was twice bombed by U.S. planes—one of many such mistakes that would be made—and suffered damage to her fuel tanks that left her trailing a broad wake of oil. At Wotje, in the Marshalls, Parks found a large Japanese transport anchored in the harbor and waited a day for her to come out. When she did, Parks set up for a daylight periscope attack—a disapproved tactic—and launched four torpedoes, two more than he should have. The *Pompano* then went deep, and when Parks brought her back to periscope depth he saw the enemy ship listing on the port beam and apparently settling. With the *Pompano* still leaking oil, Parks returned to Pearl Harbor and, like Anderson in the *Thresher,* claimed a sinking. He too was mistaken; the transport succeeded in making it back into the harbor of Wotje. In fact, the U.S. submarines sent to the Marshalls had sunk not a single Japanese vessel.

While the futile Marshalls forays were going on, Withers dispatched three submarines to prowl the enemy's home waters. These boats had a much livelier and somewhat more successful time.

The *Gudgeon,* under Elton W. Grenfell, was first off the mark, leaving Pearl Harbor on December 11, proceeding with great caution and spending more than three weeks before she finally arrived off Bungo Strait, the busy western entrance to the Inland Sea between the Japanese islands of Honshu, Shikoku and Kyushu. In daytime, Grenfell remained below the surface at approximately 100 feet, ascending only occasionally to peek through his periscope. Each night after 9 o'clock the *Gudgeon* surfaced in order to recharge batteries. This operation was often conducted with enemy ships in the distance, which made it an instructive experience. "For the first time," recalled Grenfell, "you realized that you could get killed."

On the afternoon of January 4, 1942, the *Gudgeon* sighted a small Japanese freighter. Grenfell, aided by his fire-control officer, Robert E. Dornin, moved in to a range of 2,600 yards. Dornin loosed two torpedoes—and missed. "It had been the almost perfect approach," Grenfell said later. "Dornin almost wept."

On the night of January 9 the *Gudgeon* hit a 5,000-ton freighter, and Grenfell claimed a sinking—mistakenly, it turned out. But on the way back to Pearl, the *Gudgeon* put a torpedo into a Japanese submarine. This time, though Grenfell doubted that he had a sinking, the submarine sank.

Of the other boats sent from Pearl to the Empire's waters, the *Plunger* patrolled off Kii Strait, the eastern entry to the Inland Sea. Her skipper, David C. White, did some of his hunting on the surface, relying on visual contacts by his lookouts. In this risky and disapproved posture he spied a Japanese destroyer that spotted him at the same time and made a swift run at the *Plunger,* dropping 24 depth charges. However, the Japanese submarine hunters had set their charges to explode at too shallow a depth, and the *Plunger* escaped with nothing worse than a severe shaking. After that, White was a bit more cautious. He was at periscope depth when, on January 18, he sighted a freighter and—obeying his instructions to conserve torpedoes when attacking merchantmen—sank it with two torpedoes.

Among all the submarines based at Pearl, the *Pollack,* commanded by Stanley P. Moseley and patrolling off the mouth of Tokyo Bay, had by far the busiest time. On New Year's Eve, Moseley made a night periscope attack against a destroyer. His two torpedoes missed. During the day of January 3 he fired one torpedo at a transport. It missed. Two days later he loosed six torpedoes against another transport and listened with vast satisfaction to the explosions. He claimed a sinking, but did not stay around to see if the ship went down (it did not). On January 7, Moseley scored two hits on another freighter—a probable sinking. Finally, on the night of January 9, Moseley fired four of his few remaining torpedoes at still another enemy freighter and felt confident of a sinking. Moseley believed that he had destroyed three ships, but postwar analysis based on Japanese records reduced the figure to two.

In all, the first patrols of the 11 Pearl Harbor boats had produced the disappointing total of only four ships sunk, and when the submarines returned to base, their skippers were subjected to scathing critiques—some ill-tempered and inconsistent—from Admiral Withers and his staff.

The *Argonaut's* Barchet was rebuked for making a night sonar approach, an approved tactic; Withers even suggested that Barchet might better have attacked from the surface, a tactic the admiral had vigorously disapproved. The *Triton's* Lent was singled out for his inclination to dive "immediately upon seeing or hearing anything," a tendency shown by several other skippers who went by the book. The *Gudgeon's* Grenfell had taken too long in arriving on station: "More surface cruising could have been done, reducing the terrific overhead in time." Grenfell, along with David White in the *Plunger,* was criticized for expending more than one torpedo on a freighter. Of Anderson's *Thresher,* it was said: "The percentage of time utilized in productive effort was all too low." And the unfortunate Gordon Rainer was sent back to the States.

Like the Pearl Harbor boats, the submarines of the U.S. Asiatic Fleet produced little more than a long list of woes and mistakes on their first patrols, which took place while their base was being moved from Manila to Surabaya, in the Dutch East Indies. The 22 boats available for war patrol were deployed in a desperate manner meant to protect the Philippines. Thirteen were sent by Captain Wilkes to scout and harass invasion fleets expected to come in from the west and northwest; five patrolled east of Luzon, and four took station to the south. Only one of the southern boats found a target, and the single torpedo she fired hit nothing.

To the east, the old *S-39* patrolled without finding a target, but the other four had even worse luck. While the *Tarpon* was maneuvering to attack an enemy ship, a torpedoman frightened it away by firing one fish accidentally. In the *Sculpin,* Lucius H. Chappell ran into such rough seas that—unable to fire with any accuracy—he could only watch helplessly while enemy shipping scuttled in and out of Lamon Bay on Luzon after successful Japanese landings there.

On Christmas Day near the Palau Islands, the *Skipjack's* Lawrence Freeman sighted precious game: a Japanese aircraft carrier—and, better yet, one with only a single destroyer escort. Freeman took the *Skipjack* down to 100 feet and moved in to a range that was estimated by his sonar operator at 2,200 yards. He fired three torpedoes from his bow tubes (the fourth was inoperative). Evidently, all of the torpedoes missed; the sonarman later admitted that he may have underestimated the distance by as much as 800 yards. That was as close as the *Skipjack* came to a score on her first patrol.

In the *Seawolf,* Frederick Burdette Warder, a tough, daring skipper who was appropriately nicknamed Fearless Freddy, suffered an experience that sorely tested his notoriously short temper. At Aparri, on the northern end of Luzon, Warder found a lone Japanese destroyer standing guard and managed to slip unseen into the harbor. There at anchor lay a fat and delectable seaplane tender. From 3,800 yards, Warder fired four torpedoes. Silence. Preparing to leave the harbor, Warder backed off to 4,500 yards and sent four stern torpedoes at the tender. Again silence. Warder had achieved the seemingly impossible feat of missing a large, motionless target with eight torpedoes at a good range. As he escaped from the harbor, Freddy Warder was in a profane rage. But he concluded self-confidently—and correctly—that it was not his fault. There had to be some other explanation, and it had to involve the torpedoes.

Of the 13 submarines that were headed westward, the *Searaven* and the *Sturgeon* were assigned to hunt prey in the Formosa-Pescadores area. The skipper of the *Searaven,* Theodore C. Aylward, who had long suffered from high blood pressure, experienced dizziness and chest pains; his executive officer took over most of his duties and brought the boat home after an otherwise fruitless patrol. Aylward fired three torpedoes at two Japanese ships—with no hits. In the *Sturgeon*, skipper William L. Wright completed his patrol having fired only four torpedoes at a single merchant ship, all of which missed.

The *Pike*, off the coast of Hong Kong, fired one torpedo at a freighter and missed from 3,000 yards. No further targets were sighted.

On the western coast of Luzon, the *Sailfish* made half-hearted sallies under Morton Mumma Jr., a lieutenant commander with a reputation as a stickler for discipline. On December 13, after a submerged sonar attack on two Japanese destroyers, the *Sailfish* lay deep while nearly 20 depth

On the deck of the submarine Grayling, Admiral Chester W. Nimitz (center, with braided visor) assumes command of the U.S. Pacific Fleet at Pearl Harbor on December 31, 1941. The choice of a submarine for the ceremony was a grim makeshift: The change of command would normally have taken place on a battleship, but all eight battleships at Pearl had been either sunk or damaged in the attack 24 days earlier.

charges exploded harmlessly above her. Under the strain, Mumma came completely apart and, at his own request, was locked in his stateroom. The *Sailfish's* executive officer, who assumed command, sent a radio message to headquarters: COMMANDING OFFICER BREAKING DOWN. URGENTLY REQUEST AUTHORITY TO RETURN. Permission was granted.

The *Permit* stayed for nine days off Subic Bay and cut short her patrol after her captain contracted a skin disease and a crewman's hand was caught and mangled in machinery. The *S-36*, patrolling in the Lingayen Gulf area, found plenty of targets; Japanese ships began putting troops ashore here on December 11. But the old boat did not sink anything and ended her patrol after a communications breakdown caused by a flawed radio receiver.

The *Swordfish*, under Chester Smith, made the first confirmed sinking by a U.S. submarine in this or any other war. But at first, the same problems that frustrated most of the submarines were visited copiously upon the boat. On the night of December 9, while patrolling the southern coast of Hainan Island, the *Swordfish* chanced upon a big Japanese convoy screened by destroyers.

Attacking on the surface, Smith sent a torpedo streaking toward a large supply ship. Then he had to dive to escape a destroyer bearing down on him fast. During the dive the sonar operator reported hearing the torpedo detonate. But when Smith came up to periscope depth, he saw the ship steaming along unscathed. Apparently the torpedo had exploded prematurely. Smith fired another torpedo at the ship and dived again. Again a loud explosion in the sonar, but no sinking and perhaps no hit.

The *Swordfish* tracked the convoy southward for two days and made another surface attack on the night of December 11. Smith aimed two torpedoes at a ship. Both missed. He then lost contact with the convoy.

In the predawn darkness on December 14, while at periscope depth, the *Swordfish* found the convoy again—or another one just like it. Smith brought the boat to the surface and fired two torpedoes at a freighter. Two loud explosions clattered in the sound gear. Smith later reported a sinking, but could not confirm it. (He was mistaken.)

That afternoon Smith made a submerged attack and carefully fired three torpedoes at two freighters. He scored two hits that only damaged the freighters. Then he had to dive deep and commence evasive action to escape a posse of vengeful destroyers.

Finally, on December 16, Smith caught sight of his historic victim, a big freighter off the coast of Hainan. He made a submerged approach and fired three torpedoes at 2,800 yards. One fish exploded prematurely, but the others hit. Then, from the sound gear, came the freighter's death rattle—muffled explosions as cold water drowned her boilers, followed by the crackling noises of steel plates and pipes buckling and tearing. Through his periscope Smith saw the freighter aflame and going down stern first. He had sunk the *Atsutusan Maru*, 8,663 tons.

The crewmen of the *Swordfish* were overjoyed by their kill and quickly forgot their many misses. But in fact, as Smith and other skippers sensed, the misses were more significant than the sinking.

Of all the U.S. submarines that took to the sea during that dismal December, the boat whose patrol was the most significant in the long term was, paradoxically, the one that endured the greatest frustration. The submarine was the *Sargo*, and she was sent by Captain Wilkes from Manila Bay to Camranh Bay in southern Indochina.

As it happened, the *Sargo's* skipper, Tyrrell Jacobs, had seen peacetime service with the Bureau of Ordnance, the virtually autonomous branch of the Navy that designed the torpedoes and all other weapons for the fleet. Though Jacobs was no torpedo expert, he probably knew more about the secret innards and workings of the vaunted Mark 14 than any other man aboard the boats.

The Mark 14 differed in many respects from the old Mark 10. The Mark 10 was 16 feet long, weighed 2,215 pounds, including 497 pounds of TNT in the war head, and could travel 3,500 yards at 36 knots. The Mark 14 was four and a half feet longer, about half a ton heavier and could run 4,500 yards at 46 knots or twice as far at 31.5 knots. The Mark 14 was also considerably more powerful than the Mark 10. Early versions of the Mark 14 carried 507 pounds of TNT in the war head. Later, with the development of a more potent explosive called Torpex (a compound of TNT, an explosive called RDX and aluminum powder), the warhead load was raised to 668 pounds.

There had been no attempt to change the basic propulsion system of the Mark 14. As in the Mark 10, the passage of the fish out of the tube (the Mark 14 was built to the same 21-inch diameter of the Mark 10 so that it could be fired from old submarines) tripped a starting lever, which caused water to be sprayed into a flame generated by alcohol and air carried in flasks inside the torpedoes. The resultant steam spun a turbine, which in turn drove the missile's propellers.

Before firing, the directional gyroscopes inside both models were set for the desired course. The fish were expelled from the tube by a surge of compressed air, after which they were supposed to run at a preset depth, controlled by a hydrostatic device.

The most important difference between the two torpedoes lay in their detonating devices. The Mark 10 was detonated by a contact exploder that was as straightforward as a sledge hammer. The Mark 14 was equipped with a secret and complicated new exploder that worked on magnetic principles. This exploder, designated the Mark 6, had been specifically designed to detonate the war head when the torpedo came within the magnetic field of an enemy ship.

The Bureau of Ordnance, or BuOrd as it was commonly called, had developed the Mark 6 detonator for a sound reason. Over the years, the flanks of warships had been encased in ever thicker steel plating. The old torpedoes might hit a heavily armored battleship on or just below the water-line and do little damage. However, the steel plating on a warship's underbelly was kept relatively thin, for to increase the thickness of armor there would add great weight and thus cut down critically on speed.

The Mark 6 was supposed to make it possible for the Mark 14 torpedo to get at a warship's vulnerable underbelly with maximum effectiveness. For good measure, just in case the Mark 14 failed to detonate as it entered the target ship's magnetic field, the torpedo was also equipped with a contact exploder.

The weapons designers at BuOrd had based their new exploder on a mechanism that the Germans had employed to trigger mines during the First World War. Known as a magnetic pistol, the device consisted of a magnetic compass whose needle swung and tripped off a detonator as a ship came within its range.

Experimental work on the new torpedo with its sophisticated exploder had begun in 1922, when BuOrd allocated an initial $25,000, a whopping sum at the time, to the Naval Torpedo Station at Newport, Rhode Island. The torpedoes turned out to be fiercely expensive; they cost $10,000 apiece, and the frugal officers in BuOrd regarded it as the height of extravagance to blow them up in a test program. Instead, they were tested with water-filled war heads so that they could be retrieved from the sea and used for subsequent tests and practice.

In tests performed with dummy war heads, the Mark 14s ran straight and true. But BuOrd never tested a live war head on a Mark 14 torpedo—it seemed unnecessary. The Mark 14 torpedo and the Mark 6 exploder went into limited production—but were kept secret by BuOrd from all but a handful of high-ranking officers. The line officers and men in the submarines learned little or nothing about them until the autumn of 1941, when the first few skippers and torpedo officers were sketchily briefed on the weapon that would gradually be substituted for the Mark 10 and its trusty old contact exploder.

Because of his earlier duty at BuOrd, Tyrrell Jacobs was one of the few submarine skippers who knew how the secret Mark 6 exploder was supposed to work. Since the instrument had several precise operations to perform, it was both bulky and complex; it weighed 92 pounds and was nested in the underside of the war head. To set off the war head at the right instant, its mechanism had to complete three steps in a fraction of a second. First, the firing pin, released by the target ship's magnetic field, struck a primer cap. This, in turn, exploded a detonator set into a cavity in a booster charge. The explosion of the booster created shock waves powerful enough to detonate the main war-head charge of TNT, a material normally so stable that neither heat nor minor shock would set it off.

To prevent any fatally premature detonation, the Mark 6 was designed to hold the war head unarmed and inert while the weapon was in the submarine's torpedo tube and immediately after firing. This was accomplished by keeping the detonator charge withdrawn from its nest in the booster until a spinner, set in motion by the torpedo's rush through the water and working through a gear chain, inserted the detonator charge into firing position. This action was completed only after the torpedo had traveled 450 yards, an interval

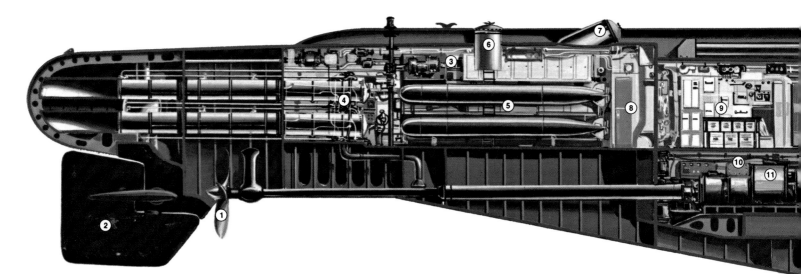

THE ANATOMY OF A FORMIDABLE FIGHTING MACHINE

1 Propeller
2 Rudder
3 After torpedo room
4 Torpedo tubes (4)
5 Reload torpedoes (4)
6 After-torpedo-room hatch
7 Torpedo loading hatch
8 Engineer's office
9 Maneuvering room
10 Motor room

11 Main motors
12 After engine room
13 Main engine
14 Main generator
15 Auxiliary engine and generator
16 Forward engine room
17 Crew's washroom
18 Crew's quarters
19 After battery compartment
20 Ballast and fuel tanks

The improved U.S. fleet submarines that came into service during the war in the Pacific had a range of 10,000 miles and cruised on the surface at 20 knots. They could dive to periscope depth at 63 feet in less than a minute, could travel underwater at a top speed of almost nine knots and could, at reduced speed, stay under for 72 hours. This remarkable performance was made possible by the design and equipment illustrated on these four pages in cross-section views of a typical fleet boat.

The core of the 1,525-ton submarine was her pressure hull; this tough steel cylinder, 16 feet in diameter with tapered ends, could withstand the crushing weight of the sea—14 tons per square foot—at half again her approved operating depth of 300 feet. Later versions had an operating depth of 400 feet and were designed to resist the awesome pressure of 19 tons per square foot at 600 feet.

Compartments at each end of the pressure hull housed the torpedo tubes, four in the stern, six in the bow. Extra torpedoes were stored on reloading racks and under the deck, for a total of 24. In the remaining space forward and aft were bunks and lockers for nearly half the 70 enlisted men.

Most of the after part of the submarine was filled with propulsion machinery. Below the main deck just forward of the after torpedo room was the motor room, where the four electric main motors were connected to the twin propellers. When the boat was submerged, these motors drew power from tiers of storage-battery cells —252 all told—arrayed below the decks of the forward and after battery compartments. On the surface, the current came from generators turned by the boat's four oil-burning diesel engines.

Above the motors was the maneuvering room, where thick electric cables converged behind rows of massive switches that shunted current between generators, batteries and motors to change speed or shift the power source from engines to batteries. Forward of the maneuvering room were two engine rooms, each with two 1,600-horsepower diesel engines, located on either side of a narrow catwalk. Below the walkway were the 1,100-kilowatt generators, used for charging batteries as well as powering the main motors. A smaller diesel generator set below the after-engine-room catwalk ran the boat's auxiliary pumps and compressors, and could also charge the batteries.

Forward of the engine rooms was the after battery compartment, which also contained living quarters for 36 of the crew. Meals prepared in the tiny 6-by-11-foot galley were served in the crew's mess; officers ate the same meals in the wardroom, located in the officers' quarters in the forward battery compartment. Between the two battery compartments were the control room and conning tower—the nerve center of the boat (overleaf).

The fleet submarine's bulging outer hull was topped by vertical sides that supported the decking and formed the knifelike bow. Rows of open ports perforated the sides for most of the submarine's 312-foot length, and allowed rapid flooding during a dive. The structure around the conning tower reduced drag and formed the bridge and gun platforms. The forward diving planes, rigged out horizontally during a dive, folded up for surface running.

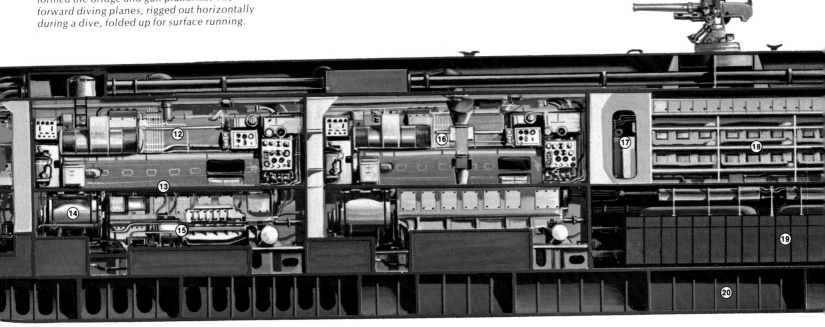

21 *Crew's mess (4 tables, 8 benches)*
22 *Galley*
23 *Ammunition magazines*
24 *Fresh-water tank*
25 *Main induction valve*
26 *SD air-search radar*
27 *SJ surface-search radar*
28 *Periscopes*
29 *Bridge*
30 *Ready ammunition locker*
31 *Main steering station*
32 *Conning tower*
33 *Radio room*
34 *Control room*
35 *Diving station*
36 *Hydraulic manifold*
37 *Christmas tree*
38 *Pump room*
39 *Forward battery compartment*
40 *Chief petty officers' stateroom*
41 *Officers' stateroom*
42 *Wardroom*
43 *Wardroom pantry*
44 *Retractable sonar unit*
45 *Forward torpedo room*
46 *Forward hatch and escape trunk*
47 *Torpedo tubes (6)*
48 *Anchor windlass*

The submarine's control room housed the main systems for diving and surfacing. Levers at the hydraulic manifold controlled vents at the tops of the ballast tanks; when opened, the vents allowed air to escape, to be replaced by tons of water rushing in through flood ports in the bottoms.

Above the hydraulic manifold was the "Christmas tree," a panel of red and green lights that showed the status of every hull opening: Green all around meant the boat was watertight and ready to dive. Two wheels at the diving station changed the angle of the bow and stern planes, the horizontal fins used to maintain depth. The trim manifold controlled the amount of water in the trim tanks to keep the boat level, while the air manifold regulated the high-pressure air used to empty the tanks when surfacing. Below the control room, the pump room was filled with machinery for the compressed-air, hydraulic refrigeration and air-conditioning systems.

The boat's command center was the conning tower, a tiny auxiliary hull above the main pressure hull, reached by a hatch from the control room. Here the skipper could draw on data obtained from the boat's eyes and ears—periscopes, radar (both SD air-search and SJ surface-search) and sonar—and bring to bear one of the War's deadliest fighting machines.

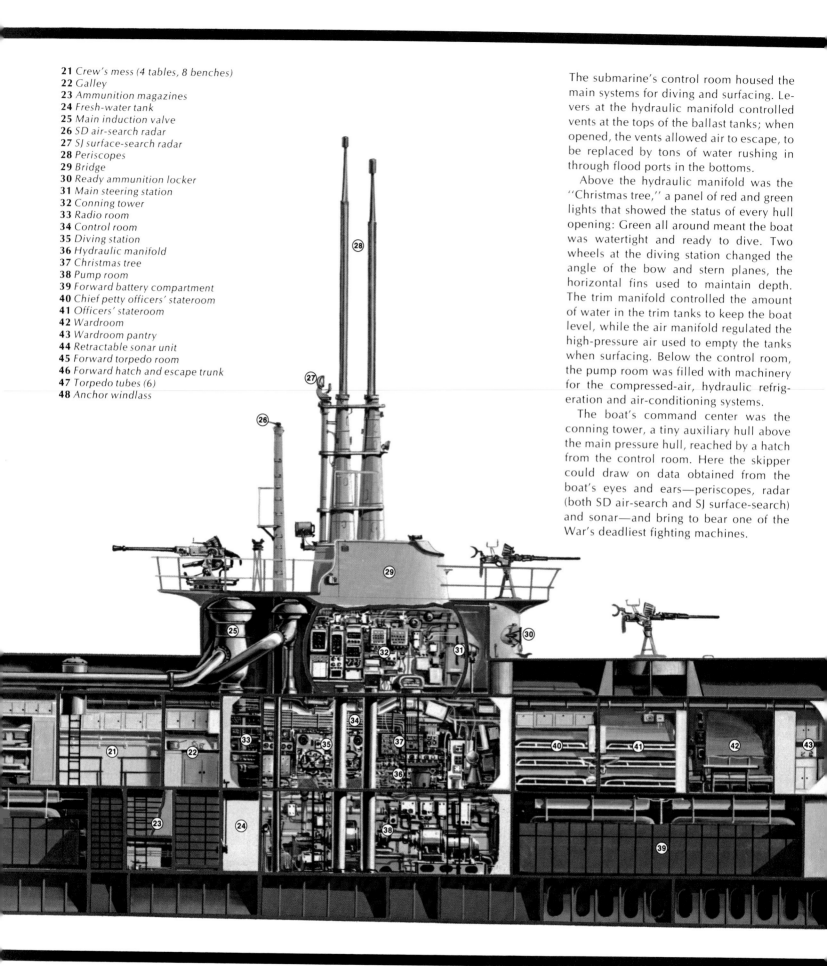

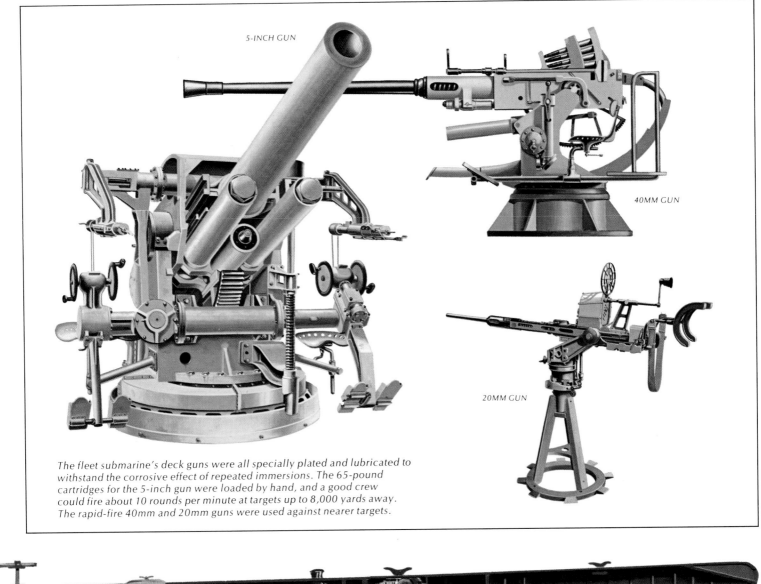

5-INCH GUN

40MM GUN

20MM GUN

The fleet submarine's deck guns were all specially plated and lubricated to withstand the corrosive effect of repeated immersions. The 65-pound cartridges for the 5-inch gun were loaded by hand, and a good crew could fire about 10 rounds per minute at targets up to 8,000 yards away. The rapid-fire 40mm and 20mm guns were used against nearer targets.

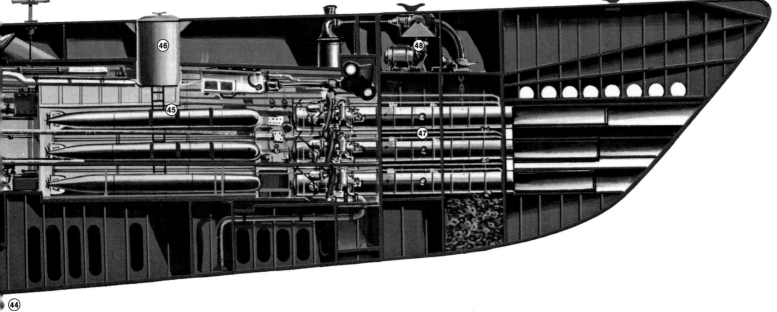

calculated to enable the fish to get safely clear of the submarine, to stabilize its initial gyrations and to give the Mark 6's electrical innards time to warm up.

One other attachment, called an anti-countermining device, was included. Using a sea-pressure diaphragm, it kept the firing pin immobilized during the torpedo's race toward the target. This prevented any nearby explosion, or the magnetic field of a mine or another torpedo, from detonating the war head prematurely.

As thus devised by the finest engineering minds in the Bureau of Ordnance, the torpedo was theoretically a perfect weapon. But Tyrrell Jacobs realized that the Mark 14 was a dismal failure, and he became the first man to attempt to correct its many complicated faults.

On December 14, Jacobs and the *Sargo* made their first contact with a Japanese ship, a 4,000-ton cargo vessel. Jacobs ordered the torpedoes set to run at a depth of 15 feet, which would carry them under the enemy ship; when they detonated in the ship's vertical magnetic field, the explosion would smash the vessel's keel, sinking her swiftly.

Jacobs fired one fish at a range of about 1,000 yards. It ran only 450 yards and then exploded, the concussion rocking the *Sargo* violently. This failure was more clearly a premature explosion than those the other skippers experienced, for Jacobs' torpedo had traveled barely the distance needed to arm its magnetic exploder.

At first Jacobs thought that some new Japanese antimagnetic apparatus had exploded the torpedo prematurely. But when other torpedoes went off at different distances from his target, he reconsidered. More likely, he decided, the premature explosions were caused by some built-in flaw in the Mark 6 exploder.

Jacobs discussed the problem with his torpedo officer, Lieutenant C. Douglas Rhymes Jr., and decided to deactivate the Mark 6's magnetic feature—a procedure expressly forbidden by the submariners' orders. Under Jacobs' direction and Rhymes's supervision, the torpedomen removed the Mark 6 devices from the torpedoes, cut a number of electrical wires, replaced the exploders in the war heads and sealed them securely. The Mark 14s would now be detonated only by their contact exploders, which presumably would make them just as reliable as the old Mark 10s.

The *Sargo* patrolled for 10 days before Jacobs found a target for his modified torpedoes. Sighting two enemy supply ships, he fired three fish set to run 15 feet deep. But the targets zigzagged and the torpedoes missed. Somewhat reassured because the fish had not gone off prematurely, Jacobs set two more to run at 10 feet and fired them at one of the ships at a range of 1,900 yards. They did not explode, but neither did they hit.

His puzzlement deepening, Jacobs found another target on December 27. This time he fired two torpedoes at a range of only 900 yards. Both fish missed.

At this point Jacobs realized that without a doubt the Mark 14 torpedo was deeply flawed. He decided to spend the rest of his patrol assembling evidence to convince his superiors that the torpedo, and not any mistake in his judgment or the torpedomen's performance, was responsible for the Mark 14's baffling behavior.

Late in the afternoon of the 27th, the *Sargo* sighted two more enemy ships. They were steaming at about nine knots on a course that permitted Jacobs to approach with great care and fire straight ahead. He would thus, he thought, eliminate the possibility of any miss caused by a torpedo launched at a more difficult angle.

Jacobs spent 57 minutes making a textbook approach. He and the crew double-checked every element involved in the firing—the targets' course and speed, the *Sargo's* course and speed, the range, bearing and the 10-foot depth setting of the torpedoes.

Then, with all conditions perfect, Jacobs fired two torpedoes at the first ship, range 1,200 yards. Both fish missed. Minutes later the second ship slipped into the periscope, and Jacobs fired two more torpedoes at a range of 1,000 yards. Again both missed.

Utterly frustrated, Jacobs conferred again with Rhymes and came to the conclusion that the torpedoes were missing because they were traveling considerably deeper than their depth setting and were passing harmlessly under the targets. Jacobs deduced—accurately—that this was happening because the depth settings had been calibrated for the dummy war heads; clearly the explosives in his live war heads were heavier than the water in the dummies, and the added weight caused the fish to run too deep.

Jacobs tried one more time to adjust a torpedo to work

right, but when he fired it at a tanker it, too, missed. At that point, having done all he could under combat conditions, Jacobs spread the alarm. He radioed Captain Wilkes, who was then en route to the new Surabaya base in Chester Smith's *Swordfish,* and informed him that he had fired 13 Mark 14s at six different targets under ideal conditions, that he had disobediently disarmed the magnetic feature and that he was convinced the torpedoes were missing because they were running much deeper than set.

Jacobs' message was also addressed to the headquarters of Wilkes's boss, the commander in chief of the Asiatic Fleet, and the ordnance expert there quickly rose to the defense of BuOrd's handiwork. He alleged that the torpedoes were failing because Jacobs had not tightly resealed the Mark 6 exploders after he had canceled their magnetic features and replaced the devices in the war heads. Sea water, he suggested, had seeped into the war heads and had flooded the exploders.

While Jacobs was heading toward Surabaya, the ordnance officer alerted the Bureau of Ordnance in Washington, and that body immediately sent winging to Surabaya a lieutenant commander named Walker to look into the charges. He placed all blame for the *Sargo's* torpedo problems on the boat's captain and crew who, he claimed, had mishandled the weapon.

Many months would pass before any sort of official testing of the Mark 14 was initiated. Nevertheless, Jacobs had accomplished something. His complaints touched off a litany of laments about the Mark 14's performance from the commanders of U.S. submarines.

In January 1942, with the Japanese swarming south from Indochina to Malaya, William E. Ferrall's *Seadragon* was sent to the enemy staging area at Camranh Bay, where Jacobs before him had met with such perplexing misfortunes. Within two weeks Ferrall made eight attacks, firing a total of 15 torpedoes; he scored only one hit, which damaged but failed to sink a Japanese merchant ship. Ferrall surfaced and

all war diaries thus far submitted has convinced me that among the causes are bad torpedo performance."

As a first step toward a solution, Lockwood asked the Bureau of Ordnance if it had recently conducted any tests that might indicate whether or not the Mark 14 torpedo was running deeper than its settings specified. BuOrd's reply once again blamed any torpedo malfunctions on improper maintenance or procedures by the men in the submarines.

Lockwood was annoyed. "I decided," he wrote later, "to take matters into my own hands." He planned a test that BuOrd should have conducted years before.

Lockwood bought an enormous deep-sea fishing net, 500 feet long, and had it rigged from the surface to the bottom in quiet water outside the harbor at Albany, Australia, south of Perth. The Skipjack, now under a new skipper, James Coe, prepared a batch of Mark 14s with dummy war heads—weighted to match live war heads. One fish, set to run 10 feet deep and fired at the net from a range of 850 yards, punched a hole at 25 feet below the surface. Another torpedo, also set for a 10-foot depth, went through the net at 18 feet. A third, set to run on the surface, sliced the net at 11 feet underwater.

Lockwood concluded that he had tracked down the torpedo's flaw and so reported to the Bureau of Ordnance. BuOrd responded that no reliable conclusions could be drawn from the Skipjack's inadequate tests.

Observing proper service protocol, Lockwood suggested that the bureau make tests of its own. In the meantime, he repeated his experiment with Mark 14s. This time the Saury, under skipper Leonard S. Mewhinney, set three Mark 14s to run 10 feet deep and fired them at the net at ranges of 850 to 900 yards. All three cut the net at a depth of 21 feet. Lockwood notified BuOrd, again urging the experts to make their own tests.

At this point the submariners acquired another, less diffident ally. The Chief of Naval Operations, Admiral King, received a copy of Lockwood's dispatch and brusquely commanded BuOrd to make the tests. With no other choice, the bureau set to work, firing fish from a submarine in Narragansett Bay off Newport. Finally, in August of 1942, almost eight months after the Pacific war began, the U.S. Navy Bureau of Ordnance admitted that its mechanical wonder chronically ran at least 10 feet deeper than set.

That seemed to settle the question, and the submarine commanders at both Fremantle and Pearl Harbor were instructed to subtract 11 feet from whatever depth setting they chose for an attack; if they wanted a fish to run at 15 feet, for example, they should set it for four feet. The magnetic exploder was left untouched.

Almost at once the submarine skippers discovered that correcting the depth settings failed to stop the torpedoes' premature explosions. On the contrary, the solution to the depth-setting problem actually increased the number of early explosions. By the spring of 1943 these had reached dismaying proportions.

Typical was the experience of the Tunny. The submarine was on patrol in the Caroline Islands archipelago when she received a report of a Japanese carrier task group southwest of Truk. The skipper, John Scott, moved to intercept, and the next night, at 10:28, he made radar contact with the group moving his way at 18 knots. A short time later he found himself at periscope depth in the middle of the Japanese formation. On one side loomed a big carrier; on the other two small carriers steamed in column. Turning the Tunny to the right, Scott fired his four stern tubes at the leading small carrier from a close-in range of 880 yards, and moments later fired the six forward torpedoes at the big carrier at a range of only 650 yards.

To a submarine skipper's mind it had been a setup to dream about. It was also very nearly a dead loss. Although all four stern-tube shots and three from the forward tubes were heard to explode, only the small carrier was actually hit, and the damage done to her was disappointing. The other torpedoes had blown up short of their targets.

Admiral Lockwood was galled by the patrol reports of prematures from the Tunny and other boats, and his mood was hardly relieved by a letter from Rear Admiral Ralph Waldo Christie, who had been largely responsible for development of the Mark 6 magnetic exploder. Christie expressed bitter resentment at the aspersions being cast on his creation. He started out by saying, "We are definitely not in accord with the opinions expressed in various patrol endorsements," and then went on at length to criticize the critical reports.

Lockwood's reply was blistering: "Thank you for your let-

PUGNACIOUS INSIGNIA FOR DEADLY BOATS

Each American submarine crew went to war with a fanciful emblem, usually one that caricatured the fish or sea creature after which its boat was named. The men took the same pride in their identifying design that U.S. air crews did in the gaudy figures they painted on their bombers.

There was a difference, however. The submarines, whose very survival depended on stealth and concealment, were denied any exterior decorations or markings that might attract the enemy's attention. Instead, the crewmen put their emblem on specially printed stationery, on patches that adorned their foul-weather jackets and on their battle flags (pages 180-181), which the boats displayed only as they neared the safety of their home ports.

Since the emblems were unofficial, the origins of many went unrecorded. But the Walt Disney Studios donated insignia for a number of boats, and Ray Young, a designer for the Manitowoc Shipbuilding Company, created 14, including the three that are shown on this page. Young submitted his emblems for the approval—and sometimes the signatures (below)—of the crews at the time of their boat's commissioning. All the crews were delighted by the pugnacious look of the fish. "The more vicious you could make them," Young recalled, "the better they liked them."

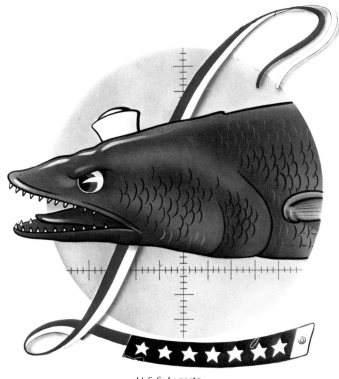

U.S.S. Lagarto

U.S.S. Lamprey

U.S.S. Lizardfish

ter. From the amount of belly-aching it contains, I assume that the breakfast coffee was scorched or perhaps it was a bad egg. You boys may figure the problem out to suit your favorite theories but the facts remain that we have now lost six valuable targets due to prematures so close that the skippers thought they were hits."

Lockwood, who had meanwhile been tranferred to the Pearl Harbor command, was called to Washington for consultations. There, at last, he let his indignation boil over in public. Addressing a group of submarine officers from several Navy bureaus, he declared: "If the Bureau of Ordnance can't provide us with torpedoes that will hit and explode, then for God's sake get Bureau of Ships to design a boat hook with which we can rip the plates off a target's sides."

The remark offended one of Lockwood's old friends, Rear Admiral W. H. P. "Spike" Blandy, Chief of the Bureau of Ordnance. When the two men later met, Blandy said, "I don't know whether it's part of your mission to discredit the Bureau of Ordnance, but you seem to be doing a pretty good job of it."

"Well, Spike," Lockwood retorted, "if anything I have said will get the bureau off its duff and get some action, I will feel that my trip has not been wasted."

By now it was apparent to everybody but BuOrd that the magnetic feature of the Mark 6 was at fault. After much investigation, it turned out to be a matter of physics and the supersensitivity of the Mark 6 exploder. Every steel-bottomed ship was encased in a magnetic field that radiated in all directions. This field was presumed to extend an equal distance in all directions—and to form a perfect hemisphere under the bottom of a ship. Thus, a torpedo set at the proper depth would intersect this hemisphere at its deepest point—precisely under the keel of the target ship. The Mark 6 magnetic exploder would then touch off the torpedo war head, and the broken-backed ship would sink.

But there was a flaw in the principle—a flaw that no one was aware of at the time. What was not understood was that the magnetic field encasing a ship varied in shape depending on circumstances. Near the Equator this magnetic envelope flattened out until it resembled a thick disk more than a hemisphere. Thus a torpedo would enter the magnetic field some distance from the side of a ship—where it would explode harmlessly.

Acting on these discoveries, Admiral Nimitz in June 1943 ordered the Pearl Harbor submarines to deactivate the magnetic feature of the Mark 6. But that remedy was not adopted in Australia; the new commander of the submarine force there, appointed in February 1943, was none other than Rear Admiral Ralph Christie. Far from bowing to the obvious, Christie waged a vendetta against skippers who slurred his torpedoes. One critic, William Millican, who had replaced the original skipper of the *Thresher,* was sent back to the States. Another, the *Grouper's* Rob Roy McGregor, was relieved of his command and shunted into staff work.

But the end of the magnetic exploder was at hand. It came with the arrival of Vice Admiral Thomas Kinkaid as commander of naval forces in the southwest Pacific, formerly known as the Asiatic Fleet and now renamed the U.S. Seventh Fleet. Kinkaid was not a man to countenance failure, and he ordered that the magnetic exploder be shelved.

Upon hearing the news, Admiral Christie noted in his diary: "Today the long hard battle on the Mark 6 magnetic feature ends—with defeat. I am forced to inactivate all magnetic exploders. We are licked."

The problem of depth was settled, the magnetic exploder was laid to rest, the U.S. submarines were now firing the Mark 14 to explode on contact—and now another flaw made known its baneful presence: duds.

Torpedoes that failed to explode on contact were of course a recognized phenomenon. Even the reliable old Mark 10 had its fair share of duds. The trouble with the Mark 14 was that much more than a tolerable number of torpedoes turned out to be duds.

After much renewed confusion there came a patrol that finally brought the problem of duds to a head. The submarine *Tinosa,* under Lawrence R. Daspit, sailed from Pearl Harbor and began combing the Carolines. She carried 16 torpedoes, and the crew prepared to use them when the radar operator reported a contact at a little more than six miles. Closing the range, Daspit discovered to his immense satisfaction that his target, as identified in the submarine's silhouette books, was one of Japan's two biggest tankers: the *Tonan Maru No. 3,* a 19,000-ton converted whale factory. A sinking should be a certainty, since the big ship was steaming unescorted at a modest 13 knots.

Daspit ran ahead and submerged to lie in the tanker's course at periscope depth. The Japanese ship plowed on, and when she reached the right position, Daspit fired a spread of four torpedoes. At least two hit but failed to explode: Daspit saw geysers of water spout up between foremast and mainmast, and the *Tonan Maru* continued on her way, apparently undamaged.

Daspit fired the remaining two fish in the forward tubes. Both hit, and this time there were heavy, solid explosions; the *Tonan Maru* stopped dead in the water and appeared to settle astern. The *Tinosa* was now in position to finish her off at leisure. Daspit worked into position squarely on the beam. At only 875 yards, he fired one. It hit—water splashed up to the main-deck level—but there was no explosion. Another dud.

For the next 90 minutes, Daspit carefully fired one torpedo after another against the *Tonan Maru's* towering flank at point-blank range. Not a single one exploded. Daspit had fired 15 torpedoes and at least 11, possibly 13, had proved to be duds. He decided to quit, leaving the *Tonan Maru* very much alive, and took his last torpedo home for study.

Back at Pearl the experts disemboweled the *Tinosa's* exhibit; they could find nothing wrong. Nevertheless, Admiral Lockwood decided to run another test—one that the Newport station might have tried months or years before. He ordered the firing of live torpedoes, the target being the submerged cliffs at Kahoolawe Island. The first dud would be retrieved and examined. The first two fish functioned perfectly, exploding on contact. There was some opposition to wasting another $10,000 torpedo, but Lockwood ordered it fired. It was a dud. Then came a ticklish business.

A volunteer diver went down through 55 feet of murky water, found the torpedo and shackled a line to its tail. It was worth the risk, for the sunken dud yielded the clue that, at long last, made it possible to exorcise the bedeviled Mark 14. The subsequent autopsy revealed that impact had properly released the firing pin but that the pin had not traveled far enough and fast enough to strike the primer. Now the only question was why.

Lockwood ran another experiment. To approximate the forces at work on a fired torpedo, his technicians fashioned dummy war heads of concrete, fitted them with exploders and dropped them 90 feet from a cherry-picker crane onto a steel plate. When the war heads hit the plate head-on, seven out of 10 firing pins failed to do their work. This was the reason that square hits often ended up as duds. But when the plate was tilted 45 degrees, the firing pins in half of the war heads traveled far enough to ensure an explosion.

It was a plain case of jamming. The firing pin in a Mark 6 was a mushroom-shaped piece of steel, and its direction of travel ran cross the axis of the torpedo. A torpedo hitting square against the side of a ship at its 46-knot speed expended a force about 500 times that of gravity. Lockwood's experts figured that such a square hit imposed about 190 pounds of inertial friction on the firing pin, and the heavy steel pin was incapable of responding fast enough and traveling far enough to set off the primer cap on contact.

The cure was ridiculously easy—a lightweight firing pin. Soon several machine shops at Pearl Harbor were turning out trimmed-down pins. The ideal metal for the job turned out to be the tough steel in the propeller blades of Japanese planes shot down in their attack of December 7, 1941.

And so, the last of the many mysteries of the Mark 6 exploder and the Mark 14 torpedo was finally solved. The first boats to carry thoroughly modified fish reported better than 50 per cent hits—and no duds. The *Haddock* sank two ships with four hits, the *Trigger* sent three ships down with eight hits, and the *Seahorse* made three kills with seven hits.

At last, nearly two years after the attack on Pearl Harbor, U.S. submarines went to sea with a torpedo that worked.

BUILDING THE UNDERSEA NAVY

The Robalo, one of 28 submarines produced by Wisconsin's Manitowoc Shipbuilding Company, is launched into the Manitowoc River on May 9, 194

PUTTING THE SERVICE ON A WARTIME FOOTING

A student officer practices working with a periscope in a simulator, one of a number of training devices that freed submarines for combat duty.

Fully a year and a half before the Japanese attack on Pearl Harbor, the United States had begun an enormous effort to build boats and train men for the undersea navy. Congress, alarmed by the fall of France in June 1940, voted to add 67 submarines to the six already authorized under its normal naval building program for fiscal 1941.

At first the new orders swamped the only three American submarine-building yards, which possessed scarcely a dozen construction ways among them. Immediately these yards initiated a crash program to add more ways, and the U.S. Navy's Bureau of Ships pressed into service two firms that had never built submarines before.

The Cramp Company, a Philadelphia shipyard that had been closed since 1926, reopened under new owners and was soon laying keels two at a time on the long ways that once had been used for building cruisers. The second company, Manitowoc Shipbuilding, was inconveniently located in Wisconsin, which meant that its boats had to be towed some 1,000 miles down the Illinois and Mississippi Rivers to the Gulf of Mexico. But these companies quickly caught on to the special techniques of submarine construction, and their boats proved to be among the best-built and tightest in the Navy.

As boat construction accelerated, the Navy's Submarine School near New London, Connecticut, struggled to keep pace in training new crews. The officers' six-month peacetime course was condensed into just three months; the enlisted men's six-week course was greatly intensified, with study and practice continuing past midnight.

The number of enlisted men accepted for each course was boosted from 336 in 1940 to a wartime high of 4,734 in March 1944. The increase in the school's output of officers was even more dramatic, soaring from 50 or so graduates each prewar year to 995 at the peak of the 1944 build-up.

The first of the boats authorized by Congress in 1940 started arriving with their new crews at Pearl Harbor in early 1942. By mid-year, the new fleet boats were going into combat at the rate of four a month.

A RACE AGAINST TIME AT THE SHIPYARDS

In their race to build more submarines faster, American shipyard managers scoured the country for metalworkers, machinists, pipe fitters, electricians and welders. In spite of the lively wartime competition for skilled workers, the managers were remarkably successful. In New Hampshire, the staff of the Portsmouth Navy Yard, which numbered 4,200 workers in 1940, swelled to 20,000 by June 1943, when the yard was turning out a new submarine every month.

The building firms did all they could to increase their efficiency. Huge banks of floodlights were set up in the yards so that three shifts could work round the clock. When a shift was shorthanded, men and women alike volunteered to work overtime. In the Portsmouth yard, workers gave up holidays for two months to set a speed record—building the *Cisco* from keel laying to launch in just 56 days.

Even more important, the yards increasingly used assembly-line production techniques. The Portsmouth yard cut the building time for each hull by prefabricating large sections of boats even before the keels were laid; then once the keel was down, the boat was quickly assembled on it. Builders at Manitowoc ingeniously used huge jigs to rotate whole hull sections so that welders could always work with their torches directed downward in the most efficient way.

Assembly-line efficiencies were made possible when Navy experts became convinced that the fleet boat had reached a sufficient level of development in the submarine *Gato*, No. 212 in the class; they froze the design at that point, prohibiting any major alterations. And, as the workers built boat after boat to the same plans, they increased their speed at each complicated operation. Within three years, the average man-hours needed to construct a submarine had been reduced from more than two million to less than 650,000.

Perched precariously atop the skeleton of the Gato, workers prepare to gird the ship's ribs with the heavy plating of her pressure hull.

Ready for launching at the Electric Boat shipyard, the completed hull of a submarine towers over a worker tightening bolts on a hull section (foreground). After launching, submarines were towed to a fitting-out pier (opposite) where technicians installed interior equipment, final wiring and trimwork.

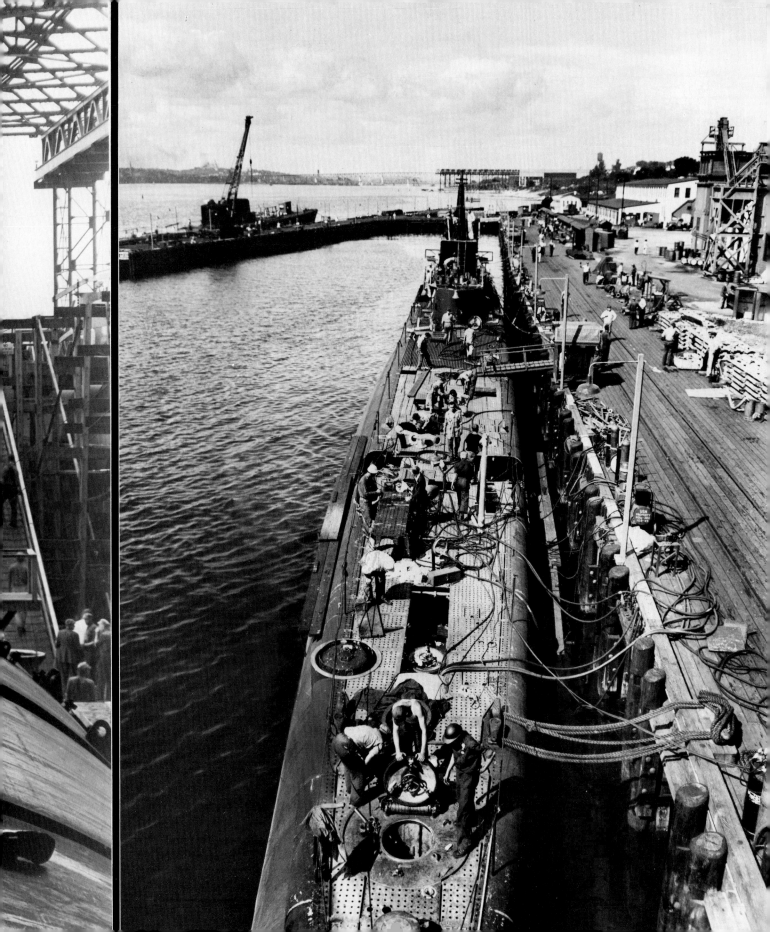

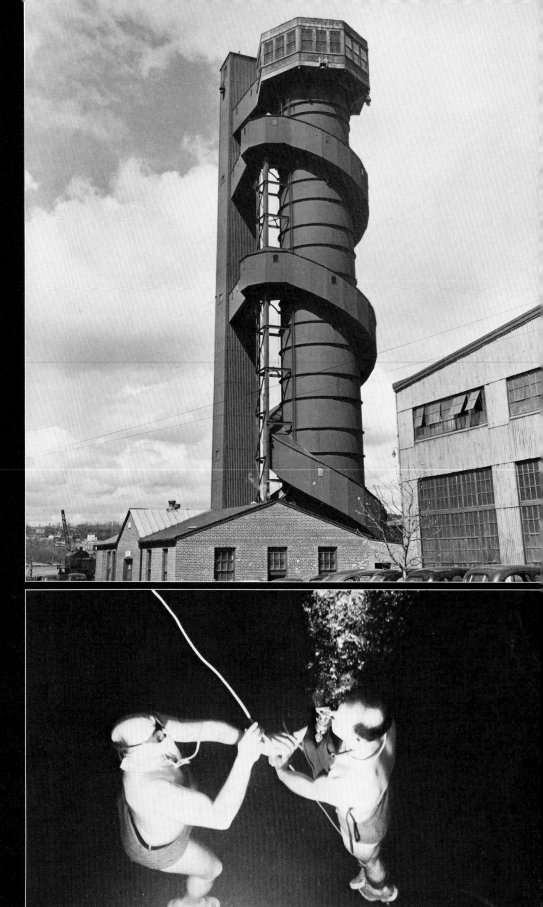

The escape training tank at New London was 118 feet deep and held 250,000 gallons of water. The students entered through four locks, at levels of 18, 50, 100 and 110 feet.

REVOLUTION IN THE SUBMARINE SCHOOL

Early in the War, the Navy's Submarine School near New London was short on almost everything—teachers, classrooms, training equipment, laboratories and barracks—needed for a student body that was increasing by leaps and bounds. The school did not even have a submarine instruction manual. Such difficult subjects as hydraulics and electricity were taught from general college texts or Navy manuals written chiefly for surface ships.

In haste, all that was changed. Building crews swarmed over the grounds, constructing dormitories and classrooms. The school brought in technical writers and professional educators to develop sound courses of instruction. The new curriculum struck a student from a prestigious college as "the toughest academic program I've ever undertaken."

At first the school had only one training device, known as an "attack teacher." This was an outdated World War I periscope simulator with such a limited field of vision that it could focus on only one ship at a time. Soon, however, new equipment arrived—complicated devices that gave students the feel of diving controls, hydraulic systems and sonar equipment.

The improved quality of the course ensured infinitely better submarine crews. When the *Tunny* put out of San Francisco in August of 1942, diving officer Henry Cappello had only three men who were familiar with the electrical gear in the maneuvering room. "Every time I had to take my diving station in the control room, I worried that someone would improperly operate the controls and cause an electrical fire," Cappello recalled.

But by the time Cappello became executive officer of the *Macabi* for her sea trials in 1944, the boat was manned by a different sort of rookie submariner. Cappello said, "It was a new crew but the men did their jobs like veterans. I didn't have to worry any more."

A student breathes through a Momsen Lung as he makes a slow ascent under the watchful eye of a free-diving instructor. The breathing device consisted of a small bag of oxygen and a soda-lime filter, which removed carbon dioxide as the wearer exhaled into the bag.

The attack trainer, a replica of a submarine's conning tower, stands ready for use at the Submarine School. The target, a ship that could be moved around by the teacher to simulate attack problems, was housed one floor above, where it was viewed through a periscope.

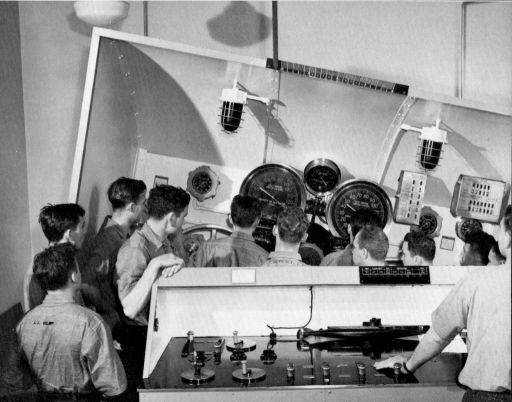

Practicing a dive on an Askania Diving Trainer, seamen steady their hands on duplicates of the instruments that controlled a submarine's exterior planes, which in turn controlled the boat's angle of descent. The large gauges, like those that registered depth on a real boat, show readings that are monitored by the instructor standing behind the console.

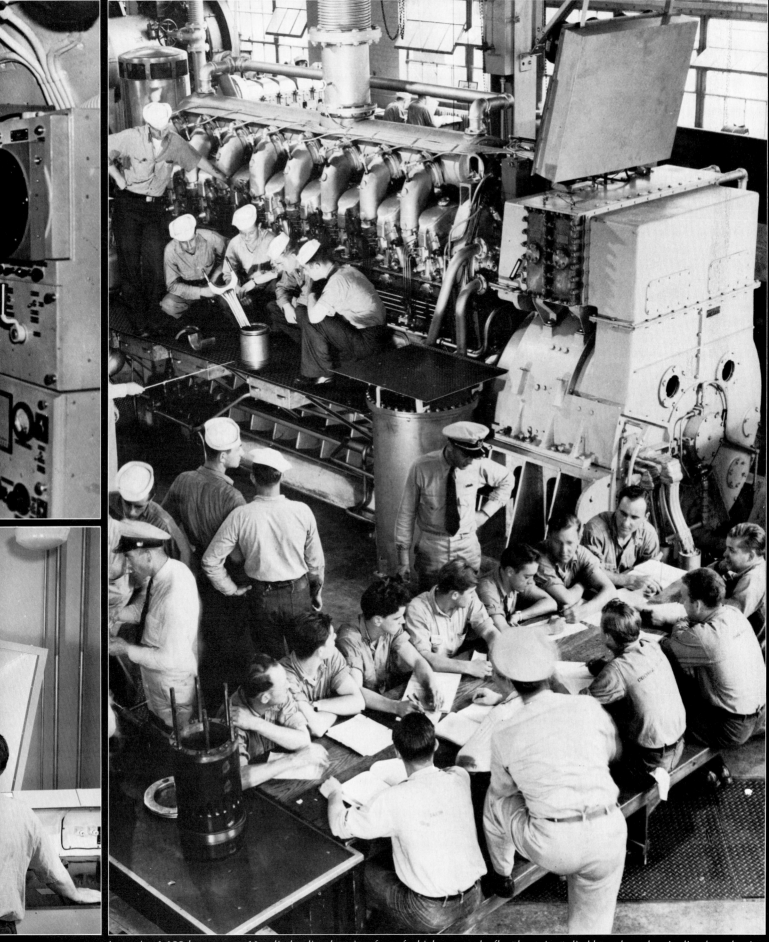

A massive 1,600-horsepower 16-cylinder diesel engine, four of which powered a fleet boat, is studied by a shop class in diesel mechanics.

A boat and a crew are officially joined
in a ceremony that was repeated on 220 U.S.
submarine decks during the Second World
War: Lieut. Commander Joseph Francis Enright,
skipper of the newly built Dace, reads the
order commissioning his boat at New London
on July 21, 1943. The civilian in the party is
L. Y. Spear, president of the firm that built the
submarine, the Electric Boat Company.

To the submariners, stealth was a weapon and secrecy a key to survival. A careless newspaper story could do great damage; for example, the mention of a couple of American submarines that had escaped depth charges might suggest to the Japanese that their destroyers were attacking with their depth charges set to explode too close to the surface to be fully effective. "In an effort probably intended to bolster public morale at home," Admiral Charles Lockwood recalled later, "great pressure was being put on the Navy Department to publish play-by-play accounts of the war. We of the submarines wanted no part of this.

"To keep the enemy guessing about what became of his ships which never reached port would, I felt, not only wear down his nerves but would deny him information on which to base changes in his routings or improve his antisubmarine measures. We wanted him to think that his existing methods were highly effective and that every time he dropped a depth charge, another American submarine went to Davy Jones's locker."

American war correspondents, accustomed to accompanying the surface fleets and hearing the exploits of captains and crews, were with rare exceptions denied access to submarines and submariners. It was primarily because of this that the American press gave to the undersea force the name Silent Service.

Shrouded thus by anonymity, fighting and sometimes dying in secrecy, imperiled not only by their foes but by friends who mistook their identity, sticking together in isolation even during their sojourns ashore, the men of the Silent Service formed the tightest of closed societies.

Within that tiny world, some men soon loomed larger than life, others were inspired by the occasion of crisis and the presence of danger, and a few won immortality by their manner of dying. The boats themselves took on character as individuals, and the stories of particular patrols became sagas of the war under the Pacific. All this was fuel for a spirit that remained unflickering, as the United States submarine force, still struggling to improve its faulty torpedoes and tactics, entered its second full year of combat.

In January 1943, the Pacific war hung briefly in suspended animation. After the great naval battle at Midway, the Japanese, in tacit admission that their empire had reached its far-

2

THE YEAR THAT TURNED THE TIDE

thest expansion, had turned their energies to the urgent business of strengthening the defenses of an island-dotted front that stretched 11,000 miles from Sumatra through the Solomons to the Aleutians. But in a series of vicious surface battles at sea and nightmarish jungle campaigns ashore, American forces had breached the enemy line in two places: Guadalcanal in the southeast Solomons and, some 900 miles to the west, the northeast coast of New Guinea. Now, both sides paused to gather breath and strength for the next phase of the struggle.

For the men and boats of the American submarine service, however, there was no surcease. In January, for example, the *Growler* and the *Wahoo* slipped out to sea from Brisbane, Australia, which had recently been established as a base. Headed for widely separated destinations, they were commanded by vastly different men—each of these men would in his own way contribute greatly to the lore and legend of the Silent Service.

Lieut. Commander Howard W. Gilmore was a relative rarity: He was a onetime enlisted man who had qualified by competitive examination for Annapolis and who had risen to the command of a submarine. "Howard was one of the finest men I ever knew," recalled a fellow officer, "but he was born under an unlucky star." Gilmore still bore the scars left by a peacetime incident in Panama, where thugs had attacked him and slashed his throat. His first wife had died of a crippling disease, and when Gilmore took the *Growler* to war in the Pacific, his second wife was still unconscious from injuries she had suffered in a fall down a flight of stairs.

Dramatic happenings seemed to follow the steady Gilmore. Assigned to the *Growler* in June 1942 on patrol duty in the brutal waters of the Aleutians, Gilmore one day came upon three Japanese destroyers anchored off the Alaskan coast at Kiska. Rather than trying to pick off one destroyer, Gilmore decided to go after all three with a single salvo. In what ranks among the submarine war's more remarkable assaults, Gilmore emptied his bow tubes, loosing one torpedo against each of the two nearer warships and two fish at the other. By a rare piece of good luck in those days of flawed fish, all Gilmore's torpedoes hit—and exploded. The *Arare* sank almost instantly; the *Kasumi* and the *Shiranuhi* were so badly damaged that they had to be towed back

to Japan. In a later 1942 patrol, this time to the East China Sea, Gilmore and the *Growler* sank four enemy ships for a total of 15,000 tons.

Now, at the beginning of 1943, the *Growler* was probing Rabaul, the main remaining Japanese stronghold in the Solomons. Early in the patrol she had sunk the *Chifuku Maru*, a 6,000-ton passenger-cargo vessel. And with six kills now to his credit, Howard Gilmore ranked among the leading American submarine skippers.

Then, early on the morning of February 7, Howard Gilmore's dark star rose in the sky. At 1:10 a.m. the *Growler's* radar raised a blip indicating a small vessel at a distance of 2,000 yards. Gilmore was on the bridge with six of his crew—the officer of the deck, his assistant, the quartermaster and three lookouts. Believing the contact to be a Japanese patrol boat that he had attacked and missed before, Gilmore ordered the *Growler's* crew to battle stations—just as the enemy ship suddenly changed course and came barreling toward the submarine. By the time the men of the *Growler* detected the enemy's charge, the two vessels were on a collision course and closing fast.

"Left full rudder!" shouted Gilmore. But the order came too late. The *Growler* and the *Hayasaki*, a 900-ton Japanese provision boat, came together with a shuddering crash, the submarine striking the Japanese vessel amidships at 17 knots. The boat heeled 50 degrees, flinging men from their feet. Almost at once the Japanese poured heavy machine-gun fire down onto the bridge of the submarine, killing the junior officer of the deck and a lookout. The two other lookouts and Howard Gilmore were wounded.

Below, at the foot of the bridge ladder, the *Growler's* executive officer, Arnold Schade, heard Gilmore's cry through the stuttering roar of the machine gun: "Clear the bridge!" The officer of the deck and the quartermaster came down the ladder above Schade, dragging the two wounded lookouts through the hatch. Gilmore did not appear. Instead, Schade heard only the shouted command by which Gilmore, seeking to save his submarine, sealed his own fate: "Take her down!"

Schade hesitated. But Gilmore's order was clear, and it was Schade's duty to do his best for the *Growler*. He closed and dogged the hatch and sounded the required two blasts of the diving alarm. The *Growler* went under, leaving

Howard Gilmore still on deck; he was last seen clinging to a bridge frame.

Schade quickly assessed the damages. Salt water was pouring in through bullet holes in the *Growler's* conning tower. The pump room and the engine room were beginning to flood. In addition, when the wounded boat finally surfaced, Schade found that 18 feet of the bow had been crushed and slued to port at a right angle. The crew's makeshift repairs kept the boat going, and although she was exceedingly difficult to handle, the *Growler* managed to limp back to Brisbane.

For sacrificing himself so that his boat might fight again, Gilmore was posthumously awarded the Medal of Honor, the first submarine officer to be so recognized. American submariners never forgot Howard Gilmore's last words: "Take her down!"

The other Brisbane boat that made submarine legend that January of 1943 was the *Wahoo*. She was a veteran of two wartime patrols, both of them disappointing. It had seemed, recalled an officer, as though the *Wahoo* and her crew had "waited in the wrong places at the wrong time like unlucky fishermen." The submarine's first commander had been relieved and replaced by a skipper who, on the basis of his record up to that time, seemed unlikely to improve the fortunes of the *Wahoo*.

He was a big man from Kentucky named Dudley W. Morton and he was referred to as "Mush" after a rawboned Kentuckian with that name in the *Moon Mullins* comic strip. Morton had taken command of the old *Dolphin* after skipper Gordon Rainer suffered a breakdown on his disastrous first patrol and was sent home. Morton did not in the least like what he found. "The *Dolphin* is a death trap," he told the executive officer. "I'm going to try to get off her. I advise you to do the same."

Morton got off, all right, although not by choice. After the *Dolphin's* return from postrepair sea trials, her division commander found that the boat was still in poor condition and declared that "Morton was incompetent to fix it." Mush Morton was removed from command. He was headed out of the submarine service when he was saved by the intervention of a superior officer, the *Wahoo's* squadron commander, John H. Brown. Brown had greatly admired Mush

Morton as a Naval Academy football star. Besides, said Brown, "I like the way Morton shakes hands."

Brown's instinctive judgment was to be proved eminently right. Saved for the service, Morton eventually got the *Wahoo*, where he quickly set about reviving the spirits of the discouraged crew. Among Morton's first acts, he assembled the boat's company on deck and dictated the terms under which his men would serve. "*Wahoo* is expendable," declared Morton. "We will take every reasonable precaution, but our mission is to sink enemy shipping. Now, if anyone doesn't want to go along, under these conditions, just see the yeoman. I am giving him verbal authority now to transfer anyone who is not a volunteer."

There were no requests for transfer. Moreover, recalled an enlisted man, the *Wahoo* thereafter seemed to be a better boat: "I could feel the stirring of a strong spirit growing in her. The officers acted differently. The men felt differently."

On this first patrol as the *Wahoo's* commander, Morton showed an easy, confident style. Lieutenant George Grider, the *Wahoo's* engineering and diving officer, later wrote: "He was always roaming around the narrow quarters, his big hands reaching out to examine equipment, his wide-set eyes missing nothing. He was built like a bear, and as playful as a cub. His authority was built-in and never depended on sudden stiffening of tone or attitude. Whether he was in the control room, swapping tall tales with Russell Rau, the chief of the boat, or wandering restlessly about in his skivvies, talking to the men in the torpedo and engine rooms, he was as relaxed as a baby. The men were not merely ready to follow him, they were eager to."

Considerably less confidence was inspired by the *Wahoo's* executive officer, Lieutenant Richard Hetherington O'Kane, with his tight lips, burning eyes and noisy ways. "He talked a great deal—reckless, aggressive talk," wrote Grider, "and it was natural to wonder how much of it was no more than talk. One day he would be a martinet, and the next he would display an over-lenient, what-the-hell attitude that was far from reassuring."

The crew's initial uneasy feelings about O'Kane were only increased when Morton placed upon him an unusual responsibility. It was Mush Morton's firm conviction that the executive officer, not the skipper, should handle the submarine's periscope. Morton's system, Grider explained,

Amid the symbols of victory, two exultant crewmen stand on the ice-caked deck of the S-32 as she enters the U.S. naval base at Dutch Harbor, Alaska, after a 1943 war patrol in the Pacific. The broomstick lashed to the forward periscope indicated that the boat claimed a clean sweep— the sinking of all enemy ships attacked—while the Japanese flags on her flank tallied the claimed kill: three warships and two merchant vessels. The lacy pennant pinned to the after periscope was probably a woman's garment, suggesting that the crew's shore leave was long overdue.

"left the skipper in a better position to interpret all factors involved, do a better conning job, and make decisions more dispassionately."

Morton's orders were to patrol in the Caroline Islands. On the way to his station, he was to look in at a New Guinea harbor called Wewak, where the Japanese reportedly had a supply base. But at the time, American charts of those remote seas and shorelines were rudimentary, and the *Wahoo's* officers could find no mention whatever of Wewak. The problem was solved by a motor machinist's mate, D. C. Keeter, who went to Grider with a high school geography book he had bought in a Brisbane shop. Keeter pointed to a map of the New Guinea coast and asked, "Hey, is that the Wewak we're going to?"

Using the latitude and longitude references given in Keeter's book, the *Wahoo's* officers placed Wewak at a previously unmarked point on their Navy chart. Then they contrived a blowup of the area by using an enlarger made from a signal lamp and the lens from George Grider's old Graflex camera. "It might have made a cartographer shudder," Grider later said, "but it was a long way ahead of no chart at all."

On the morning of January 24, the *Wahoo* submerged to periscope depth and crept into Wewak harbor with Dick O'Kane taking frequent brief peeks through the periscope. As O'Kane called directions, the *Wahoo* dodged patrol boats and narrowly avoided a reef. At one point O'Kane saw a Japanese in a white shirt squatting under a coconut palm; by good fortune the lookout did not see the boat. After taking the *Wahoo* nine miles into the harbor, O'Kane sighted a destroyer, apparently at anchor, and got a bearing.

"Down scope!" snapped O'Kane. Morton called the crew to battle stations and ordered the forward torpedo doors to be opened. Then O'Kane flipped his thumbs up to indicate that he wanted one more look. What he saw was the enemy destroyer, now under way, gathering speed—and heading out of the harbor.

Morton fired three torpedoes. All three missed, and then the destroyer turned toward the *Wahoo*. Morton fired another. It missed. Morton fired his next to last forward fish at the narrow, onrushing bow. It missed. He fired the last one and yelled, "Take her deep!"

The *Wahoo* went under, her crewmen in a kind of frozen calm. They were trapped, fearful of going too deep; lacking good charts, they had no way of telling how much water lay under the keel.

In the confined harbor, the destroyer had to know precisely where they were. A tremendous explosion shook the submarine; light bulbs shattered and bits of cork broke away from the bulkheads. It was, the men knew, the first of many depth charges sure to come. "We waited for the second blast," Grider recalled, "each man lost within himself, looking at objects rather than other men, no eyes meeting."

They waited. There was no second blast; 10, 20, then 30 seconds passed, and finally a dazed voice came from the pump room, saying, "Jeez. Maybe *we* hit *him*."

From the conning tower came Morton's yell of laughter. "Well, by God, maybe we did. Bring her up."

At periscope depth, the crew took turns crowding to the eyepiece to watch the destroyer slowly going under, men swarming over deck and rigging. A gun crew was still firing at the *Wahoo's* periscope as the warship went down. Morton claimed the sinking and received credit for it. However, the Japanese later were able to raise the destroyer and restore her to service, and after a review of Japanese records the credit was canceled.

For Dick O'Kane, the terrifying experience had been one of fulfillment. Recalled Grider: "It was as if, during all the talkative, boastful months before, he had been lost, seeking his true element, and now it was found. He was calm, terse and utterly cool. My opinion of him underwent a permanent change. It was the most dramatic example I was ever to see of a man transformed under pressure from what seemed almost adolescent petulance to a prime fighting machine."

Once out of Wewak, Morton set course for the *Wahoo's* patrol station in the Carolines. He never got there. Two days later, slightly north of the Equator, smoke was sighted over the horizon. The *Wahoo* tracked on the surface, submerged to wait and intercepted what at first appeared to be two freighters. Morton fired four fish, heard three hits and went deep to reload. When the submarine ascended to periscope depth four minutes later, one freighter was sinking and the second, crippled, was steaming slowly toward the submarine, obviously attempting to ram. To O'Kane's surprise, a third ship, a huge transport, came up in the periscope eye only 1,800 yards away. Morton made a quick setup on the transport, fired three forward tubes, then turned and fired one fish head-on at the oncoming freighter. Then the Wahoo dived to 100 feet. During the descent she felt the shock of explosions as her torpedoes struck.

Morton, now down to nine torpedoes, reloaded and resurfaced. The wounded freighter had turned and was now trying to get away. The transport was dead in the water. Morton, a fierce joy in his eyes, prepared to finish her off. The job took two torpedoes. The first, as so often happened, was a dud, but the second hit under the stack and blew the midship section into the sky. As the big ship rolled ponderously, hundreds of men fell, jumped, slipped and slid into the sea. The bow dipped, the stern rose and the ship went to the bottom.

Morton turned the Wahoo to pursue the crippled freighter, but the submarine, her batteries depleted during hours of submerged running, lost ground. Morton returned and surfaced where the transport had gone down.

"The water was so thick with enemy soldiers that it was literally impossible to cruise through them without pushing them aside like driftwood," recalled Grider. "These troops we knew had been bound for New Guinea to fight and kill our men." Some of the soldiers did fight, firing machine guns and small arms at the Wahoo from motor launches, cabin cruisers and lifeboats. Morton ordered his deck guns manned and told the men to open fire on the Japanese boats. The gun battle went on for about 20 minutes. Then Morton quit and set off, still on the surface, in pursuit of the damaged freighter that had managed to get away.

He found the ship about sundown, now in company with a tanker. The Wahoo fired three torpedoes at the tanker, scoring at least one hit. That left the Wahoo with only four torpedoes, all aft. The two enemy ships were still trying to get away, zigzagging wildly. At last Morton solved the pattern of the tanker's zigs and hit her with two torpedoes. The freighter continued to evade the submarine until a searchlight—probably from still another Japanese ship—suddenly appeared on the horizon. Evidently thinking help was on the way, the freighter's captain stopped zigging and headed straight for the light.

Morton fired his last two torpedoes at long range. Within moments, both fish hit and the freighter, dying swiftly after its daylong struggle for survival, sank at last.

That night, Morton got off a laconic report that he had sunk an entire convoy of four enemy ships. Admiral Lockwood sent a reply: COME ON HOME, MUSH. YOUR PICTURE'S ON THE PIANO.

When the Wahoo returned to the submarine base at Pearl Harbor, she flaunted a broom lashed to her mast—symbolic of her clean sweep. Two weeks later she was out once more, heading for the Yellow Sea, between Korea and the coast of China. She returned early in April, once again out of torpedoes and once again displaying a broom. She had sunk nine ships in 10 days and Admiral Lockwood began calling her "the one-boat wolf pack." O'Kane and Grider, moving up in rank toward commands of their own, were transferred to other boats.

In October 1943, only 10 months after Mush Morton's meteoric career on the Wahoo had begun, it ended. On Oc-

Running at high speed, a U.S. submarine reveals her presence with 12 feet of periscope, extended to search for Japanese ships in the distance. As a boat closed in on her target, she normally showed less than one foot of her periscope; the submarine would be all but invisible to enemy lookouts at a distance of about 1,200 yards, the average range at which American skippers fired their torpedoes.

IDENTIFICATION INDEX

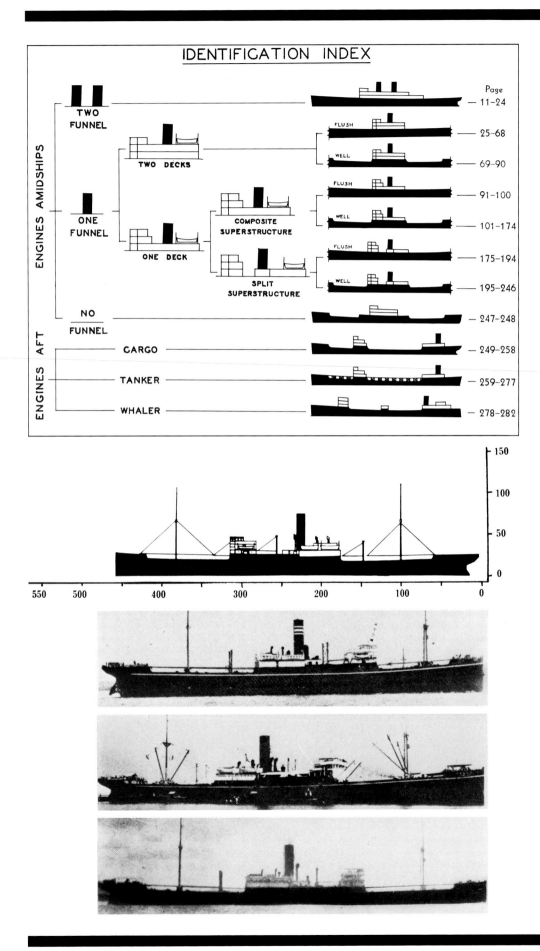

			Page
TWO FUNNEL			11–24
ONE FUNNEL	**TWO DECKS**	FLUSH	25–68
		WELL	69–90
	ONE DECK — **COMPOSITE SUPERSTRUCTURE**	FLUSH	91–100
		WELL	101–174
	SPLIT SUPERSTRUCTURE	FLUSH	175–194
		WELL	195–246
NO FUNNEL			247–248

ENGINES AMIDSHIPS

ENGINES AFT

	Page
CARGO	249–258
TANKER	259–277
WHALER	278–282

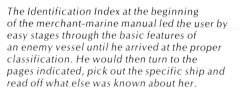

The Identification Index at the beginning of the merchant-marine manual led the user by easy stages through the basic features of an enemy vessel until he arrived at the proper classification. He would then turn to the pages indicated, pick out the specific ship and read off what else was known about her.

For each class of merchant ship, the manual provided a silhouette, with scales showing the height and length of the vessel, as well as photos that disclosed such other characteristics of the class as cargo-handling gear and bridge details. According to the Identification Index above, the vessel shown here is a one-funnel, one-deck, split-superstructure freighter—a group dealt with in a 50-page section. She is one of a class of three 7,000-ton ships (left), built in 1920, with a cruising speed of 12 knots and operated by a crew of 65.

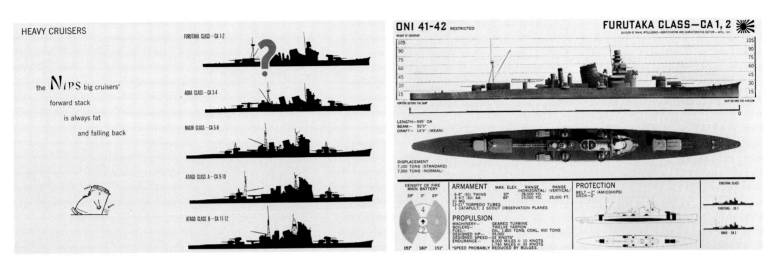

HEAVY CRUISERS

FURUTAKA CLASS—CA 1-2

the N*ips* big cruisers'

forward stack

is always fat

and falling back

AOBA CLASS—CA 3-4

NACHI CLASS—CA 5-8

ATAGO CLASS A—CA 9-10

ATAGO CLASS B—CA 11-12

ONI 41-42 RESTRICTED

FURUTAKA CLASS—CA 1, 2

DIVISION OF NAVAL INTELLIGENCE—IDENTIFICATION AND CHARACTERISTICS SECTION—APRIL 1943

LENGTH—595' OA
BEAM— 50'9"
DRAFT— 14'9" (MEAN)

DISPLACEMENT
7,100 TONS (STANDARD)
7,500 TONS (NORMAL)

DENSITY OF FIRE MAIN BATTERY	ARMAMENT			PROTECTION
	6-8" (50) TWINS MAX. ELEV. 30° RANGE (HORIZONTAL) 28,000 YD. RANGE (VERTICAL)	BELT—2" (AMIDSHIPS) DECK—2"		

ARMAMENT
6-8" (50) TWINS MAX. ELEV. 30° RANGE (HORIZONTAL) 28,000 YD.
4-4½" (50) AA 85° 19,000 YD. RANGE (VERTICAL) 25,000 FT.
10 MG
12-21" TORPEDO TUBES
1 CATAPULT; 2 SCOUT OBSERVATION PLANES

PROTECTION
BELT—2" (AMIDSHIPS)
DECK—2"

PROPULSION
MACHINERY— GEARED TURBINE
BOILERS— TWELVE YARROW
FUEL— OIL, 1,800 TONS; COAL, 400 TONS
DESIGNED HP— 95,000
DESIGNED SPEED—33 KNOTS*
ENDURANCE— 8,000 MILES @ 10 KNOTS
1,740 MILES @ 33 KNOTS
*SPEED PROBABLY REDUCED BY BULGES.

The submarines' warship-recognition manual included several pages of memory aids in doggerel. The question mark indicates a class of two heavy cruisers that may have been sunk.

A page in the manual summarizes all the essential information on the two-ship Furutaka class. Built in 1926, these heavy cruisers weighed 7,500 tons and carried 8-inch guns.

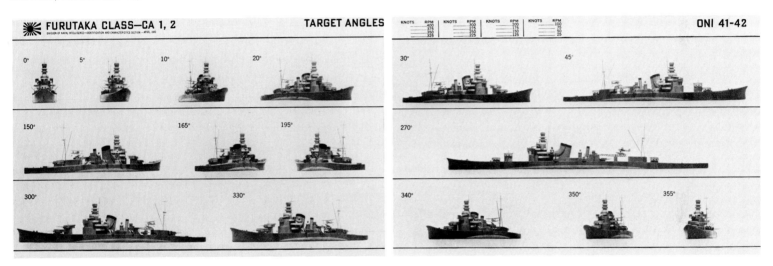

FURUTAKA CLASS—CA 1, 2
DIVISION OF NAVAL INTELLIGENCE—IDENTIFICATION AND CHARACTERISTICS SECTION—APRIL 1943

TARGET ANGLES

ONI 41-42

KNOTS	RPM	KNOTS	RPM	KNOTS	RPM	KNOTS	RPM

0°   5°   10°   20°   30°   45°

150°   165°   195°   270°

300°   330°   340°   350°   355°

Detailed models of each warship class were shown at various angles; this aided quick recognition of a target not seen in full profile, and helped to establish torpedo-firing data.

A PERISCOPE'S-EYE GUIDE TO ENEMY SHIPS

While stealthily pursuing a Japanese warship or merchant convoy, the skipper of an American submarine periodically ran his periscope up and called out a description of the vessel or vessels ahead. To identify the target the commander described, the tracking party in the conning tower thereupon searched through two recognition manuals: thick, loose-leaf notebooks that contained silhouettes, photos and specifications of every known type and class of Japanese vessel.

The books, supplied by Naval Intelligence, did not compare enemy vessels with U.S. ships, as did aircraft recognition manuals; the submarines almost always hunted in waters traveled only by Japanese. However, precise target identification served two useful purposes. It enabled the Navy to keep an accurate tally of the types and tonnage of ships sunk. And it provided the skippers with valuable attack information.

The 294-page book devoted to the Imperial Navy illustrated and described nearly 600 warships; their specifications forewarned the skippers of the armaments they would confront in the attack. The second

book, only slightly less bulky, helped the skippers choose the larger of two targets of similar design and size, and thus use their 24 torpedoes to best effect. The merchant-ship manual was conveniently arranged according to the number of funnels and the type of superstructure—the first distinguishable parts of a distant target. Other details narrowed the identification to a specific class and even a single vessel.

Identification had to be done quickly. Once the American torpedo hit, Japanese escorts would come roaring after the submarine. The skipper would have to dive and—as one commander said—"get the hell somewhere else in a hurry."

tober 5, the Japanese news agency Domei announced the loss of the 8,000-ton transport *Konron Maru,* with all 544 men aboard, to a submarine off the west coast of Honshu, where Morton was patrolling. Morton did not report the sinking. No word ever came from the *Wahoo,* and the U.S. Navy never learned her fate—whether she was lost to some unrecorded enemy action or perished in a tragedy at sea.

As 1943 wore on, the submarine force, fortified by the success of such men as Morton, grew steadily bolder. Night attacks on the surface became the preferred tactic. One version of the tactic was named after a football play—the "end around." In the maneuver, the submarine would run past the target on a parallel course but out of sight, and lie in wait for the victim to come up within range. This move was made possible by the fleet boat's high surface speed, up to 21 knots in a newer submarine. This was considerably faster than most merchantmen could steam and faster than many warships usually cruised. The great advantage, of course, was that once the boat had reached her ambush position ahead of the target, the skipper could line up a perfect shot at his leisure. Often a single fish perfectly placed sent the enemy to the bottom.

Along with new techniques, the submariners were getting new tools. One of them was the so-called SJ radar, which supplemented the outmoded SD model.

The SJ's beam was more powerful and therefore its range was greater. In addition, its parabolic reflector antenna was beamed for surface vessels, not for aircraft as that of the SD had been. Good as it was, the SJ became even better when its capabilities were enhanced by the plan position indicator (PPI), a viewing scope that showed the relative positions and distances of all blips within reach of the radar impulse more or less as a geographical presentation on a cathode-ray tube. If, for example, the submarine found herself near a convoy, the skipper could see the disposition and the relative sizes of all enemy units, and he could select his targets with an almost godlike omniscience.

Another attack aid that underwent steady refinement was the target bearing transmitter (TBT). In earlier days, the only way for a skipper on the bridge to advise the plotting crew in the conning tower of the bearing of a target was to yell this intelligence down the hatch. Finding the bearing was doubly difficult in the dark, and some skippers, particularly on the ill-equipped old S-boats, tried to make do with a crude arrangement of brads nailed around the circumference of a pelorus, or bearing circle. To use the device, a captain would sight the darker blob of darkness that was his target, then feel out the bearing by running his fingers around the circle of brads.

The TBT was a vast improvement. The mechanism consisted of a pair of powerful night binoculars fixed to a rotating base, whose bearing was continuously and automatically transmitted to a repeater in the conning tower. The captain on the bridge would press a button located on the base of the binoculars, signifying that he had focused on the target. The operator of the torpedo data computer (TDC) would then enter the exact bearing, and the TDC would calculate the proper firing angle and automatically feed the information into the directional gyro mechanism in the torpedo itself. When the submarine was underwater, the bearing was read off the periscope.

Another device, the bathythermograph, made life in a combat submarine safer. The submariners had known for a long time that two layers of water might differ sharply in temperature, and that this phenomenon would bend or even reflect sound waves, thereby throwing off an enemy's echo-ranging sonar gear. Therefore it was distinctly beneficial to find and get below a layer of water that was either colder or warmer than the one above it. The bathythermograph provided the necessary information. It permanently registered on a graph the degrees of temperature changes and the depths at which they occurred. In so doing, it pointed out possible thermal hiding places for skippers and their submarines.

Some of the submarines in the Pacific were seriously handicapped by engines of a type that had never worked satisfactorily. The flaw in the HOR engine—which was manufactured by the Hoover-Owens-Rentschler Company, an American subsidiary of a German firm—lay in its gear train: The gear-wheel teeth constantly broke, causing wild vibrations that eventually knocked out the engine. Far better engines made by General Motors and Fairbanks Morse had long been coming into service, but a few of the HORs (the submariners had come to call the engines by a phonetic nickname describing an ancient profession) still remained.

"Whiskers," the title of this photograph from the scrapbook of skipper Creed Burlingame, shows the Silversides' bearded crew on their return to Pearl Harbor from war patrol in January 1943. Though beards and mustaches were not officially banned in the U.S. Navy, most captains of spit-and-polish surface ships frowned on facial hair. Informality was the rule on the boats (note the man at rear with an Australian digger's hat).

One of the last submarines equipped with HOR engines made an outstanding patrol in spite of their usual malfunctioning. The boat was the *Gurnard,* and her mission began in June of 1943 under Charles Herbert Andrews. Hardly had the *Gurnard* left Pearl Harbor to patrol the Palaus when the gears on her HOR engines began to strip. Andrews probably should have returned to port for repairs but he kept the boat going, for he had something to prove to himself.

Andrews was a small man, only five feet four inches tall. "When I was a little kid" he said, "I was considered a sissy. I was the only boy in a house with three older sisters. My mother dressed me in velvet pants and Buster Brown collars." As a consequence, when he found himself going into combat many years later, "I felt a strong drive to carry my own weight."

After reaching the Palaus, Andrews enjoyed playing a sort of silent tag with the Japanese destroyers that moved in and out of the harbor entrances; he would surface to taunt them, then dive to elude them. By this method, recalled Andrews, "I worked up a little contempt for them."

One morning, while Andrews was playing his dangerous game near a lagoon entrance at 90 feet, the *Gurnard* was rocked by two depth charges. "It was a hell of a blast," An-

drews said later. "They went off under us, blowing us upward with a terrific up angle." The *Gurnard* was in imminent danger of broaching. "Flood everything," shouted the executive officer. "Flood! Get her *down!*"

The submarine refused to respond properly—the blasts had knocked out electrical connections and with them automatic control over the diving planes. There were manual controls, but the heavy wheels were spinning so wildly that no one could handle them. When the engineering officer, a 225-pounder, tried to grapple with the wheel for the bow planes he was hurled across the control room and knocked unconscious.

Andrews, desperately trying to lower the bow, sent 50 men rushing to the forward torpedo room, an uphill climb as the boat lay. "That did it," he later reported. "We started down like a rock."

Now the nature of peril was reversed: The *Gurnard* was diving at a steep angle and going fast into dangerous depths. Andrews ordered Executive Officer Robert E. Ward to get the men back out of the torpedo room and send them aft. The gasping crewmen climbed to the stern and the *Gurnard* again overreacted. With the bow now pointing up steeply, the depth gauge in the control room showed 495 feet; Andrews estimated the aft torpedo room must be nearly 530

feet down—and in imminent peril of being crushed by the immense pressure of water outside.

The *Gurnard* was sorely in need of a savior and at this critical moment one came to her rescue. He was an electrician, Chief W. F. Fritsch, and he came up with an inspired improvisation to supply power to the submarine's useless diving planes. Lacking any other tool at the moment, Fritsch grabbed a wet toothbrush and shoved it between two severed electrical connections. Current flowed. The planes worked again and the *Gurnard*, at last, righted herself. Somehow, making further patchwork repairs as best they could, Andrews and his *Gurnard* submariners lasted out the depth-charge attack.

Soon after her time of greatest crisis, the *Gurnard* came up and sighted a Japanese convoy emerging from a lagoon. Andrews attacked in the face of numerous escorts. He hit two freighters and a destroyer and believed that all three sank. With the remaining escorts charging, Andrews prudently took the *Gurnard* deep.

Even as the submarine endured depth charges, her crew worked to reload. But only three forward tubes were ready when Andrews impatiently rose to periscope depth—and, to his delight, saw a Japanese aircraft carrier standing out of the harbor. "I was surprised," Andrews said later, "because the Japs knew we were sitting right out there." The *Gurnard* fired the three forward fish at 1,800 yards, then swung around and let go a torpedo from the stern. Andrews thought he had got two solid hits, and when he put the periscope up again he saw the carrier dead in the water, listing and smoking. Escorts saved the damaged carrier by preventing the *Gurnard* from attacking again.

Without further mischance, the *Gurnard* returned to Pearl Harbor. Andrews received a Navy Cross for what his division commander called "one of the finest, most aggressive first patrols on record." Chief Fritsch got a Silver Star for his expert use of the toothbrush, and best of all, the submarine base commanders scheduled the *Gurnard* to receive new engines in place of her troublesome HORs.

By July of 1943, the only major tract of enemy water still unmolested by U.S. submarines was the Sea of Japan, between the home islands and the Asian mainland. The Sea of Japan was accessible by four straits: Tsushima in the south, Bungo between Kyushu and Honshu, Tsugaru between Honshu and Hokkaido, and La Pérouse in the far north between Hokkaido and Sakhalin Island. Admiral Lockwood had long cast an enterprising eye on the Sea of Japan, reasoning that its protected waterways must certainly be used by enemy ships galore.

The problem was how to penetrate the narrow gateways. Both the straits of Tsushima and Tsugaru were believed to be heavily mined against both surface and undersea vessels. La Pérouse, frozen in the winter months, was probably mined deep against submarines. But since Japan and the Soviet Union were at peace and Soviet surface ships used La Pérouse Strait, it seemed unlikely that any mines would be set shallow enough to endanger surface ships. On this assumption, Lockwood proposed to send a submarine expedition through La Pérouse on the surface at night. If successful, the mission might mark a significant advance in the submarine strategy of the United States. In the event—although the basic fact would remain unrecognized until almost the end of the War—the first thrust into the Sea of Japan disclosed that Japan, still seemingly formidable in the farthest reaches of its empire, was pathetically weak within its citadel waters.

On the night of July 4, three submarines—the *Lapon*, commanded by Oliver Kirk, the *Plunger*, under Raymond Bass, and Wreford G. Chapple's *Permit*—made the much-feared penetration. It was a watchful, nerve-racking trip, but an anticlimactic one. The boats got through the narrow passage with only a small incident: The *Permit* hit the bottom and damaged her sonar head.

Now the three boats deployed for an attack plan that was calculated to sample the hunting and get them out of the area before the enemy could organize countermeasures. The *Lapon* peeled off from the little group and moved toward the southern end of the Sea of Japan. To give her time to reach her position, the *Permit* and the *Plunger* were to hold their fire in northern waters until midnight of July 7. At that point, the three boats would commence hunting and, after exactly 96 hours, bolt for the exit.

While waiting for the *Lapon* to reach station, the *Permit* and the *Plunger* saw numerous targets, invitingly lighted up and steaming along without zigzagging. The crews looked forward to a turkey shoot. But when the appointed attack time arrived, the Japanese shipping—for no discernible reason—had virtually vanished.

The *Lapon,* far to the south, was plagued by fog and radar malfunctions; she saw little and got nothing. The *Plunger* sank a small freighter. The *Permit* got a merchant ship but, while surfacing after the attack, she had an accident. A huge wave flooded the conning tower and control room and wrecked the SJ radar. Thereafter the boat was electronically blind, and she sank only one more small vessel.

The short hunting season drew to a close and the three boats headed for the exit. The journey was uneventful for the *Lapon* and the *Plunger*. But as the *Permit* made her way out on the surface, she fired several shots from her 4-inch deck gun at what Chapple took to be a Japanese picket boat. His gunners soon scored a hit, at which point the ship broke out a white flag. Chapple brought the submarine alongside the sinking vessel—and discovered to his consternation that he had an international crisis on his hands: He had been shelling a Soviet trawler. One man was dead and another dying. There were five women in the crew and they had shrapnel wounds.

Chapple took aboard 13 passengers, including the dying man, and once out of the strait radioed headquarters for permission to land them on Soviet soil. Admiral Lockwood, fearing Soviet reprisal, ordered Chapple to take his guests to Dutch Harbor in Alaska. En route, the *Permit's* crew treated the Russians as royally as a submarine's limited facilities allowed, and the women became so fond of their hosts that they wept when they were put ashore. As for the Russian captain, he gratefully reported to his government that he had been attacked by an unidentified submarine—and that the *Permit* had come nobly to the rescue.

The material results of the first American foray into the Sea of Japan were meager indeed. But a trail had been blazed into a rich hunting ground; it would later be exploited to the full. And for the present, the submariners' morale was given a big lift by their invasion of what they called "the Emperor's wading pool."

Soon after the mission into the Sea of Japan, there arrived on the watery battlefield a new fleet boat, the *Puffer*. She was sleek and deadly. Yet her first patrol proved, if any proof were needed, that a modern boat was still terribly vulnerable, and that every submarine and her crew were locked in an unbreakable life-or-death relationship.

The trouble began when the *Puffer* reached Makassar Strait between Borneo and Celebes. Skipper Marvin Jensen attacked an apparently unescorted merchantman and hit her with two torpedoes. The ship was severely damaged. Jensen was maneuvering the *Puffer* for another attack when his soundman reported the pinging of enemy sonar. As Jensen went deep, a half-dozen depth charges exploded nearby, springing some of the hatches. Sea water gushed into the submarine. Miraculously, this problem lasted only a few seconds; the hatches settled back onto their gaskets. But another, more critical, problem loomed. A sea-valve plug in the after torpedo room was loosened and a thin, flat stream of water the size of a knife blade jetted into the boat. The crewmen were helpless; they dared not tighten the plug for fear of rupturing the valve. The *Puffer* was still seaworthy, but her troubles were just beginning.

The attacking vessel was a 500-ton *Chidori*-class submarine chaser, and the Japanese captain was dismayingly persistent. Hour after hour he circled around, dropping his depth charges often enough to fray the nerves of the *Puffer's* crew, relentlessly pursuing and countering every evasive action Jensen took.

At 5:25 a.m. on October 9, the skipper went down deep to wait out the pursuer. Shutting off the air conditioning and the blowers to reduce every giveaway noise, he descended far beyond the boat's 300-foot test depth. When the *Puffer* finally leveled off, she had 500 feet of water above her conning tower—and plenty of water inside her as well. The boat was slowly flooding and getting heavier aft—her trim pump had stopped working. As time passed, depth control became barely manageable.

The air grew hot and foul. Carbon dioxide built up steadily, and even the use of bottled oxygen failed to make the air fit to breathe. The men sweated profusely; they wiped themselves with towels, but were immediately drenched by fresh rivulets of perspiration. Moisture dripped from the hull and the decks grew slippery.

After 12 hours, around 6:00 p.m., the *Puffer's* tormenter was joined by another Japanese submarine chaser. The depth charges came faster.

Throughout the boat, the crewmen's one overwhelming

A submariner reads in his torpedo-room bunk. Nearly half the crew slept among the tin fish.

EIGHTY MEN LIVING CHEEK BY JOWL

Surface sailors viewed submarines as cold, dank, seagoing dungeons. This was slightly inaccurate. Though a 1940s fleet boat might have more than 80 men crammed into an equipment-filled space no bigger than three boxcars, the crewmen made that space remarkably livable, ate the best food in the Navy and, except when the boat was battened down for combat, went about in air-conditioned comfort.

The men put up with annoyances, of course. Everything aboard, including their clothes and bedding, was covered with a smelly film of oil. And new submariners had to resign themselves to dodging pro-

In the crew's head, a sailor uses a washer run on water condensed from the air conditioning.

Motor machinist's mates monitor the two huge

jecting valve handles, waiting their turn at the three heads and getting along without a moment's privacy through a two-month-long patrol. Yet for all the inconvenience there was surprisingly little friction among the crew members.

On patrol, the men often contended with weeks of boredom between periods of furious action. But there was ample recompense. Daily routine was easy and discipline was only strict enough to maintain the efficiency and teamwork of the tight-knit little society. The crewmen slept a lot and whiled away the hours reading, playing cards and acey-deucey (a version of backgammon), and trading ribald stories about everyone aboard. They made, as one skipper noted, "a damn good time out of practically nothing."

A card game draws an off-duty crowd in the mess, a 24-hour center for coffee and snacks.

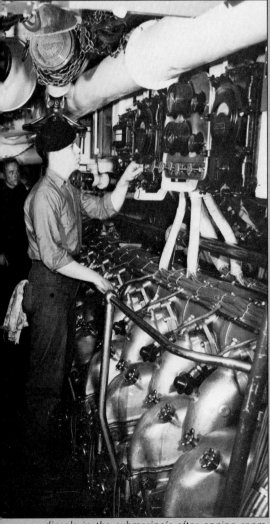

diesels in the submarine's after engine room.

A pair of crewmen overhaul a 20mm gun while others relax inside the after torpedo room.

emotion was anger. Their fury was both general and specific. They hated themselves for getting into this fix, despised themselves as fools for volunteering in submarines. They hated the Japanese captains and discussed ways of getting at them. They conceived of such bizarre notions as somehow surfacing and spreading the sea with acid to eat the bottoms out of the Japanese vessels. But they were imprisoned and helpless in their brand-new boat.

Time ceased to exist; the crew knew nothing but agonizing thirst. By now the men were dehydrated and suffering from heat exhaustion. In this condition, they could not replenish their body fluids; everything they drank they immediately vomited up again. Some men sank into a stupor so deep they could not be roused to stand watch. The men who were still mobile suffered under the slightest temperature change; when they moved from the maneuvering room, where the thermometer read 125° F., into the cooler after torpedo room, where it was over 100°, they were wracked by chills and shivering.

The *Puffer's* harrowing ordeal finally ended at 7:10 p.m. on the 10th of October, 37 hours and 45 minutes after it began, when Jensen took a chance and surfaced. He found that the enemy ships had given up the submarine for dead and departed. The *Puffer* had gone deeper and stayed longer than her designers had conceived in their most optimistic estimates. Thereafter her skipper and crew had an almost superstitious faith in her ability to survive. They would not be disappointed. The boat would live through the War and sink eight enemy ships totaling 38,707 tons.

Even as the *Puffer* was undergoing her lonely trial, Admiral Lockwood was readying an experiment in which groups of submarines would support one another and work in concert. The idea was not new, of course. The wolf packs of German U-boats commanded by Admiral Karl Dönitz had been the scourge of Atlantic shipping all through 1942 and well into 1943. Now that more submarines were coming from U.S. shipyards, Lockwood decided to try the tactic in the Pacific, and he put his skippers to work rehearsing their moves in an odd setting—on the one-foot-square black and white tiles of the dance hall in the officers' club at the Pearl Harbor submarine base.

Some senior officers were dubious about the whole no-tion, especially since the Allies, by dint of their massive convoy system, were now gaining the upper hand over Dönitz' U-boats. "Wolf packs are all right," an admiral wrote to Lockwood, "when used against sheep, but they are duck soup for the opposition if he is ready for them."

Very much to the point, Lockwood believed that the Japanese were not nearly as ready as the Americans and British in the Atlantic, and he had in mind some modifications to the German method. Since the Japanese convoys were small ones, he figured that a few of his boats could operate far more effectively and more safely than the large groups Dönitz sent into action. Moreover, Dönitz personally directed his U-boats by radio from his headquarters in Kerneval near Lorient on the French Atlantic coast, and the result was nearly incessant chatter that Allied radio trackers used to find and defeat the boats.

By contrast, Lockwood planned to cut his packs loose. He would send the boats to sea under the direction of a group commander who went with them; they would communicate only by short-range radio—and sparingly at that. Unlike the U-boats, the American submarines would attack one at a time, thereby reducing the possibility of hitting one another. After one boat was done, she would drop back while the others were attacking seriatim, and would stand ready to pick off cripples.

The submariners soon learned that wolf-packing was more difficult at sea than on a dance floor. Under the overall command of Captain Charles Momsen, the first group of boats, the *Cero*, the *Shad* and the *Grayback*, went to the East China Sea near Okinawa, where they fanned out to seek a likely target for a coordinated attack. They were hampered, however, by their reluctance to use their radios, and in their first efforts each submarine wound up assaulting without coordination.

The *Cero*, skippered by David C. White, found a three-ship convoy on October 12 and damaged one vessel. The next day John Moore in the *Grayback* made contact with a convoy escorted by two light cruisers. Unable to get set for a shot at the cruisers, he sank a 7,000-ton transport. Next the *Shad*, under Edgar MacGregor III, intercepted a task force of three or four heavy cruisers and what appeared to be an escort carrier. MacGregor got off five torpedoes at the cruisers and believed he made three hits. Destroyers drove him deep and kept him down with a prolonged but harmless depth charging. When he finally surfaced, MacGregor tried to call in the other two boats, but they were out of range, chasing contacts of their own. A day later Moore in the *Grayback* sank a 7,000-ton transport. The results of the first wolf-pack expedition were not bad but they were hardly what Lockwood had in mind.

Five days later, in something that more closely approximated a real wolf-pack assault, the *Grayback* and the *Shad* made a simultaneous attack on an unescorted four-ship convoy. Both boats, however, unwittingly fired fish at the same ship. The *Fuji Maru,* a 9,100-ton transport, was the hapless victim of overkill, and each boat later received official credit for half a sinking.

A second wolf pack made up of Samuel D. Dealey's *Harder,* the *Snook* under Charles Triebel, and the *Pargo,* commanded by Ian Eddy, set out in late October for the Marianas, where they hoped to interdict Japanese shipping during the invasion of Tarawa. The pack commander, who sailed in the *Pargo,* was Fearless Freddy Warder, whose earlier heroics had won him a post on Lockwood's staff.

For Warder, Triebel and Eddy, the cruise produced some exceedingly confused and worrisome days. For Dealey, it was the journey in which he came into his own. A member of a wealthy Texas family, Dealey had been considered something of a Navy dilettante: He had flunked out of the Naval Academy, somehow managed to get back in, and finally graduated in 1930. Shunted from one dreary peacetime job to another, he had often talked about quitting the Navy. Shortly before the attack on Pearl Harbor, he was given command of the *S-20,* a toothless old boat that would never see combat. Finally he was transferred to the *Harder.*

On his only previous war patrol, he had sunk just one Japanese ship in seven attacks before returning to Pearl with an engine out of commission.

Now, Dealey in the *Harder* tasted the wolf pack's first blood. On November 12, Dealey fired three torpedoes at a small freighter. Later the same night, he surfaced and sank one of the freighter's small escorts with gunfire.

After a week without contacts for the pack, the *Harder* scored again. The target she picked up was a convoy of three big freighters and three escorts. Before attacking, Dealey radioed the course of the convoy to his mates in the *Snook* and the *Pargo.* But in his haste, he neglected to transmit another piece of vital information. ''Received enemy's true bearing from *Harder*,'' Triebel wrote in the *Snook's* log, ''which was worthless as we did not know *Harder's* movements during the last three hours.''

Operating on his own, Dealey shot 10 fish into the convoy and counted seven hits. One freighter sank, one was damaged so badly that she later went down, and one got away. As the Japanese escorts raced down the torpedo tracks bent on vengeance, Dealey took his boat down. Nearby, but still unable to locate the battle, Triebel noted: ''Heard depth charges or torpedoes all morning. This was the most frustrated I have ever felt. On the surface, at full speed, hearing explosions, and we couldn't make contact.''

The Japanese depth charges—Dealey counted 64 of them—kept the *Harder* down until nightfall. Then Dealey surfaced to chase the freighter he had missed. Three hours later, he found her but had trouble sinking her; though he did not realize it at first, his remaining Mark 14 torpedoes came from an old batch that had been manufactured before the causes of their malfunction had been corrected. Dealey

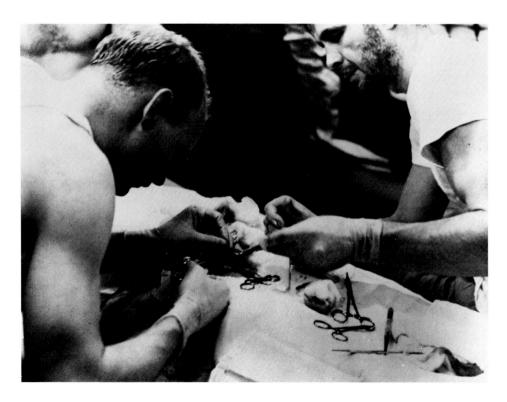

On a hastily rigged operating table aboard the submerged Silversides, Pharmacist's Mate Thomas A. Moore (left) performs an emergency appendectomy on crewman George Platter, with the help of Radioman Richard Stegall. Submarines carried no medical officer, but the service's pharmacist's mates performed 11 successful appendectomies during the War.

had to fire seven fish to make the two hits that stopped the enemy ship dead in the water.

Dealey was now down to four torpedoes and he was determined to use them all if necessary to put the damaged ship under. He brought the *Harder* in to 600 yards, so near he could watch the Japanese crewmen swarming over the ship, evidently trying to save her. He fired a single fish, and it ran wild. He fired another; it too was erratic. He fired the third—and watched it streak off toward the horizon on a course nowhere near the target. The fourth boomeranged and came rushing back toward the *Harder*. Dealey dived to evade his own torpedo.

Out of torpedoes, Dealey departed the pack and headed for port. He was bitterly disappointed at having left a cripple afloat (in fact, it later sank). But by the determination of his attacks he had started toward a fame that would soon inspire the Silent Service.

With Dealey gone, the *Pargo* and the *Snook* patrolled more or less in company, 20 to 30 miles apart. On November 28, the *Pargo* made a contact and Eddy called Triebel on the radio. The skippers had by now learned at least a partial lesson about the wolf pack's need for coordination. This time the *Snook* homed in on the *Pargo's* radar pulses; Triebel later wrote, "I believed they knew where the convoy was and I didn't want to get left chasing my own shadow 10 miles on a flank again."

Both submarines closed in on the convoy, four big cargo carriers. Once again, a wolf-pack principle was forgotten in the heat of the hunt. Triebel picked a target and was about to fire his bow tubes when flame and water spouted up beside the freighter. Eddy had fired first.

Triebel fired a spread of six anyhow and watched one hit Eddy's victim and a second slam into another ship. When both submarines were out of torpedoes, they turned for home. There each boat was credited with two ships sunk and two damaged.

In spite of that pleasing result, wolf-packing was clearly an art that the Americans had yet to perfect. But the first patrols, however confused and confusing they might have been, were at least a start—and within a few months' time American wolf packs, using improved techniques, would be working against the Japanese with devastating effect.

Two 80-ton pontoons rise to the surface on July 13, as the bow of the *Squalus* churns up a foaming whirlpool. Cables attached to each end of the pontoons were fastened to heavy chains under the *Squalus'* keel.

The bow of the *Squalus* surfaces briefly before plunging back down. The abortive surfacing wrecked 13,600 feet of air hoses running from the salvage ship to the pontoons to the ballast tanks of the *Squalus*.

RAISING THE "SQUALUS" FROM FORTY FATHOMS

The world regarded it as a marvel of modern technology when, on May 24, 1939, a U.S. Navy diving bell rescued 33 men from the submarine *Squalus*, sunk in 240 feet of water off New Hampshire. But that was just the beginning. Two days later, a 400-man salvage team began the task of raising the *Squalus* from her resting place 40 fathoms down.

The salvage operation was complicated and lengthy. A 50-man team of Navy divers worked round the clock for 45 days; using hydraulic gear, they pulled heavy chains under the *Squalus'* keel and then positioned huge pontoons above and to either side of the boat. The lifting, begun on July 13, was done by expelling water from the interior compartments—and also by pumping air into the *Squalus'* ballast tanks. But the *Squalus*, jolted from her resting place, shot to the surface—and then slid back to the bottom.

The salvage men started from scratch. On August 12, they began the tedious job of lifting and dragging the boat until she was grounded in 96 feet of water. On September 13, they finally raised her to the surface and towed her 10 miles to dry dock at Portsmouth, New Hampshire.

After 11 months of refurbishing, the *Squalus* was recommissioned as the *Sailfish*. But superstitious submariners let no one forget the new boat's tragic past: They nicknamed her the *Squailfish*.

Samuel Dealey, as it turned out, had been among the last skippers to be frustrated by a wholesale batch of bad torpedoes. Of course, the many modifications now being built into the Mark 14s were no guarantee of perfect performance; there would always be some faulty fish—that was only to be expected in a delicate weapon doing rugged duty. For the most part, however, the torpedoes behaved admirably from that time on. If the men of the United States submarine force did their part, the torpedoes would bring down their prey.

On November 30, shortly after U.S. Marines landed on Tarawa, three Japanese carriers, the *Zuiho*, the *Unyo* and the *Chuyo*, sortied from Truk and headed home to Japan. In Pearl Harbor the code breakers picked up news of the departure and Admiral Lockwood put out an alert to U.S. submarines in the area.

Among those receiving the message was the *Sailfish*, a boat with a notorious history. Originally named the *Squalus*, she had been training near the Isle of Shoals off Hampton, New Hampshire, in May 1939, when the lid on her main induction line failed to close during a dive. The *Squalus* sank and lay helpless beneath 240 feet of water. But a sister boat, the *Sculpin*, located her on the bottom, and a diving bell known as the McCann Rescue Chamber was brought out and clamped onto the hatches of the *Squalus'* two torpedo rooms. Thirty-three men were saved but 23 perished. Now, four years later, the *Squalus*—refloated, refurbished and renamed the *Sailfish*—lay under the sea off the coast of Japan, awaiting enemy carriers.

On the evening of December 3, skipper Robert Ward (formerly the executive officer of the *Gurnard*) took the *Sailfish* to the surface, where he found weather conditions that could scarcely have been worse. The *Sailfish* was in the middle of a winter typhoon, with mountainous seas, gale force winds and visibility that varied from nothing to 500 yards. The seas were so rough that the submarine was not able to make more than 12 knots on the surface.

In a way the typhoon was a boon. Since the weather was as bad for the enemy as it was for the *Sailfish*, the Japanese carrier commander, evidently doubting that a submarine could attack in such a sea, had permitted his big ships to cease zigzagging.

At 12 minutes before midnight, the *Sailfish* got a major radar contact 9,500 yards distant. Ward, certain that his boat could not be seen in that wild sea, closed in on the surface to 2,100 yards and, at 12 minutes past midnight, fired four fish from the forward tubes. As he swung the boat to port to bring her stern tubes to bear, Ward heard his first and fourth torpedoes hit. Then he took the boat down into quiet water to reload. Two depth charges exploded nearby and then, farther away, 19 more.

Around 2:00 a.m. the *Sailfish* surfaced again in the wild night. The radarscope showed blips in several directions; a big one, presumably the unidentified ship Ward had already damaged, was circling slowly, as if hurt.

At 5:50 a.m. Ward made an entry in the log: "Morning twilight and visibility improving fast, rain has stopped but bridge is still shipping water, target's tracking with speed varying from one to three knots, range 3,500 yards. With visibility improving so rapidly must fire soon." Two minutes later he fired three forward tubes at 3,200 yards, a fairly long shot. But he both heard and saw two of the torpedoes hit, although in the raging sea he still could not identify the nature of his target.

The Japanese vessel began firing with a dozen guns, and the *Sailfish* dived once more. At 7:48 a.m. she was up again and now, for the first time, Ward got a look at his victim. "Finally see something," he wrote in his log. "Aircraft carrier, range about 10,000 yards. Dead in the water. Nothing else in sight."

A few minutes later Ward wrote, "Am passing carrier down port side, range 1,500 yards. He has many planes on deck forward and enough people on deck aft to populate a fair size village."

At 9:40 a.m., after carefully working himself into position, Ward fired three more torpedoes at 1,700 yards and heard two of them hit. "Although I had the periscope up anticipating the pleasure of watching the hits, depth control was so lousy that we were at 60 feet when the torpedoes hit and all I could see when the scope was out of the waves was a skyful of tracers being shot up into the air from the carrier's bearing."

Ward maneuvered the *Sailfish* with the intention of administering the death blow. But there was no need for another torpedo. The submarine's sound gear reverberated with the grinding, tearing, explosive noises of a ship breaking up. The *Chuyo*, 20,000 tons, was on her way to the bottom. She was the first Japanese aircraft carrier to be sunk by an American submarine.

There was a bitter aftermath to the *Sailfish's* triumph. Much later, her men learned that *Chuyo* had gone down with 20 Americans aboard. They had been taken prisoner two weeks earlier when an American submarine was sunk by a Japanese destroyer in the Gilberts. That submarine was the *Sculpin*—the same boat that had, back in 1939, rescued the *Squalus,* now the *Sailfish.*

The year, one of learning, of testing, of perseverance and promise, was nearing an end. But one more fancy prize remained to cap the submarine fleet's progress.

Late in December, the code breakers flashed word that the 68,000-ton battleship *Yamato,* along with her twin sister the *Musashi,* the biggest warships afloat, had put to sea from Japan. Admiral Mineichi Koga, commanding the Japanese Combined Fleet, had pressed the mighty *Yamato* into service as a transport, and she was now carrying troops to Kavieng.

Among the American submarines that answered the call was the *Skate,* on patrol off the north side of Truk. Her commander, Eugene McKinney, was convinced that he would never see the monster. He later wrote, "I was the last guy on the line, the last to get a crack at her. She was due in my area Christmas Day. Lockwood warned me that the escort-

ing destroyers had excellent radar and not to get within 30,000 yards of *Yamato* on the surface."

McKinney turned the *Skate* toward the projected track of the Japanese battleship. The other submarines missed connections and—right on schedule before dawn on Christmas Day—the *Skate's* radar picked up the approaching task group at 27,000 yards. McKinney took his boat down and began to make his approach. For a while, he despaired of getting close enough to shoot. But then the battlewagon zigged toward him.

"I put up the periscope and saw this huge mound," McKinney said. "It looked as big as Alcatraz island."

He fired four stern fish, two of which hit. The *Yamato* did not sink, but she was damaged badly enough to abort her mission and had to be laid up for repairs for six months.

McKinney got off a coded radio report, carefully saying only that he had damaged "a ship." Had he mentioned the *Yamato* by name and had Japanese code breakers read his message, they might have concluded—correctly—that the battleship had been intercepted because the Americans were reading the Japanese code.

"When I got back to Pearl Harbor," McKinney recalled, "Lockwood raised holy hell with me." The admiral had planned, for once, to break the silence of his service. "I hadn't mentioned *Yamato,*" McKinney said. "He had been all set to put out a Christmas press release stating that a U.S. submarine had damaged *Yamato* but since I hadn't said *Yamato* he couldn't claim it."

By the end of 1943, U.S. submarines had gone on about 350 patrols and, for the expenditure of 3,937 torpedoes, had sunk 335 ships with a total tonnage of 1.5 million. (At the time, they were credited with higher totals, but postwar accounting and a review of Japanese records reduced the figures.) That record would soon improve dramatically. But it was better by far than the record of 1942. And, by an order of magnitude, it outmatched the performance of Japanese submarines. In fact, though the Americans could hardly know it, they had already won the war under the Pacific.

FIND 'EM, CHASE 'EM, SINK 'EM

On war patrol in the western Pacific, the American submarine Batfish slices ahead at high speed while an officer scans the horizon for Japanese ships.

"STAY WITH HIM 'TIL HE'S ON THE BOTTOM"

"Captain, you put us into position and we'll blow her out of the sea." This confident assurance, spoken by a torpedo-man aboard a U.S. submarine in the Pacific, captured the essence of what made a war patrol successful—expert teamwork by about 80 crewmen secure in the knowledge of their specialized jobs. Teamwork and one thing more. "Tenacity," a skipper said—tenacity in pursuit of the enemy. "Stay with him 'til he's on the bottom." Indeed, it took determination to patrol for several weeks, as many a submarine did, before finding an enemy ship to shoot at.

The chase, when there was one, followed a fairly standardized ritual. It usually began while the submarine was cruising on the surface. The crew was galvanized by a lookout who spotted smoke on the horizon, or by a radar operator who reported a blip on his screen. At the skipper's command, the tracking team in the control room (right) and the operator of the torpedo data computer (TDC) in the conning tower began plotting the enemy's speed and course from the ranges and bearings the skipper supplied. The TDC added in the boat's speed and course, and automatically computed and set the proper angle of fire on the torpedoes' controlling gyroscopes. The angle of fire changed with every deviation in the course of both the submarine and the target, which began zigzagging as soon as it spotted the attacker.

The skipper, angling the boat to intersect the target's course, slowly closed the gap. The process, according to one skipper, was like a "slow-motion football game": The enemy ship was an open-field runner, and once the submarine got into a good position, her torpedo made the tackle.

As the submarine approached her target the crewmen fell silent. Even though 20 miles or more might separate them from the target at first, they concentrated with deadly intensity on the complex problems of preparing for the attack. But they also thought ahead—especially those crews who had not sighted a target for weeks—to the instant when they would fire their first fish at the target. "There's no better morale booster," said a veteran skipper, "than the sound of your own torpedo exploding against an enemy ship."

Ready to depart for Japanese waters, crewmen of an American submarine receive Communion from a priest standing between racks of torpedoes.

Their faces etched with tension, the members of a tracking team plot the course of their Japanese target so that the submarine can close in for the kill.

SIZING UP THE TARGET

Well after the initial contact, a pursuing submarine often discovered that the distant smoke or radar blip was not a single enemy ship but a tight convoy of several vessels. The telephone talker, standing at the skipper's side, relayed this information to other talkers who repeated the words to crewmen in all parts of the boat.

The sound men, bent over their sonar gear, listened for the slow *thump, thump, thump* of freighters' propellers, which they could distinguish from the rapid *swish, swish, swish* of an escorting destroyer's screws. On learning of an escort, the skipper would keep a sharp eye on the radarscope so that he could plan his approach to avoid the destroyer.

Then the skipper ordered, "Take her down," and the talker alerted the crew. As the boat submerged, the order "Battle stations" was passed quietly through the boat, sending everyone to his post.

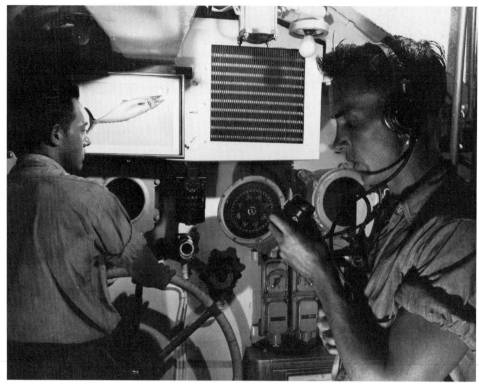

Chasing an enemy ship, the helmsman in the conning tower of the Cero receives a course change.

In the Wahoo's control room, the bow planesman (right) carefully maintains periscope depth as the boat closes in on a Japanese convoy off New Guinea.

A crewman on the Sea Dog stands by the valve controls, which eject water from the negative ballast tank to level off the submarine at the ordered depth.

Watching electric meters in the maneuvering room of the Batfish, an electrician grasps the propeller control lever that changes the direction of the boat.

Torpedomen in the Cero make ready the forward torpedo tubes after receiving from the telephone talker (left) the captain's orders to prepare to attack.

MAKING READY AT BATTLE STATIONS

As the submarine closed in on the target, the report came to the skipper, "All stations manned and ready."

In the maneuvering room *(left)*, the electrician and his helpers at their control levers tensely awaited orders from the engineering officer in the control room. Theirs was the vital task of directing the boat's electric current wherever it was needed. Monitoring the amperage closely was essential because a skipper often drove the electric motors hard in order to gain extra speed in the approach, and this put a severe drain on the storage batteries.

Next, the torpedo officer gave the order, "Make ready the bow tubes." The men in the forward torpedo room, knowing that their six fish would be the first fired, let compressed air—600 pounds per square inch—into tanks for use in firing each torpedo, and flooded the tubes. Then came the command, "Open the outer doors."

After complying with this order, one man at each torpedo stood with his hand over the firing pin he would use if the automatic firing control in the conning tower malfunctioned. Now the torpedomen awaited the final order to fire.

Lieutenant Richard H. O'Kane, executive officer of the Wahoo, sights through the periscope at the height of a battle in which his submarine sank an entire Japanese convoy of four ships off New Guinea in 1943.

AT LAST, THE KILL

The chase, which often lasted for hours and sometimes for days, climaxed as the submarine finally reached the captain's chosen attack position. An instant before firing the torpedoes, the skipper took a last look through the sea-splashed periscope, placed its hairline sight on the middle of the target (MOT) and gave the command, "Bearing—Mark!"

Then the TDC operator pressed a button that locked the last-minute bearing of the enemy ship into the torpedo data computer, which in turn automatically set the final firing angle on the torpedo.

"Set!" responded the TDC operator.

"Fire!" At this command, the torpedo officer at the firing panel in the conning tower hit the plunger that sent the torpedo off with a jolting whoosh. The submarine shuddered as compressed air forced the fish out of the tube. Sea water immediately flooded back into the tube, and the diving officer then had to angle the boat's bow planes down to maintain an even keel.

Other torpedoes followed, each aimed at a different section of the same target. The sonar operator tracked the course of the fired fish. "All hot, straight and normal," he said, indicating that each torpedo was speeding on its programed course.

The quartermaster counted the seconds as the torpedo raced toward the target at a speed of 46 knots: "53, 54, 55, 56. . . ."

The crewmen waited with bated breath. Then, Whoom! A hit! The explosion sent shock waves through the submarine's hull.

On virtually every attack, the crewmen in the bowels of the boat missed the satisfaction of viewing the result of their handiwork. Even the skipper often missed the spectacle; after observing the first hit, he usually dived the boat to escape pursuit.

But the crewmen could hear, through the sound gear and the hull, their victim's death agony: the grating sounds of twisting and rupturing steel. It was cause for rejoicing but also a warning that the submarine could meet the same fate. That sobering thought was enough, said a skipper, to "keep any lookout on his toes for weeks."

A torpedo launched from the Puffer explodes aft of the stacks on the Teiko Maru, a 15,100-ton Japanese troop transport, off the coast of Borneo in February 1944. Thousands of enemy soldiers went down with the ship.

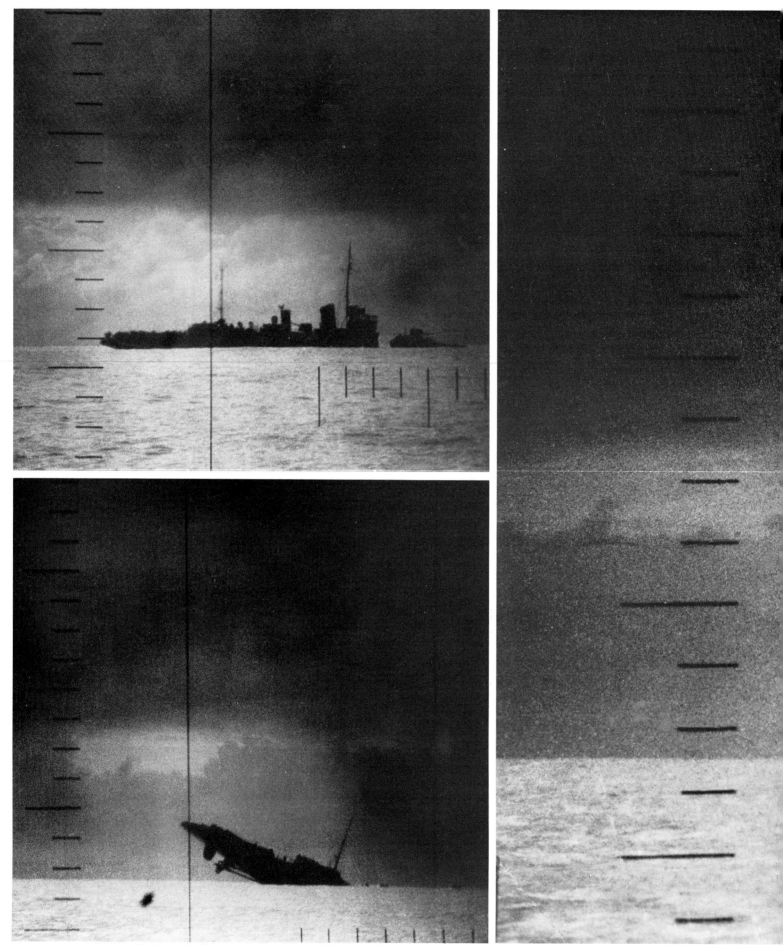

A periscope camera records the death throes of a Japanese patrol boat torpedoed off Formosa by the submarine Seawolf in May 1943. The sequence began

(upper left) shortly after the fish struck the target's forward quarter. Minutes later, the enemy ship pointed her fantail skyward and plunged to the bottom.

Periscope photographs taken from U.S. submarines record the violent deaths of assorted torpedoed Japanese vessels—warships, freighters, troop transports and

tankers. On a destroyer (bottom, far left) burning off an island north of New Guinea, the sailors line the deck waiting for rescue or preparing to swim for shore.

3

THE ENEMY BELOW

Like the rest of the Japanese military services, the Imperial Navy's submarine force had based its strategic plans on a thunderclap war brought to lightning decision. But from the first, high-placed Japanese recognized the enormity of their gamble. "For six months or a year, I can run wild," said Admiral Isoroku Yamamoto, Commander in Chief of the Imperial Combined Fleet, shortly before the War. But Yamamoto, who knew and respected the productive powers of United States industry, added soberly: "After that, I don't know."

As the Japanese saw it, they had no choice but to wage war in a desperate race against time. Natural circumstances had decreed that the island nation of Japan must import nearly all its strategic raw materials—among them rubber, tin, iron, copper, bauxite, rice and, most critically, oil. Before the War, Japan had purchased about 88 per cent of its oil products from foreign nations; of that amount, some 80 per cent came from the United States. By July 1941, when an American-British-Dutch embargo on the sale to Japan of oil and other strategic items took full effect, the Japanese had, through long and laborious stockpiling, managed to accumulate 43 million barrels of oil—enough to wage war for a little more than one year.

To Japanese planners, therefore, the strategic imperative was to seize with utmost speed the natural treasures of Borneo, Celebes, Malaya and the Dutch East Indies, especially Java. Once this was accomplished, the Japanese could establish a defense perimeter in the hope that the Americans would soon prove unwilling or unable to wage a two-ocean war against both Germany and Japan, and would negotiate a peace in the Pacific, leaving the Empire in possession of its precious new conquests, euphemistically called the Greater East Asia Co-Prosperity Sphere.

In the minds of Admiral Yamamoto and his fellow strategists, this vision of swift expansion depended on the destruction of the U.S. Navy in the Pacific. To plot the ruin of that navy and to plan the seizure of Southeast Asia, about 40 of Japan's top Navy officers met in September 1941 for a two-week conference at Tokyo's Naval war college.

Much as their American counterparts had envisioned in Plan *Orange*, the Japanese officers foresaw that the Pacific conflict would be decided by a single great naval battle. But as a prelude to that historic clash of fleets and the Japanese drive to the south, Yamamoto conceived an idea that would attempt to tilt the odds heavily in Japan's favor. "Our best course of action," he declared, "is to deliver a knockout blow to the American fleet at the very start." He meant, of course, the surprise attack on Pearl Harbor—which would, he hoped, so damage the American fleet that when it was later brought to battle "we can destroy it completely."

In achieving that destruction, Japanese submarines would play a part. As the fighting arm of the Sixth Fleet, which consisted solely of submarines and their auxiliaries, Japanese fleet boats were organized into three front-line squadrons. Zenji Orita, an officer in Submarine Squadron One (SubRon One), recalled: "Basic prewar strategy centered around my squadron's advancing deep into enemy waters, and keeping watch on his naval ports. Should he sally forth to attack the Japanese homeland, we were to attack him, then use our high surface speed of 23 knots to dash away and set up a second ambush for him, repeating this tactic until we were out of torpedoes.

"If in spite of the damage we did to his fleet, the enemy kept advancing toward Japan, our Combined Fleet would sortie to meet him with SubRon Two and SubRon Three screening far ahead of it. Those submarines would repeat the tactics of SubRon One. Theoretically, by the time the enemy closed with our main body for the decisive sea battle admirals dream of, he would be so weakened that he could be crushed. Japan would win control of the Pacific Ocean!"

Implicit in this plan was a fact later explained by Mochitsura Hashimoto, who ended the War as one of Japan's few successful submarine captains. "The Japanese policy was to use submarines primarily for attacking enemy naval forces," Hashimoto wrote. "Merchant ships were legitimate targets only when there were no warships to be considered." In line with that thinking, submarine commanders were given a schedule for torpedo expenditure that was even more restrictive than the original American quota: Enemy battleships and aircraft carriers were worth the firing of all torpedoes; cruisers rated three torpedoes, but a single torpedo had to suffice for destroyers and merchant vessels.

While the American submariners honored their torpedo priorities mostly in the breach, the disciplined Japanese would stick to their policy long after it had demonstrably failed, and at no point would they turn their concentrated attention to merchant shipping—the natural prey of the submarine. In retrospect, a number of Naval officers speculated on the reason for this blind or stubborn impracticality. Atsushi Oi of the Japanese Naval General Staff ventured to guess that "maybe at the bottom of our naval tradition there was a problem of racial temperament." Compared with Europeans, Oi continued, "the Japanese are generally said to be more impetuous and less tenacious. They preferred colorful and offensive fighting. The picture of a fleet action is colorful."

In any case, the Japanese submariners never thought in terms of a slow war of attrition against commerce; they went to war single-mindedly determined to send U.S. warships to the Pacific floor with all possible haste. And for this task they were thoroughly trained.

Submarine officers were graduates of the Naval Academy at Etajima, which modeled itself so closely after Great Britain's Dartmouth that bricks for the buildings had been imported from England, along with a lock of Admiral Horatio Nelson's hair. On active duty, the ensigns served until they rose to the rank of lieutenant, junior grade, before they could apply for submarine service. Then came two years aboard submarines. After this stint, they were sent to specialized service schools ashore for six-month courses in torpedoes, navigation, communications, diesel engines and electrical engineering—followed by another four months of instruction in submarine diving techniques. Finally, if after three to five years they had proved themselves worthy, they might be sent to a school for submarine commanders.

Enlisted men were selected from the various service schools (torpedo, gunnery, engines), and there was never a dearth of candidates; crewmen and officers alike received an extra 30 per cent in pay, and even in peacetime service on submarines counted double when figuring retirement benefits. Physical qualifications were strict, with special emphasis placed on keen eyesight and good hearing. Like the Americans, the recruits underwent psychological tests for their capacity to function efficiently over long periods in confined space. Then, after six months of submarine school, they were assigned to boats.

Even before the War, training exercises were made as realistic as possible, regardless of the risk of accident. Indeed, during the 20 months before Pearl Harbor, the Japanese lost three submarines—two in collisions and another during fleet maneuvers. The accidents, a submarine captain wrote later, were "due to the rigors of intensive training that was standard policy." Tough as it already was, the training schedule was stepped up between June and August of 1941, as submarines maneuvered vigorously from the bleak Kuriles to such tropical islands as Truk. And in exercises that would have horrified the U.S. Navy's cost-conscious Bureau of Ordnance, each Japanese submarine was permitted to fire a live Model 95 torpedo against the steep shores of Oshima, a desolate island south of Tokyo Bay.

That torpedo was a paragon. Adapted for submarines from the Model 93, which was fired from surface ships and was to become famed as the "Long Lance," the Model 95 could travel at 49 knots for a staggering distance of nearly 11 miles, leaving no telltale wake. It packed an explosive charge of 1,000 pounds—almost twice that of American torpedoes. It detonated on impact, with none of the troubles the Americans had with their magnetic exploder.

The torpedo's secret lay in its propulsion system: It was driven by oxygen. This gas, with which the Japanese had been experimenting since the 1920s, made a treacherous propellant. The British had tried oxygen and discarded it because of its nasty habit of exploding without apparent provocation. But Japanese designers had discovered that the problem lay in the twists and turns of fuel lines leading from the oxygen tank to the combustion chamber, and in rough spots that formed pockets inside the fuel lines. When the angles were too sharp, oxygen massed at the turns and in the pockets; this built up pressure in the lines, thereby increasing temperatures and causing explosions.

The Japanese solution was simple, at least in concept. "We redesigned the fuel lines into smooth curves, eliminat-ing all sharp angles," explained Captain Sadaharu Otsuka, a Navy torpedo specialist. "Also, during torpedo assembly, we cleaned the lines with a potassium compound, to eliminate all oil and grease. Finally, to overcome the chance of oxygen still massing when an engine was first started, we used compressed air to start the torpedoes, and introduced oxygen only after the cycle was 'open.' All that remained was to handle each torpedo with care and respect."

From their other equipment, Japanese submariners received mixed performances. Their optical gear was of superior quality—a fact somewhat muddled by a folklorish debate in which Americans held that Japanese had naturally poor vision and the Japanese insisted that brown eyes could see better at night. It made no difference. The lookouts of Japanese submarines were expert by any standard—and they were certainly helped by their excellent binoculars.

Japanese underwater listening apparatus was adequate, with an echo-ranging feature more or less accurate up to 3,400 yards and hydrophones that could give bearings at more than 5,400 yards. But in other areas of electronics the Japanese began the War significantly behind the Americans—and as the conflict continued the gap would widen.

Most notably, Japan had a deficiency in radar that was disastrous. Plagued by an inability to develop a high-powered transmitting tube whose centimeter microwaves tracked enemy ships accurately, the Japanese Navy entered the War without radar of any sort. Surface warships received their first crude radar apparatus only after the Battle of Midway in June 1942. And not until almost two years afterward would Japanese submariners, despite much beseeching, get radar. "The submarine crews in the forward areas," recalled Mochitsura Hashimoto, "were longing for radar as farmers look for rain in a long drought. In our despair we were almost

Radiating good cheer, Japanese submariners soak up the sun on the return leg of a 1942 war patrol. Submarine duty, at least at the start of the War, was favored by enlisted men for its informality and lack of the fierce discipline that characterized the surface navy. One veteran boasted that officers and men ate the same food, and that he never saw an officer exercise his right to strike an errant sailor.

driven to the view that a single radar set would be of more value than a hundred submarines."

In that, the submariners may have been right, for in the most basic item of all—the boats themselves—Japanese quality was questionable. Perhaps the most dispassionate appraisal came later from a German admiral named Paul Wenneker, who served throughout the War as his country's naval attaché in Tokyo. "The Japanese," Wenneker said succinctly, "had poor types of submarines in this war."

At the outbreak of the War, Japan's submarine force was numerically a shade larger than the American strength of 56 boats assigned to the Pacific. But of Japan's 60 submarines, 14 were obsolete RO, or second-line, boats (comparable to the American S-boats), incapable of diving more than 245 feet and usable only in coastal waters. Although all the others were designated I-class, or first-line, they varied greatly in size and purpose. Four, for example, were minelayers. Because of their special construction they were dangerously unwieldy, tending to sink if at all overloaded and to pop to the surface when lightened. They were known throughout the service as "the dreaded submarines."

The backbone of the Japanese undersea force lay in these versatile I-class fleet boats. They displaced from 1,600 to 2,200 tons, carried up to 20 torpedoes, had a maximum range of 16,000 miles and top speeds of more than 20 knots on the surface and seven to nine knots underwater. On the average, they were slightly larger and faster than the American fleet boats—and much harder to handle when submerged. They were also handicapped with needlessly complicated control systems, and they vibrated excessively, thereby making underwater noises that could be—and often were—disastrous.

Nevertheless, these I-boats were Japan's best, and 27 of them figured in plans for the surprise attack on Pearl Harbor. That fateful mission would also engage five boats of another, secret type—the midget submarine.

The inspiration for the miniature boats had come from a Japanese submarine officer who had seen a rudimentary one-man submersible used by fishermen, presumably to search for good fishing grounds. Various types of midgets were developed, the first in 1934. The model produced for the Pearl Harbor attack was a two-man, two-torpedo version, 78.5 feet long. This peculiar little vessel was driven by a 600-horsepower electric motor whose storage batteries could not be recharged once the midget was weaned from her mother boat. The midget could travel 55 minutes on the surface at a top speed of 23 knots or 19 knots submerged. By drastically cutting speed, the crew could extend her range to approximately 100 miles.

In the original attack plan, several midgets were to be carried aboard a converted seaplane tender sailing with the Combined Fleet; as the fleet entered battle, the undersized boats would be launched and, with their low susceptibility to detection, bustle about in the midst of the melee, mystifying the enemy warships and doing them harm.

But as the moment for war approached, midget enthusiasts importuned the commanders of the Imperial Navy for a chance at greater glory. Why, they asked, could not several midgets be carried aboard regular fleet submarines, then be let loose to penetrate and wreak havoc in the enemy anchorages? Most particularly, why could they not participate gloriously in the Pearl Harbor attack?

The scheme went all the way to Admiral Yamamoto, who questioned it, partly out of fear that premature attacks by the midgets might warn the Americans of the main strikes by carrier aircraft. Yamamoto also thought that the proposed midget venture smacked of a suicide mission—a measure for which Japan was as yet unready. Finally, under continuing pressure from the midget advocates, Yamamoto acquiesced—but only after receiving promises that every attempt would be made to retrieve the little vanguard boats and their crews. Detailed arrangements were made for the midgets' post-attack rendezvous with the mother submarines that would carry them piggyback to the threshold of Pearl Harbor and then carry them home.

Thus, a scant six weeks before they actually set out on the long trek to Hawaiian waters, round-the-clock work began on the five I-boats that were to carry the midgets, secured by heavy clamps to their pressure hulls. The specific nature and purpose of that work was kept secret from the I-boat skippers and even from their squadron commander; they were told only that their submarines were being given "special fittings."

With these belated amendments, the submarines' role in the Pearl Harbor attack finally jelled and the boats themselves got under way. Twenty-seven fleet I-boats, 11 of them carrying small reconnaissance floatplanes, slipped out of the Kure and Yokosuka naval bases between November 10 and 21, 1941. Each boat carried provisions for 90 days; except for the diesel-engine room, all available interior deck space was covered to a depth of two feet by bags of rice and containers of other foods; to get from one place to another the men walked on top of the foodstuffs. On the night of November 18, five more I-boats left Kure, each carrying a midget abaft her conning tower. This was a so-called Special Attack Unit.

While the Japanese Navy was on its way to a smashing victory, its undersea complement was heading for a dismal reverse that would, for much of the War, cast a pall over the entire submarine force.

The journey toward Pearl Harbor started out well enough for the midgets. The mother boats traveled in line abreast at 20-mile intervals, remaining mostly on the surface but running submerged while passing within range of American patrol planes based on Johnston, Howland and Wake Islands. But as the submarines neared Hawaiian waters, the weather worsened. On the I-22, Lieutenant Naoji Iwasa, a zealous young career officer who was to command one of the midgets, disobeyed orders requiring a life line for everyone topside on the rolling boat; fearing for the safety of his midget, Iwasa ventured onto the deck to look after her and was nearly swept overboard. He was ordered by the I-boat's irate captain to remain below for the rest of the trip.

The roaring seas caused abject misery for the men below. A surfaced submarine breathes by sucking air through an induction valve on its bridge. Now, as huge waves repeatedly drowned their induction valves, the submarines' engines gasped for air within the boats, and the frequent sharp changes in internal atmospheric pressures afflicted the men with agonizing earaches.

At last the storm abated, and shortly after sunset on December 6 the five mother submarines gathered about 100 miles south of Pearl Harbor. Then they cautiously crept to within 10 miles of the great anchorage and deployed in a fan-shaped formation outside its mouth. After midnight they surfaced. Cloaked by darkness, the Japanese could see the glow of neon from signs on Waikiki Beach, the beam of

automobile headlights moving in the hills beyond, the steady glare of landing lights at Hickam Field and John Rodgers Airport. On their wireless sets they heard the all-night jazz on Honolulu's station KGMB, on whose beam the Japanese carrier planes would, a few hours later, home in.

On the I-24, the midget's gyro compass was found to be broken and, though technicians worked on it frantically for two hours, it could not be fixed. The I-boat's commander asked the midget's skipper, Ensign Kazuo Sakamaki, if he wished to cancel the mission. Replied Sakamaki: ''Captain, I am going ahead—on to Pearl Harbor!''

Around 3:30 a.m. on December 7, the five midget submarines began to float free of their mothers and head for the antisubmarine net guarding the harbor entrance. They were supposed to attack targets of opportunity in the interval between the first and second waves of torpedo planes from the Japanese carriers, which took up positions about 200 nautical miles north of the big island of Oahu.

At 6:30 a.m., Hawaiian time, the net opened to admit the U.S.S. Antares, an old freighter that had been converted to target-towing duty. Casually watching the Antares puff past, a helmsman on the nearby U.S. destroyer Ward noticed a strange object—it appeared to be a buoy—following in the

Nobuo Fujita, the submarine-based aviator who bombed the mainland of the United States, had been near a Japanese target that was attacked by one of Lieut. Colonel James H. Doolittle's airmen in April of 1942. ''That pilot had bombed my homeland for the first time,'' Fujita said later, ''now I was bombing his. It gave me a great deal of satisfaction.''

Antares' wake and maintaining a steady distance. When summoned, the *Ward's* captain immediately identified the object as the conning tower of a submarine—in an area where submerged submarines were assumed to be hostile. Her alarm blaring, the *Ward* opened fire with her 4-inch guns; the intruder rolled over and vanished beneath the water. The *Ward* followed up with a depth-charge attack that was probably unnecessary: The midget lay dead on the bottom of Pearl Harbor.

The *Ward* at 6:53 a.m. flashed a message to headquarters of the 14th Naval District: WE HAVE ATTACKED, FIRED UPON AND DROPPED DEPTH CHARGES ON A SUBMARINE OPERATING IN THE DEFENSIVE SEA AREA.

At 7:55 a.m., the first wave of Japanese planes roared over Pearl Harbor. The attack was still going on when the destroyer *Monaghan,* just north of Ford Island in Pearl Harbor, spotted the U.S. seaplane tender *Curtiss* flying a signal that warned of an enemy submarine in the vicinity. Almost at once, another midget submarine launched a torpedo at the *Curtiss*—it missed and passed on to explode against a dock. The *Monaghan* roared in to ram, struck the midget a glancing blow, then dropped depth charges so close that they almost blew off her own stern. The midget was finished. Later, her wrecked hull was retrieved and used as fill in the construction of a new pier at Pearl Harbor's submarine base. The bodies of Lieutenant (jg.) Shigemi Haruno and Petty Officer Harunori Yokoyama were still entombed within.

The Japanese planes finished their devastating work at 9:45 a.m. Later, the destroyers *Blue, Helm* and *Monaghan,* the destroyer-minelayers *Breese* and *Ramsay,* and the light cruiser *St. Louis* all reported attacking submarines outside Pearl Harbor. It is entirely likely that one of them sank the *I-22's* midget with Lieutenant Naoji Iwasa and Petty Officer Nahoharu Sasaki aboard. At any rate, they were never seen after leaving their mother boat.

The destroyers may also have got the *I-20's* midget, carrying Ensign Akira Hiroo and Petty Officer Yoshio Katayama. The boat vanished, and her disappearance would years later give rise to one of Pearl Harbor's most intriguing mysteries. In June 1960, Navy SCUBA diving trainees were practicing outside the Keehi lagoon near Pearl Harbor. In 76 feet of water, they found a midget submarine—its coral-encrusted hull apparently undamaged, its torpedoes still in the tubes, its hatch unlatched, necessarily from the inside. The divers found not the slightest trace of the boat's onetime occupants. Almost certainly, Hiroo and Katayama had left the midget through the hatch, and they might well have ascended safely to the surface. If they were still strong enough to swim a mile to shore, they may somehow have managed to mingle with Oahu's large Japanese population—and might, conceivably, have still been alive.

Whatever the fate of Hiroo and Katayama, one of the 10 men who embarked in midget submarines on that morning of December 7 most certainly did survive. He was Ensign Sakamaki, who had set off with his gyro compass still out of commission. Ironically, he had been selected for the mission because, in the not-unlikely event of his death, he would not be missed as much as many other officers: He was one of eight sons—and if he died, his family would still have seven left.

As it happened, Sakamaki did not die, but he suffered a series of nightmarish experiences. Hardly had he and Petty Officer Kiyoshi Inagaki left the *I-24* than their midget lost trim and began to sink, nose down. While Inagaki desperately shifted 11-pound lead ballast weights toward the stern, Sakamaki threw the boat's counterrotating propellers into reverse and backed up to the surface. When he got there he saw Honolulu behind him; he had been heading in the wrong direction.

Correcting his course, Sakamaki worked his way back toward the harbor entrance; there, southwest of the Pearl Harbor entrance buoy, he found his way blocked by a small minesweeper, the *Condor,* and the ubiquitous destroyer *Ward.* Sakamaki tried to run between them submerged, but was depth-charged by the *Ward.* Although the charges missed, their concussion was so violent that Sakamaki lost consciousness. When he recovered, he saw through his periscope that the *Ward* was behind him. The midget's way into the harbor was presumably clear.

But near the harbor's entrance, the boat struck an underwater coral reef, which lifted her bow out of the water and left her stranded. After several tries, Sakamaki backed off and started on his way again—only to hit another reef.

Now Sakamaki and Inagaki crept back and forth, shifting ballast aft within the submarine; electrolyte fumes were

I-BOAT EMISSARIES TO THEIR GERMAN ALLIES

Crewmen of the Japanese I-30 salute their German allies at Lorient after a voyage from Malaysia, which included a refueling stop off Madagascar.

German and Japanese sailors swap hats as souvenirs of the visit.

The German U-511 (far right) lies tied up with various Japanese types at Penang.

On August 6, 1942, the first Japanese submarine to reach Atlantic waters arrived at the German U-boat base at Lorient on the coast of France, thereby completing a 15,000-mile journey halfway around the world from her home port in Penang, Malaysia. The visit of the *I-30* was fraught with ceremony and symbolism—a linking of arms between Axis allies. But there was much more to it than that.

In her capacious hull, the *I-30* carried tons of tin, tungsten, zinc and other raw materials desperately needed to fuel Germany's war machine. The Japanese had these critical resources in abundant supply in their conquered Far Eastern territories, but an Allied naval blockade had prevented their shipment to Germany—except by long-range submarine. In return, the Germans offered technology: advanced designs for artillery weapons, for aircraft engines and particularly for submarines.

The voyage of the *I-30* ended in disaster for the Japanese. Returning home with plans and samples of the latest German sonar, the *I-30* struck a British mine off Singapore and sank, with the loss of 14 of her crew and all of her precious cargo. It was a bad beginning. Nevertheless, the Japanese and Germans persisted in believing that a regular strategic exchange could be effected by submarine.

In the months that followed, the Japanese dispatched five more I-boats to occupied France; only two reached Lorient, and none returned to Penang. The Germans were even more ambitious—and just as unlucky. In June 1943, they sent a "Monsoon Group" of 11 long-range U-boats and three submarine tankers heading for the Far East. More than half of this force was lost to Allied submarine hunters before it even cleared the Atlantic. Other groups fared worse; indeed, only 20 or so U-boats made the round trip to Penang successfully during the entire War.

There was a final disappointment. In 1943, Adolf Hitler gave his Asian allies the latest and most sophisticated U-boat—the *U-511*—in hopes that they would copy it and thus increase the effectiveness of their undersea force. But the design proved to be too complicated for Japanese technicians, and the superb long-range attack boat spent the War languishing as a training vessel in the Sea of Japan.

seeping from the tilted batteries, and both men suffered shocks as they crawled on the flooded deck. At last, the midget floated free of the reef.

Inspecting the damage, Sakamaki found that the torpedo-launching mechanism was broken and the tubes would no longer fire. But Kazuo Sakamaki was dauntless: His torpedoes were still in their tubes, and he decided to explode them by ramming the first enemy ship he could find.

By now it was past noon, and the midget was foul with battery fumes. Both Sakamaki and Inagaki passed out from lack of oxygen—and the boat drifted out to sea. Eventually the fumes cleared and Sakamaki revived. He had no notion where he was, but when he opened the hatch that night to breathe fresh air, he saw an island not far away. Trying to make for it, he ran the midget onto an outlying coral reef.

The hang-up, the third of the day, immobilized the little boat for good. Sakamaki and Inagaki tried to swim to land, which lay about a mile away. Inagaki struggled as long as he could and then went under. Sakamaki, too, seemed to be done for; exhausted by the effort, he lost consciousness. But he was washed ashore, a full 50 miles from Pearl Harbor. There he was found by a U.S. Army sergeant and became the Americans' first Japanese prisoner in World War II.

In sum, the midget mission against Pearl Harbor was a total loss. As for the fleet boats of the main submarine force that had sailed from Japan in high hopes of fighting a great sea battle, they fared little better than the midgets. The 14 fleet boats out of Yokosuka had been positioned in three tiers north of Oahu as a screen for the carrier strike force; another 12 were arranged in two arcs to the south of Oahu, ready to attack American warships attempting to escape from Pearl Harbor. There they waited—and waited.

The day of the great Japanese air attack on Pearl Harbor passed without incident for the impatient submarines. So did the next day. Not until the evening of December 8 was there a sighting. Then, Commander Tsuso Inaba, in the *I-6* to the north, reported seeing an aircraft carrier and two cruisers heading northeast. From his headquarters on the old cruiser *Katori* at Kwajalein, Vice Admiral Mitsumi Shimizu, commander of the undersea fleet, ordered his submarines to "pursue and sink."

Eight boats took up the hunt—only to find that their quarry had a lethal sting. She was, in fact, the carrier *Enterprise,* and on the morning of December 10, one of her planes caught and bombed the *I-170* on the surface. The Japanese submarine was so badly damaged that Commander Takashi Sano dared not submerge. That afternoon another *Enterprise* plane found the *I-170* and sank her with all hands.

On December 14, Admiral Shimizu gave up the chase and ordered the pursuing submarines to proceed to the U.S. West Coast to cut off any supplies and reinforcements that might be headed into the western Pacific. With that, the Pearl Harbor operation came to an end. The Japanese submarine force had lost five midget submarines and one fleet boat. It had inflicted no damage whatsoever, and its failure would have a long-lasting and insidious effect on the Imperial Navy commanders' attitude toward the undersea service. The officer who later became commander of the submarine fleet, Vice Admiral Shigeyoshi Miwa, summed up the result: "Our Navy was obliged to build battleships, aircraft carriers; so the limited material was divided and we could not build many submarines."

Off the West Coast of the United States, the seven submarines that had broken off their pursuit of the *Enterprise* were joined by two others, and as they gazed shoreward the bemused submariners found themselves feeling very much like tourists. "I've never been to America," Captain Hiroshi Imazato, a division commander, told fellow officers on the bridge of the *I-15.* "If we weren't at war, this would be an excellent chance to pass in through the Golden Gate and visit that famous city of San Francisco." Off Long Beach, California, crewmen on another I-boat saw, with mixed scorn and envy, Americans relaxing under colorful beach umbrellas, just as if there were no war going on.

During the submarines' brief stay, the *I-17* claimed two merchant-ship sinkings and the *I-21* reported two others; actually, they sank one ship each. The *I-25,* under Commander Meiji Tagami, daringly pursued a cargo ship into the mouth of the Columbia River, where the merchantman went aground.

By Christmas, that group of boats was ordered to report to Sixth Fleet headquarters at Kwajalein. There, on January 15, aboard his flagship, the *Katori,* Admiral Shimizu reviewed with subordinates the progress of the submarine war to date. Balanced against their Hawaiian losses, Japanese submarines throughout the Pacific had sunk 17 ships. But these were all merchantmen, most of them small—and to the Japanese commanders, in their preoccupation with warships, they barely counted. "Vice Admiral Shimizu," recalled one officer present, "was much dismayed."

He would soon be even more dismayed: By the end of the month, three more Japanese submarines were gone. The *I-160,* attacking Singapore shipping traffic in Sunda Strait, was sunk by the British destroyer *Jupiter.* The U.S. submarine *Gudgeon* destroyed the *I-173* north of Midway. The *I-124,* a minelayer, ventured too close to the harbor at Darwin, Australia, where she was detected and successfully depth-charged by the U.S. destroyer *Edsall* and three Australian corvettes. Although claims of submarine sinkings were often later found to be mistaken, there could be no doubt about this one: Allied divers actually descended and stood on the *I-124's* hull.

By the end of February, the Japanese were ready to make another attack in U.S. waters. Under Commander Kozo Nishino, the *I-17* returned to the California coast and surfaced well offshore on the night of February 22. Genji Hara, a seaman aboard the *I-17,* noted the beginning of the daring mission in a diary full of rare and intimate glimpses of the Japanese enlisted submariner at war: "Captain Nishino told the crew of his plans. 'We are now entering Santa Barbara Strait,' he said. 'We will lie submerged tomorrow, doing reconnaissance with our periscope. Then, tomorrow night, we will surface after dark and bombard the Ellwood oil fields, inside the strait.' "

Hara was overjoyed. *"We are really going to do it this time!* I told myself. As a substitute gunner in case a gun crew member was injured or killed, I had to check over our deck weapon. About 30 knots of wind was blowing over the deck while we did it and there were plenty of white caps on the waves. There was a dull half-moon, with a hazy halo about it. I looked up into the sky and located Great Bear and the Northern Star. Then I tried to estimate the direction of Japan from where I stood. In that moment I hoped that, if I died, the people back home would know that *I-17* had reached out 4,000 miles to strike at America for them. I felt very warm and full of sentiment at that moment."

The next afternoon, the 23rd of February, the submerged

boat crept deep into American waters. Wrote Hara: "I-17 changed course and, at a slow pace, began navigating blindly through Santa Barbara Strait, not even showing her periscope for fear of making a telltale spray. I tried to calm down by reading a book, but couldn't. I had finally decided to try to eat something to distract my mind, when the word was passed, 'All hands to battle stations!' "

At about 5:40 p.m., Nishino ordered, "Battle surface! Man the deck gun!" As the boat surfaced the gun captain and his crew went on deck. Hara remained below but heard the men talking on deck. He wrote, "Captain Nishino kept calling out, asking the distance to land and the submarine's depth, giving instructions about the targets. He ordered that shells be fired only at oil tanks."

The gunners on deck began firing and the crewmen below "could only listen and imagine what it was like above from the sounds and shocks that came through the hull.

"One . . . two . . . three . . . we could imagine the gunners loading each of those rounds; the trainer and the pointer trying to sight on the target. We had counted up to 17 when the shooting suddenly stopped.

"Petty Officer Homma and I had the radio watch. We spun our receiver dials, trying to find some indication of American reaction. There was none. We heard no alarm or call for help. The California radio station programs continued as leisurely as before. Gunners dropped through the hatch and I-17 began picking up speed. Two of the crew, Onodera and Nagata, came into the radio room.

"Nagata said it was beautiful and that he could see automobile headlights. The navigator came into the radio room then. 'We started shelling right after sunset,' he said. 'There was no reply until we started speeding away. Some enemy planes dropped flares, but they were far from our position.'

"The reaction set in then. 'We are the first to bombard America!' everybody began telling one another. 'Even if we don't hit a thing, they know I-17 has been here!' All of us felt like heroes."

They were. And yet, as would happen time and again to the Japanese submarine force, the adventure had been essentially useless. The Ellwood oil field, 12 miles north of Santa Barbara, was only slightly damaged, and its workers missed not a day's production. The incident may have been

the cause of a bad case of jitters among the antiaircraft gunners in the Los Angeles area; the next night they fired off 1,400 rounds of ammunition at illusory airplanes. But wartime censorship kept the Ellwood attack out of the papers, and there was no real civilian panic.

By the end of March 1942, the Japanese had occupied Sumatra in a stunning advance, and the Greater East Asia Co-Prosperity Sphere was for all practical purposes complete—in half the time originally estimated by the Japanese commanders. Since events had outstripped plans, most Japanese warships were recalled to the home islands for refit, while preparations were being made for the War's next phase.

In spite of all the dazzling successes, Admiral Yamamoto was disturbed: Early in 1942 the United States showed unexpected signs of coming back from its catastrophe at Pearl Harbor. First, Admiral William Halsey ordered carrier strikes against the Gilbert and Marshall Islands. Then, on April 18, B-25s under Lieut. Colonel James H. Doolittle bombed Tokyo after a daring takeoff from the carrier *Hornet,* and in early May, U.S. warships checked Japanese expansion in the Battle of the Coral Sea.

Yamamoto urgently wished to lure the U.S. fleet into the single, decisive battle while there was yet time. His gaze fell upon Midway, the outermost island of the Hawaiian chain and only 3,200 miles from San Francisco. The Japanese bombers could use the strategic speck of land as a base. Surely, Yamamoto thought, an invasion of Midway would draw out the American fleet for annihilation.

The date was set for early June. Preliminary to the great battle, Japanese submarines would deploy in far-flung picket lines to give warning of the U.S. fleet's approach.

Inexplicably, however, that crucial assignment was given to SubRon Five, a second-line unit under Rear Admiral Tadashige Daigo. This force was made up of obsolescent I-boats, each of them at least a dozen years old and already scheduled for retirement to training service. At least one Navy staff officer, Commander Shojiro Iura, protested the choice to Yamamoto's chief of staff. "Those submarines," he said, "are too old and too slow for that mission. I think the Combined Fleet staff officers are taking too much for granted when they station such a worn-out group of submarines in the path the Americans are most likely to use."

Iura was overruled—and his worst fears were soon fulfilled. SubRon Five was delayed in leaving Japan because of the extensive repairs required for its aged boats. Then, further delayed by a typographical error in position orders and still 2,000 miles from Midway, the squadron stopped to refuel at Kwajalein. Thereafter, for the most part, the boats traveled submerged lest they be seen by American planes from Midway. And it was while SubRon Five labored slowly toward its station that American carriers reached their positions unseen, to lie in wait for the Imperial Combined Fleet, completely upsetting Yamamoto's plan. Among the several factors that contributed to the Japanese disaster at Midway, the failure of SubRon Five took high place.

During the furious swirl of the Battle of Midway, the Japanese submarines sailed the distant peripheries in idle frustration, sighting little and sinking nothing. But in the immediate aftermath of Midway, Lieut. Commander Yahachi Tanabe in the *I-168* did salvage some pride for the submarine force by scoring a spectacular victory.

On the 5th of June, the day after the battle, a Japanese scouting plane reported that the U.S. aircraft carrier *Yorktown* lay badly damaged and dead in the water about 150 miles northeast of Midway. Commander Tanabe received the signal: SUBMARINE *I-168* WILL LOCATE AND DESTROY THE AMERICAN CARRIER.

After running submerged for the rest of the day and on the surface through much of the night, the *I-168* spotted her helpless prey about 11 miles away at 5:30 a.m. on June 6. "It was the easiest intercept a submarine commander ever made," recalled Tanabe. "My course had not changed from beginning to end."

Diving to 90 feet, Tanabe cut his speed to six knots, then to three. He had spotted one minesweeper with a towline out to the *Yorktown,* a destroyer, the *Hammann,* close by her side, and three more patrolling the flank nearest to the *I-168.* Figuring that there must be at least two others on the carrier's far side, Tanabe calculated that he was opposed by seven destroyers. "Our screws were barely turning over," he wrote, "and I hoped they were not giving off enough turbulence for the American ships to detect us."

The U.S. warships detected nothing. Shortly after 11 a.m., Tanabe's sound operator reported that he could no longer hear the *ping, ping* of the destroyers' echo-ranging. "It appears," said Tanabe, "the Americans have interrupted their war for lunch." In fact, Tanabe had crept through the destroyer screen, and the escorts were pinging on their far side, away from him. With infinite caution, Tanabe raised his periscope—and saw the huge loom of the *Yorktown* a mere 600 yards away.

"The tension in *I-168's* conning tower had been steadily building up for six and a half hours," Tanabe recalled. "We were all perspiring heavily. My torpedo petty officer was scanning his switch panel, and a nervous helmsman wiped clammy hands frequently on his pants. Lieutenant (jg.) Nakagawa, pencil in hand, mopped his damp brow between looks at the compass and speed indicator."

Then, to the astonishment of his colleagues, Tanabe stepped back from the periscope. "Down periscope!" he said. "Right 20 degrees rudder! Maintain full silence! Maintain speed of three knots!"

The others in the conning tower stared at Tanabe as if he were mad. "What has happened, Captain?" they asked. "Aren't we attacking?"

Tanabe explained: When fired from a depth of 60 feet, his torpedoes would require time to stabilize before striking the target. "The range is too short," he said. "I'm going to open the range and try again. I want to be sure of this kill."

In a slow, perilous journey requiring nearly 90 minutes, Tanabe edged the *I-168* to the right in a circle, returning to the boat's original track about a mile from the *Yorktown*.

Incredibly, the destroyers had still failed to detect him.

Once in place, Tanabe had a novel firing plan. "If I followed the usual procedure and fired four torpedoes with a two-degree spread," he later explained, "they would cover six degrees. But I wanted very badly to deprive the Americans of this carrier. I intended to limit my salvo to a two-degree spread. I would fire No. 1 and No. 2 first and then send No. 3 and No. 4 in their wakes, on the same courses. I would thus deliver all my punch into the carrier's midsection, rather than spread it out along her hull."

At 1:30 p.m., Tanabe fired. Within a minute, explosions were heard, and the submarine echoed with shouts of "Banzai!" Two of the torpedoes hit the *Yorktown,* and one hit the destroyer *Hammann,* killing many of her crewmen and sending the rest overboard. Soon the destroyer went down.

"Go ahead at full speed!" Tanabe ordered. And then: "Take her down to 200 feet!"

But on this day Yahachi Tanabe was full of surprises, and instead of fleeing he soon shook his officers by ordering the boat slowed almost to a standstill in what he considered the perfect hiding place. "By that time," Tanabe recalled, "we were where I wanted to be, directly beneath the enemy carrier. I didn't think she would sink at once, so had no fear of her coming down on us. There would be men in the water. Her destroyers wouldn't risk dropping depth charges for a while, for fear of killing their comrades."

It was a brilliant idea, but it failed. The crewmen of the

On one of many special missions performed by Japanese submarines, the I-29 (rear) prepares to meet a string of rubber boats from the U-180 at a rendezvous off Madagascar in April of 1943. The boats' chief passenger was Subhas Chandar Bose, a violently anti-British Indian nationalist who was coming out of exile in Germany. Bose planned to raise an army among Indian prisoners of war in Japan, and attack British colonial forces in Burma and elsewhere. But the scheme failed dismally, and Bose himself died in a plane crash in 1945.

Yorktown stayed aboard, and the destroyers quickly began depth-charging for all they were worth. The *I-168,* driven from her shelter, wriggled and squirmed for her life for the next two hours. At last, around sunset, more than 12 hours after the boat had submerged, she shook free from her tormentors. And 12 hours later, the *Yorktown* finally sank, taking 81 officers and men down with her.

It was a hallmark of Japanese submariners that they clung to large dreams, even though they could translate each one into only a small reality. Shortly after Midway, with all its discouragements, they returned to the dream of attacking the continental United States—this time using a single submarine to launch a plane flown by a warrant flying officer and his observer.

By the start of the War, 11 Japanese I-boats had been fitted out to carry, in deck hangars, a single-engined, catapult-launched plane, capable of flying for three hours at up to 100 knots. While its mother submarine was in transit, the plane was stored in 12 separate parts that could be quickly assembled for flight. Called *geta* (after the Japanese wooden clogs whose shape its floats resembled), the plane was meant to extend a submarine's reconnaissance range.

But Warrant Flying Officer Nobuo Fujita, a farm boy who had been conscripted into the Navy and subsequently spent nine prewar years as a pilot, had an idea for putting the *geta* to more lethal use. Shortly after the beginning of the War, while serving as a *geta* pilot on the *I-25,* Fujita took his plan to the boat's executive officer. "If our planes were armed with bombs," he said, "I could not only locate enemy ships for *I-25,* but also join in attacks to sink them."

The executive officer was enthusiastic, and urged Fujita to put his scheme on paper to be forwarded to higher command. Fujita complied. And there the matter seemingly rested—until July 27 when the *I-25,* which had just returned to Yokosuka, received a message: WARRANT OFFICER FUJITA IS INSTRUCTED TO REPORT TO IMPERIAL NAVAL HEADQUARTERS AT ONCE.

When he arrived at that august headquarters, Fujita was ushered into the office of Commander Iura, who was waiting there with another man dressed in the uniform of a Navy commander. Fujita was stunned to recognize the officer as Prince Takamatsu, younger brother of the Japanese Emperor. "Fujita," said Iura, "we are going to have you bomb the American mainland."

At that point another officer entered the room and spread charts on a table. Recalled Fujita: "He ran his finger along the American coastline, stopping at a point just inland of the coast and about 75 miles north of the California border. 'You will bomb forests for us,' he said, 'right about here.'

"I was dumfounded! Even a cadet pilot could bomb a forest. What did they want *me* for? The aide read my disappointment, for he began to speak more rapidly.

" 'The northwestern United States is full of forests. Once a blaze gets started in the deep woods it is very difficult to stop. Sometimes whole towns are destroyed. If we were to bomb some of these forests, it would put the enemy to much trouble. It might even cause large-scale panic.' "

The mission went forward. Fujita spent weeks training and studying for his momentous task. Then came his long, slow journey to American waters in the submarine *I-25.* Fujita was cleaning his pistol at 4 o'clock on the morning of September 9, 1942, when a messenger ordered him to report to the *I-25's* skipper, Meiji Tagami, in the conning tower. There, nodding at the periscope, Tagami said, "Take a look, Fujita, and tell me what you think."

Recalled Fujita: "I grasped the periscope's handles and peered through its eyepiece at the coast of Oregon, its inland mountains wreathed by haze. I could make out the white face of Cape Blanco and could see its lighthouse flashing in the twilight. The waves, so high for the past 10 days, had flattened out. The sky was clear, too. 'Captain,' I said, 'it looks good. I think we can do it today.' "

Once again, the preparations for a Japanese submarine mission were more exciting than the mission itself. The brave Fujita and his observer, Petty Officer Shoji Okuda, did fly 50 miles inland. They did drop two bombs on Oregon's forests. They did return in the best of health. "Mission is completed, sir," Fujita reported back to the commander of the submarine. "Both bombs exploded perfectly. Two large fires are spreading."

In fact, Oregon had recently been saturated by heavy rains, and Fujita's fires quickly burned themselves out. Little damage was done and the American populace did not panic. Fujita's exploit had been a symbolic success but a practical waste of a submarine. The *I-25* could have been employed to much better effect in the Solomon Islands, where a crisis had meanwhile developed that would permanently change the major mission of the Japanese submarine force.

On August 15, 1942, when the I-25 left for the Oregon coast, other Japanese submarines were scattered far and wide: Some were operating off Australia, others in the Aleutians, some in the Indian Ocean and the Bay of Bengal. So widespread was the deployment that only two submarines, both of them RO-class coastal boats, were in the Solomons area when, on August 7, the U.S. Navy began landing 11,000 Marines on the malarial island of Guadalcanal.

Taken by surprise, the Imperial Navy reacted swiftly and furiously. By August 24, no fewer than 13 more submarines

had been rushed to the Solomons, along with strong surface forces. On that day, shortly after 8 a.m., the I-123 was patrolling in Indispensable Strait, between the eastern end of Guadalcanal and the island of Malaita, when she was spotted by the old U.S. destroyer Gamble, which had been converted into a minelayer. The Gamble depth-charged the I-123 for nearly four hours, and destroyed her and her crew.

Japanese submariners soon took revenge in full and with interest. On the afternoon of September 15, Commander Takaichi Kinashi, already one of Japan's submarine aces with six ships totaling about 40,000 tons to his credit, was in the I-19 in the waters of the Solomon Islands. Raising his periscope to reconnoiter his surroundings, Kinashi was awe-struck. There were so many American warships within

A dense pall of oily smoke mushrooms skyward from the U.S. tanker Mississinewa, set afire in the Ulithi atoll on November 20, 1944, by a kaiten—a piloted torpedo launched from a Japanese submarine. The suicide pilot in this case was one of the weapon's two designers, Lieutenant Sekio Nishina (above).

THE MANY ROLES OF THE PBYs

U.S. submarine crews in the Pacific developed a special fondness for the lumbering old flying boat everyone knew as "Dumbo," after Walt Disney's amiable flying elephant. Officially designated the PBY Catalina, this rugged twin-engined reconnaissance craft could fly for an average of 14 hours at a speed of 100 miles per hour and cover a wide swath of ocean.

For submarines on war patrol, the Dumbos were superb teammates, spotting and tracking enemy convoys and warship formations. And for boats on lifeguard duty, charged with rescuing downed fliers, the Dumbos were peerless guides, finding the men bobbing in the sea and staying with them until the submarines arrived.

But there was another side to the PBYs' personality. Armed with depth charges, the planes were also efficient hunters of enemy submarines. Each morning at bases throughout the Pacific, PBYs would take off and, flying at wavetop height, patrol their beats, circling harbors and beaches to guard against undersea intruders.

Once the enemy was sighted, the PBY would swing swiftly into its attack before the submarine dived. "We tried to drop everything on the first run," said one flier, Navy Lieutenant William Scarborough. "Everything" meant two wing-mounted, 325-pound depth charges that could be set to explode on contact as well as underwater. After the attack, a standard tactic was to call in a second bomb-carrying PBY, and then orbit some distance away waiting for the target to resurface.

Exactly how many submarines the PBYs sank in the Pacific is uncertain. They were officially credited with two of the 112 Japanese submarines known to have been destroyed by U.S. forces. But it is likely that they got some of the 19 Japanese submarines unaccounted for. In any case, the relentless patrolling helped greatly in forcing Japanese submarines away from American bases. "We kept them scrambling and below periscope depth," said one pilot. "We neutralized them."

A midget submarine, perhaps abandoned, lies aground on an unidentified island in this photo by a PBY.

110

A PBY's bomb explodes astern after an attack on a submerged Japanese submarine. A second bomb is visible under the plane's left wing.

reach of his torpedoes—23 altogether—that he could not see them all at once. There was the carrier *Wasp,* with cruisers and destroyers in escort. Beyond the *Wasp* was the carrier *Hornet,* accompanied by the new battleship *North Carolina* and other escorts.

Given the range and the crowd, Kinashi could hardly miss. He fired six torpedoes. Three smashed into the *Wasp* so violently that aircraft were hurled from her flight deck. Three others sped past the *Wasp* and the *Hornet's* group, exploding against the *North Carolina* and the destroyer *O'Brien.* In the confusion, Kinashi's *I-19* easily escaped.

Six hours and 15 minutes later, the *Wasp,* her fires out of control, went under. Although the sturdy *North Carolina* was saved, she was put out of the War for two months. The *O'Brien* was given temporary repairs and sent limping back to the United States. But her back had been broken and she finally sank between New Caledonia and California.

For another two months, savage battles raged ashore and on the sea's surface for control of Guadalcanal, with the submarines of both sides playing only a minor part. But by mid-November it was clear that the Americans were on Guadalcanal to stay, and the Japanese problem became one of keeping 15,000 troops alive until they could be extricated. On November 16, Vice Admiral Teruhisa Komatsu, who had succeeded to the command of the Sixth Fleet, held a conference at Truk—and announced that submarines henceforth would carry provisions to Guadalcanal.

The junior submariners were aghast. "How," asked one, "can submarines carry out their foremost mission—attack—when we are forced into this stupid work?" Finally Komatsu held up his hand for silence. The troops on Guadalcanal, he said, were starving. "We must help them," he insisted, "no matter what sacrifices must be made."

So began an enterprise that would preoccupy most of the Japanese submarine force until the end of the War. Supply operations expanded almost immediately from Guadalcanal to include beleaguered troops on New Guinea and other islands, and eventually reached a point where there were more boats on supply missions than on war patrols. It was dangerous and dirty nightwork; the submariners contemptuously referred to it as Operation *Mogura*—or Mole.

By early 1943 as many as 17 Japanese submarines were relegated either full- or part-time to *Mogura.* Submarines were so valuable for this unsubmarinely task that even the Japanese Army was quietly getting into the business of building boats for supply duty. Japan's wartime Prime Minister and Minister of War, General Hideki Tojo, tried to keep the secret. "If the Navy learns of Army plans to build submarines," Tojo told an associate, "it will surely oppose them. So don't tell the Navy."

The Navy not only found out, but cordially loaned the Army several technicians to help in the project. All told, some 50 Army submarines were constructed, but they went to waste: Only three actually saw service, running supplies to the Philippines in late 1944.

As for the Navy's *Mogura,* its techniques were at first both imaginative and crude. A major difficulty lay in landing supplies under the constant threat of attack by American aircraft and warships. In the early attempts, provisions were placed inside rubber bags, which in turn were encased in wooden cylinders to be fired ashore from submarine torpedo tubes. The containers blew up, strewing supplies across large tracts of water.

More practical methods were soon developed. One employed the *unkato,* or "stores-carrying tube," a 130-foot-long cylinder with ballast tanks at each end. When filled with supplies, the *unkato* had a capacity of 377 tons. Towed into shallow water by a submarine, it was then cast loose and retrieved by soldiers who waded out to haul it ashore.

More sophisticated was the *unpoto,* or "cannon carrier," so called since it was sometimes used to land artillery pieces. The *unpoto* was a raft 71 feet long and 13 feet wide that was floated on two cylinders and propelled by the power plants of two torpedoes. Like the *unkato,* the *unpoto* was towed to the landing site; from there it was driven ashore by a pilot from the submarine.

While flirting with fate in enemy-controlled waters, the *Mogura* boats suffered high casualties. On December 9, 1942, with the operation barely begun, the *I-3,* under Commander Ichiro Togami, was caught and sunk by an American torpedo boat off Cape Esperance. On December 20 near Simpson Harbor, New Britain, Lieut. Commander Toshitake Ueno's *I-4* was sighted by the U.S. submarine *Seadragon,* which fired four torpedoes and sank the Japanese boat. And on January 29, 1943, a wild fray put an end to the long career of the *I-1*, at the age of 16 the "grandfather" of the Japanese submarine fleet.

The *I-1*, under Lieut. Commander Eichi Sakamoto, appeared on the radar of a New Zealand corvette, the *Kiwi*. At 9 p.m., as Sakamoto was preparing to unload supplies in Guadalcanal's Komimbo Bay, the *Kiwi* rushed at her, firing deck guns, machine guns and even rifles. The *Kiwi* rammed the *I-1*, and then, during a battle at close quarters, rammed her twice more. Somehow, the boat remained afloat. Then the *Kiwi's* sister ship, the *Moa*, joined the brawl, and she too rammed the *I-1*.

During the struggle, Sakamoto was mortally wounded and 30 Japanese seamen were killed. But the *I-1* did not go down. Her executive officer, Lieutenant Sadayoshi Koreeda, finally disengaged the boat, ran her onto the beach and escaped with about 50 survivors. A few, Koreeda among them, joined Japanese soldiers and spent the rest of the War in the fetid jungle of Guadalcanal.

"The war in the Pacific," wrote submariner Zenji Orita, "was truly developing into a hellish one for our Sixth Fleet." And while those on supply missions might call themselves moles, those on war patrols thought of themselves as *nezumi*, or rats. "With their radar," Orita recalled, "the American destroyers were like cats in the dark, ready to pounce, and the 'rats' had to elude them." In November of 1943, the fate of a nine-submarine Japanese patrol east of the Gilbert Islands more than proved Orita's point.

By October, Japanese Naval commanders had heavily fortified the Gilberts, suspecting quite correctly that the is- land group was a target for imminent invasion. And in mid-November nine submarines were sent out on a scouting expedition. For about five weeks, all seemed placid. Then, on November 20, the waters of the Gilberts suddenly teemed with American warships in overwhelming strength, and U.S. Marines were landed on Betio, an island at the southern end of the Tarawa atoll. After that, the reports from the submarines to Japanese Sixth Fleet headquarters came thick and fast for a while and then—sickeningly—slowed and almost stopped.

On November 22, Lieut. Commander Hideo Yamamoto in the *I-35* sent a wireless message: YESTERDAY *I-35* PIERCED THE ENEMY SCREEN AND GOT WITHIN SIGHT OF TARAWA. SIGHTED LARGE ENEMY TASK FORCE AND TRIED TO APPROACH IT BUT WAS INTERCEPTED BY AIRCRAFT AND HAD TO DIVE. Yamamoto was never heard from again: The *I-35* had been detected by the U.S. destroyers *Meade* and *Frazier*. They depth-charged the *I-35* to the surface, where the *Frazier* rammed the submarine and sank her.

That same day the *I-19*—the submarine that had sunk the *Wasp*—radioed headquarters that she expected to arrive within 30 miles of Tarawa within 48 hours. That was the *I-19's* last message: She was picked up on radar and depth-charged to destruction by the destroyer *Radford*.

Other boats were heard from once and then no more. On November 25, just after Japanese land forces had been annihilated on Betio, Lieut. Commander Makio Tanaka in the *I-39* reported that he was 60 miles southwest of Tarawa and had attacked enemy ships. Then silence. On November 27, the *I-21's* commander, Hiroshi Inada, reported that he was

Japanese midget submarines sit like cigars in a box at the naval shipyard near Kure. More than 400 of these two-man craft were stockpiled to defend against an expected U.S. invasion.

30 miles southwest of Tarawa and enemy warships were in sight. Silence. Neither the *I-40* nor the *RO-38* answered a general call to report on December 3. The *Radford* had sunk the *I-40*. Thus, out of the nine submarines that had gone on patrol to the Gilberts, only three survived.

The Gilberts debacle, combined with Operation *Mogura's* continuing drudgery, had an extraordinary aftermath. Skippers of the three surviving submarines complained bitterly—and openly. "I am positive," said Lieut. Commander Nobukiyo Nambu of the *I-174*, "that all the submarines lost went down without even getting a chance to attack the enemy." The *I-169* and the *I-175*, which had also survived, had received insufficient rest from previous patrols and, as a result, their crews were exhausted. "As for *RO-38*," he continued, "she was fresh from home waters, with an inexperienced crew that still needed lots of training." Added Lieut. Commander Zenshin Toyama of the *I-169* and Lieut. Commander Sunao Tabata of the *I-175*: "Sixth Fleet headquarters required reports from us too often, again making for easy discovery through radio detection." Tabata, however, had scored a big hit in the Gilberts operation: On November 24 the *I-175* sank the U.S. escort carrier *Liscome Bay* off Makin Island, with a loss of 644 American lives.

In January of 1944, a nearly mutinous protest came from an officer who had merely heard of the Gilberts fiasco. He was Zenji Orita, by now a lieutenant commander and the skipper of the *I-177*. Orita stated his case aboard the *Katori*, facing the latest fleet commander, Vice Admiral Takeo Takagi, and his chief of staff, Rear Admiral Hisao Mito.

"As all here know," said Orita, "using submarines for transport is throwing away the reason for their construction." His men, he continued, were eager to fight but not to lug around crates of supplies.

Admiral Takagi tried to soothe Orita, then stood up to signal the end of the meeting.

"Admiral," said Orita, "I have other things I would like to add." Takagi sat down.

Among other things, Orita criticized the continuing deployment of submarines in sentry lines. When the enemy detected one boat in a line, he said, "he can detect the others even more easily. Thus, all are endangered by one."

Admiral Mito interrupted. Japan's situation, he said, was such that "sometimes we have to send our submarines out

when there is not even a 50-50 chance of their returning."

Orita, furious, pounded the table. "All submariners are willing to give their lives at sea," he cried. "What we expect of you and your staff is that you keep that 50 per cent chance in mind. Otherwise, we will lose all of our boats."

Admiral Takagi brought the astounding session to a close. Orita's views, he said, reflected "a negative attitude. No matter what the difference may be between our capability and that of the enemy, we must still carry out our orders, mustn't we? This has always been the battle spirit of Japanese submarine men, has it not?"

Orita, utterly defeated, shut up. But his negative attitude about picket lines was, all too soon, to be proved devastatingly correct.

Early in 1944, the American forces in the central Pacific were on the prowl, beginning with the seizure of the Marshall Islands in January and February. Then carrier forces went after the Japanese fleet at Truk and the Palaus, and, in April, to General MacArthur's aid in his invasion of Hollandia on the north coast of New Guinea. Now they were ready to move on the Marianas. By May 16, Japanese submarines were in place off the Marianas—as always, they were deployed in a picket line.

On May 19, the U.S. destroyer escort *England*, patrolling with the destroyer escorts *George* and *Raby*, followed up an American plane's report of sighting a submarine. The *England* found, attacked and destroyed the *I-16*.

By now well aware of Japanese tactical deployment, the three warships swung west, seeking the next submarine in the line. They missed the *I-144*, but continued on their way and found the *RO-106*. The *England* sank her. Next in line was the *RO-104*, which eluded the destroyers for what was left of the day; they found her the next day, and the *England* got her. Missing the *RO-105*, the destroyers killed the *RO-116* and, 48 hours later, the *RO-108*. On May 31 the *RO-105* went down. Within 12 days, by the relatively simple procedure of rolling up a picket line, the *England's* group had sunk six Japanese submarines.

The Japanese were now engaged in a desperate war of defense, and their submarine force reflected that bitter reality. Eighteen boats of the *RO-100* class, capable of a top surface speed of 14.5 knots and able to do only eight knots

The last major victim of Japan's submarine fleet, the cruiser Indianapolis was sunk by Lieut. Commander Mochitsura Hashimoto (inset) and his I-58 on July 30, 1945, only eight days before the first atomic bomb was dropped on Hiroshima. Ironically, the U.S. warship went down just after delivering A-bomb parts to the B-29 base at Tinian in the Marianas.

while submerged, were built as part of the Navy's replenishment program for the defense of island shorelines. Two even slower boats, at least while submerged, were the I-351-class submarines, which crept beneath the water at a snail's-pace 6.3 knots. Carrying 370 tons of gasoline in addition to their own diesel-fuel requirements, the I-351s had been designed as undersea tankers to supply distant submarine bases; in the event, however, they were used as seaplane tenders.

Toward the end of the War, the Japanese gained the distinction of producing the world's fastest submersible. Modeled after the German Type XXI U-boat and further refined, the I-201-class attack submarines had highly streamlined hulls, a narrow 12 to 1 length-to-beam ratio, improved diesels, and enormously powerful electric motors that could drive the boat for 55 minutes at a fantastic 19 knots underwater. Twenty-three were ordered, but only three were actually completed, and they were commissioned too late in the War to have any effect; there is no record of their ever having sunk a ship.

As far back as 1942, wonderful plans had been made for building giant I-400-class submarines—more than 400 feet long and displacing upward of 5,000 tons. These boats would carry two or perhaps three aircraft and span the globe, attacking New York, Washington and other ports on the East Coast of the United States. Those hopes were later reduced to a scheme for blockading the Panama Canal. And in fact, when two of the monsters were completed, they too were used for routine supply duty.

At one point in 1944, there was a plan brewing to convert existing I-boats to transport amphibious vehicles piggyback from Kure to Bougainville. The amphibians, equipped with tracks, were supposed to crawl over coral reefs into lagoons and attack enemy ships with—incredibly—torpedoes. The plan died in embryo.

Much more practical—and infinitely more sinister—were the two transport submarines of the new I-361 class, which had been completed by the late summer of 1944. These could carry 85 tons of supplies, 100 men and two small craft to land them. But they were adapted to a grim use—the very use Admiral Yamamoto had been determined to avoid when he authorized the deployment of midget submarines at Pearl Harbor. In less than three years, Japan had been so reduced in fortune that it was prepared to send men to their deaths by suicide.

The macabre idea was born in the minds of two young

midget-submarine pilots, Lieutenant (jg.) Hiroshi Kuroki and Lieutenant (jg.) Sekio Nishina. They began drawing plans for a tiny pilot's compartment with controls, a seat and a periscope, to be inserted between the war head and the power plant of a Model 93 torpedo, surface sister to the submarines' Model 95. When transported to the target area on an I-boat, the lethal little submarine would be cast free to inflict death at the cost of the pilot's life. Kuroki and Nishina called the weapon a *kaiten*—literally "sky change" and, by extension, the agent of change in Japan's fortunes.

When the *kaiten* plan was submitted early in the War, it was flatly rejected by the Navy's command. Kuroki and Nishina persisted. Finally, to impress their superiors with their sincerity, they observed the honored tradition of writing a petition in their own blood. In late 1943, upon receipt of the petition, the Imperial Japanese Navy accepted the submarine as a *tokko,* or suicide, weapon.

In the summer of 1944, a *kaiten* base was established on Otsujima, an island in Japan's Inland Sea, with several dozen young trainees who were prepared to die for their country. They would be followed by many more—there was never a dearth of volunteers, either for the *kaiten* or for its airborne equivalent, the Kamikaze program, which was established two months later.

The chief instructors at the Otsujima base were, appropriately, Hiroshi Kuroki and Sekio Nishina. But on the 6th of September, Kuroki, whose dream of glory would send other young men to death, met his own inglorious end when his controls jammed. Practicing in a *kaiten* designed to hold two men, Kuroki and a trainee, Lieutenant Takashi Higuchi, lost control and plunged to the bottom. There their submarine broke open, drowning them both.

On November 8, 1944, the *I-47,* commanded by Zenji Orita, the man who had stood up to fleet commander Takagi and his chief of staff, departed from Otsujima on the first *kaiten* mission. The submarine's destination was the Ulithi atoll in the Caroline Islands, with its enormous deepwater lagoon. Ulithi had been occupied by the Americans without a fight in September 1944 and was now being used as a major forward anchorage by the U.S. Pacific Fleet.

On their voyage, the four *kaiten* pilots on the *I-47* studied recognition silhouettes of enemy ships, played chess, and teased one of their number, a young lieutenant, junior grade, named Hitoshi Fukuda, who was so shy that he suffered through his first full day at sea rather than ask how to work the submarine's rather complicated toilet.

At noon on November 19, Orita raised his periscope just outside Ulithi's reef. He saw the lagoon dotted with dozens of American warships of every description. Said Orita: "We will launch *kaiten* in the morning."

That evening, recalled Orita, "a fine sake, a gift from the Emperor, was served in specially prepared lacquer-ware cups. Then the pilots retired to get what rest they could. I waited until 90 minutes after sunset, then took *I-47* to the surface. At a speed of 12 knots I approached Ulithi. There was no need to take a star sight. The atoll sky was bright, like a coastal city's in peacetime. I told myself that the presence of all those lights meant the enemy had no idea we were anywhere near."

By 4 o'clock on the morning of November 20, the four pilots had entered their *kaiten.* One of them was none other than Sekio Nishina, who had with him an urn containing the ashes of his coinventor, Hiroshi Kuroki.

At 4:15 a.m., Orita gave the command, "Go!"

Nishina's *kaiten* slid off the *I-47's* deck and disappeared. By 4:30 a.m., all four *kaiten* were in the water. On the bridge of the *I-47,* Orita and others waited tensely. At 5:07 a huge burst of light within the harbor was followed in seconds by the sound of an explosion; four minutes later, there was still another explosion. For the *I-47,* it was time to leave: Orita took the boat down and headed north, away from the first *kaiten* attacks.

Returning to Kure, the *I-47* was credited with an aircraft carrier and a battleship. In fact, only a U.S. fleet oiler had been destroyed; the other three *kaiten* were either sunk by U.S. defenders or were otherwise wrecked.

So far as is known, there was only one other victim of the *kaiten* during the War. A human torpedo from the *I-53* blew off the bow of the U.S. destroyer escort *Underhill* on July

24, 1945, in the Philippine Sea, damaging her so badly that she had to be sunk. The cost of the kaiten program to the Japanese was heavy: 80 pilots lost on sorties, and another 16 in training.

For Japanese submariners, the War was all but over. By 1945, only a dozen or so submarines remained fit for combat service. Among them, with kaiten aboard, was the I-58 under Commander Mochitsura Hashimoto, a veteran who had been a torpedo officer on one of the I-boats carrying midgets to Pearl Harbor.

On the night of July 29, 1945, at about 11 o'clock, the I-58 and Hashimoto, 11 days out of Kure, were on the surface between Guam and Leyte when a dark mass was sighted on the horizon. Hashimoto went to periscope depth, then submerged fully. "All tubes to the ready," he ordered. And then: "Kaiten stand by."

The dark shape grew larger and larger. "It was still making straight for us," recalled Hashimoto. "At this rate it would pass right over us."

By now, the kaiten pilots were begging Hashimoto to surface so that they might enter their craft. But Hashimoto was having none of it. He had Model 95 torpedoes in his tubes and he was determined to use them as a captain should.

"Stand by," ordered Hashimoto. "Fire!"

Six torpedoes were launched and sped from the forward tubes. Hashimoto waited.

"Every minute seemed an age," he wrote later. "Then on the starboard side of the enemy by the forward turret, and then by the after turret, there rose columns of water, to be followed immediately by flashes of bright red flame. Then another column of water rose from alongside No. 2 turret and seemed to envelop the whole ship. 'A hit, a hit!' I shouted as each torpedo struck home, and the crew danced round with joy."

The I-58 had dealt mortal blows to the U.S. heavy cruiser Indianapolis as she headed unescorted toward the Philippines. Two Japanese torpedoes had hit her, and the secondary explosions that followed ripped the ship wide open. Internal communications were knocked out immediately, and all fire mains burst. The crippled ship plowed on, scooping up tons of water that hastened her sinking.

The commander of the Indianapolis, Captain Charles Butler McVay III, ordered a distress call sent. But no ship or shore station ever received his SOS. Less than 15 minutes after being hit, the Indianapolis went down, bow first. Hundreds of stunned, badly burned sailors leaped into the oil-streaked, shark-filled water wearing life jackets but with only 12 rafts and six large rescue nets among them.

For the survivors, the real ordeal lay ahead. One day passed, and then another, and another. The sailors, burning with thirst, fired flares and watched in anguish as Army planes streamed by overhead without noticing them. They watched their mates die. Some men began to hallucinate.

"Here comes a Jap, he's trying to kill me, help!" shouted a sailor on one raft. He began swinging wildly. He kept punching thin air until his mates subdued him.

More than 80 hours after the sinking, a twin-engined Ventura, flying by chance in the area, spotted an oil slick. The plane swooped low to investigate and the pilot saw the men in life rafts. After dropping some gear to the desperate men, the pilot sent a radio message that started one of the largest rescue operations in history. Ships and planes swarmed to the area and picked up 316 survivors. But some 400 men of the Indianapolis had been killed in the torpedo blast, and about 500 more had died in the water.

The Japanese submariners who had sunk the Indianapolis did not know the identity of their victim; the cruiser was so big they thought they had sent down an Idaho-class battleship. In any case, the victory was a magnificent one, and they celebrated it with a feast of rice, beans, boiled eels and tinned corned beef. The only unhappy men aboard were the kaiten pilots. With tears in their eyes, they demanded to be taken to a good target. Commander Hashimoto obliged. On the way home in early August, the I-58 came across several enemy ships and all but one of the kaiten pilots on board were launched on glorious suicide torpedo runs. Hashimoto detected explosions, and claimed a destroyer and a merchantman sunk. But Allied records do not confirm any sinkings at that time along the I-58's track.

ALL THE EMPEROR'S BOATS

Celebrating a national holiday, Japanese submariners toast the Emperor on the deck of their I-class fleet boat, moored in the harbor at Truk in the Carolines.

MARVELS OF INVENTION AND VERSATILITY

"We overestimated our submarines," admitted Vice Admiral Shigeyoshi Miwa, commander of Japan's undersea fleet, after the War. "When it came to the test of actual warfare," added a veteran senior officer, "the results were deplorable." Yet despite flaws in their design and serious mistakes in their tactical use, the Japanese boats were marvels of versatility, performing a wider range of services than any other nation's submarines.

By the start of the war with the United States, Japan's naval designers had created or modified boats of many shapes and sizes for literally dozens of special functions. There were small HA-class and RO-class boats for defending coastal waters and midget submarines for infiltrating enemy harbors to attack capital ships at anchor. I-class boats, comparable to the U.S. fleet submarines, were equipped to transport the short-range midgets and launch them close to the enemy bases. Huge I-boats were modified to carry a small seaplane that greatly extended the surface fleet's reconnaissance range. A few experimental I-boats were adapted to carry amphibious vehicles to the reef-barred island battlefields of the central Pacific.

When the tide of war turned against Japan in 1943, the submarines were further modified to cope with harsh new realities, and here they served exceptionally well. Many I-boats, stripped of torpedoes and transformed into cargo carriers, smuggled supplies to island garrisons bypassed by the advancing Americans, and on their return voyages they served as hospital ships, bringing home the sick and the wounded. They were refitted as oil tankers at a time when, as a Japanese Naval officer said, "one drop of high-octane gasoline is as precious as a drop of human blood."

In removing the I-boats' attack gear, the Japanese high command tacitly admitted that the last chance for victory was slipping away; survival alone had become the objective. Yet the crews who had served so gallantly in a lost cause were still unready to accept defeat. In 1944, several I-boats were modified anew—their decks were rigged to carry huge torpedoes converted into suicide submarines.

In Kure harbor, two small HA-class coastal-defense submarines lie alongside a speedy I-boat and the I-106, a slow but commodious supply submarine.

THE LEVIATHANS
AND THE MINNOWS

Japan's undersea force included the leviathans and the minnows of the submarine world. The smallest Japanese submarines were only 78.5 feet long and displaced a mere 46 tons. These two-man midgets had a range of only 100 miles, and since they had no generators to recharge their batteries, they were virtual suicide craft. More than 100 were built during the War, but only a few of them saw action.

Each of the three biggest Japanese submarines was 394 feet long and displaced 3,530 tons—roughly 800 tons more than the world's next-largest boats, the French *Surcouf* and American *Argonaut*. The Japanese giants were equipped with a special breathing device also possessed by the latest German U-boats: Air tubes that could be extended to the surface enabled them to operate their four diesel engines while submerged. The fuel tanks held 500,000 gallons, enough to carry the submarines 30,000 miles, the longest range of any boat that fought in the War.

Japan's enormous I-400 displays a black surrender flag at war's end in August of 1945. The boat was designed for long-distance attack missions, but she never saw action.

A midget submarine, one of the five that attacked Pearl Harbor, wallows in the surf on the east side of Oahu. She was fitted with a self-destruct mechanism, but it failed to work.

I-BOATS WITH
AN ADDED DIMENSION

About 40 of the large I-class submarines were equipped as aircraft carriers, with a small reconnaissance seaplane. The special planes had a top speed of approximately 150 miles per hour and a range of 550 miles. Their wings, floats and fins were detachable, and the flaps and tail assemblage folded so that the plane could be stored on deck in a cylindrical hangar.

The plane was usually assembled in the early-morning hours for a reconnaissance mission at dawn and then was hurled off the forward deck by a compressed-air catapult. When the mission was completed, the pilot landed at sea at a prearranged rendezvous point and waited there for the submarine to arrive. The plane was hoisted aboard by a crane.

Both the launching and the recovery process took nearly one hour—more if the sea was rough. And the operation was hazardous indeed, for during launching the submarine lay vulnerable to armed enemy patrol planes. At least one submarine, forced to dive by a sudden air attack, had to abandon her plane and its pilot.

The submarine I-26 slices through home waters during a test run off Honshu in October of 1941. Her aircraft hangar, extending forward from the conning tower, was later used for transporting supplies to other I-boats.

On patrol off the Malay coast, crew members of the I-29 prepare to launch a seaplane from a catapult on the forward deck. The planes could carry two 170-pound bombs.

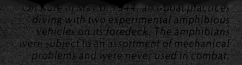

On Kure in May of 1944, an I-boat practices diving with two experimental amphibious vehicles on its foredeck. The amphibians were subject to an assortment of mechanical problems and were never used in combat.

Two Japanese submariners inspect a beached amphibious vehicle on Kure. Equipped with tanklike treads, these vehicles were designed to crawl over coral reefs and attack U.S. ships anchored in inner lagoons.

Crewmen on an I-boat load two amphibians with attack weapons: two torpedoes, one to a side. Once the vehicles were released from their submarine, they could not be recovered.

Vice Admiral Miwa exhorts kaiten pilots assembled on the deck of an I-boat at Otsujima. The pilots wear white headbands and gloves as symbols of their determination and purity.

Departing aboard the I-370 to attack the U.S. invasion fleet at Iwo Jima, four kaiten pilots brandish ceremonial swords atop their suicide torpedoes. The I-370 was sunk by a U.S. warship before she could launch her kaiten.

A "NEW, SECRET, ONE-WAY WEAPON"

In August 1944, at a secret base on Otsu-jima, in Japan's Inland Sea, more than 200 Japanese volunteers began learning to pilot a "new, secret, one-way weapon"—the *kaiten*, a 54-foot-long torpedo with a small pilot's chamber, a periscope and a 3,000-pound war head. The addition of the pilot was supposed to guarantee a hit every time. But the *kaiten* was bulky and difficult to control. "A man needed six hands and eyes," recalled a trainee.

The *kaiten* pilot received a final estimate of the target's course and speed just prior to being launched from the deck of an I-class mother submarine. After a brief submerged run, he popped to the surface for a sighting, and then barreled ahead at 40 knots to the target.

In approximately 80 missions during the final nine months of the War, *kaiten* managed to sink only three U.S. ships. Besides the 80 men who died in suicide missions, no fewer than eight *kaiten*-bearing I-boats were sunk en route to launch sites, killing more than 600 crewmen.

The U.S.S. *Narwhal* was an old and obsolete submarine, unfit for the rigors and hazards of combat patrol. She had been built in the 1920s, and could manage scarcely 16 knots surfaced and six knots submerged, far less than the newer fleet boats. What is more, she presented a fat and inviting target to submarine-killing Japanese convoy escorts, for she displaced an enormous 2,700 tons and was about as maneuverable as a coal barge.

Yet in November 1943, as she plowed her way through the Mindanao Sea, the *Narwhal* was fulfilling a role for the U.S. Navy in which she excelled. The big old submarine was on a special mission to the Philippines as part of a remarkable operation known as *Spyron*—for Spy Squadron.

Though the *Narwhal* was armed, she had been pressed into service as a supply carrier for the Philippine guerrillas; every square foot of unoccupied space in her ample interior was crammed with cargo, 92 tons of it, including radio sets, quinine and other medicines, clothing, carbines and cartridges.

The *Narwhal* also carried a special passenger. He was Lieut. Commander Charles "Chick" Parsons, an officer in the Naval Reserve who had been manager of a stevedore company in the Philippines. Taken prisoner after the fall of Manila, Parsons had persuaded his captors to treat him as a neutral on the ground that he had been filling in for the absent consul of Panama; he had been allowed to leave on the repatriation ship, the *Gripsholm*. Now, as the head of *Spyron*, he was back—commissioned by General Douglas MacArthur to organize, coordinate and supply the guerrillas. His task was to prepare for the American liberation of the Philippines, and even the matchbooks he brought ashore for the guerrillas were printed with MacArthur's famed promise, "I shall return."

Most of the *Narwhal's* crew would much rather have been in a lean and deadly fleet boat, hunting and sinking enemy ships. As it happened, the mission of the *Narwhal* was anything but a milk run, and for the submariners craving action it provided an almost fatal dose of excitement.

The *Narwhal* was 18 days out of Brisbane on the way to Mindoro when she made a night surface contact with a Japanese tanker in the Mindanao Sea. By rights, the skipper, Frank D. Latta, should have ignored the tanker; his business was elsewhere. But Latta, like his crew, was yearning for

ON SPECIAL ASSIGNMENT

combat. He executed an attack approach on the tanker and fired a spread of four torpedoes from his forward tubes. All four fish missed.

At once the rash attack backfired, for the tanker was accompanied by three destroyer escorts, which Latta had overlooked in the dark. And now they came roaring down on the *Narwhal*. Latta took the huge submarine deep and she lay there suffering as a fierce barrage of depth charges exploded all around.

When the sound and fury died down, Latta took her up again. And there were the waiting escorts, driving at flank speed toward his surfaced boat. Desperate, Latta started to run for his life, the *Narwhal's* four diesels pounding heavily.

The escorts pursued, firing star shells to illuminate their target and armor-piercing shells to sink it. Latta called for more speed. The engineering officer, a lieutenant named Plummer, grew worried about his overworked diesels and called the bridge. "Captain," he said, "if we don't slow down pretty soon we're not going to have any engines left back here." Latta eyed the oncoming Japanese and replied, "If we slow down we won't need those damn engines."

Then, incredibly, the shell splashes gradually began to fall farther and farther behind the *Narwhal's* churning wake. The ancient tub was opening the range on the Japanese escorts. With vast relief, Latta realized that the escorts themselves had to be older vessels incapable of more than 15 to 16 knots. As the star shells faded into gloom, the U.S. skipper zigged his submarine off on a new course. And after an hour's frantic race, he at last managed to elude the enemy—and back off the throttles of his overheated diesels.

From then on, Latta stuck strictly to business. Two days later the *Narwhal* lay to at an appointed spot just off the coast of Mindoro. Soon a guerrilla sailing vessel, the *Dona Juana Maru*, came alongside and took off some supplies.

A few days after that, the *Narwhal* put in at a place called Nasipit Harbor on the island of Mindanao. The guerrillas there were numerous and supremely confident that—with the help of the supplies and weapons provided by the *Narwhal*— they could hold their own against the Japanese. In fact, their village band arrayed itself onshore and, in defiance of any Japanese who might have been patrolling nearby, serenaded the *Narwhal* with "Anchors Aweigh."

Emptied of cargo, the submarine evacuated 32 refugees

and then turned back toward Australia to load up for yet another *Spyron* mission. During the rest of the War, the *Narwhal* would undertake eight more *Spyron* missions. On each trip she played a deadly game of tag with Japanese patrol boats, and her crew never knew if her appointed rendezvous would be betrayed by an informer. (It never was.)

As the many Philippine guerrilla forces grew (toward a total of a quarter million men), so did their supply requirements. Other submarines were diverted from regular patrols to carry in American intelligence agents, coastwatchers, radios, money (both genuine currency and counterfeit Japanese invasion scrip), ammunition and weapons, including bazookas, machine guns and even light cannon. The radios smuggled ashore by the submarines helped the guerrillas and coastwatchers set up more than 150 clandestine stations and report on Japanese shipping and troop movements all over the Philippines and adjacent waters.

In all, 19 U.S. submarines undertook 42 *Spyron* missions with only one loss. That boat was the *Seawolf*, which in October 1944, while carrying 17 U.S. Army agents and about 10 tons of supplies to Samar in the central Philippines, was sunk by depth charges from the destroyer escort U.S.S. *Rowell* after having been mistakenly bombed and marked by a Navy plane.

The accomplishments of the *Narwhal* and her companion boats in the *Spyron* operation epitomized a wholly different aspect of the U.S. submarine campaign in the Pacific. Though the primary business of the undersea fleet was to sink enemy vessels, the very qualities that made the submarine a fearsome weapon—its stealth and long range—made it ideal for any number of exotic missions. These missions, for all their basically noncombat nature, were filled with risks of every sort. From the start, they called up uncommon courage and endurance from the crews; and any skipper who was not a master of improvisation when he set off on a special mission soon became practiced in the art.

As the War progressed, the types of special missions assigned to U.S. submarines told much about the course of the fighting. At first, the submarines were hastily drafted for desperate errands—anything to stave off disaster. Later, as the fortunes of war shifted in favor of the United States, the special missions became large, confident, well-organized oper-

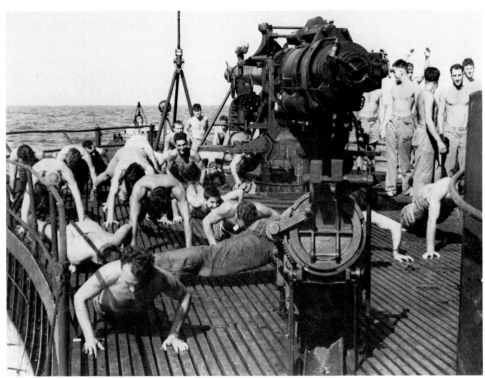

Marines take their 10 minutes of daily exercise on the deck of the Nautilus during the trip to Makin.

SUBMARINES ON A BOLD HIT-AND-RUN RAID

It was a small-scale operation, and the sort of thing not often repeated as the U.S. gained the upper hand in the Pacific. But it was yet another occasion on which the submarine proved its wonderful versatility.

On August 8, 1942, the *Nautilus* and the *Argonaut* left Pearl Harbor carrying 222 Marine Raiders. The submarines were to land the leathernecks for a hit-and-run attack on Makin, a speck of coral just above the Equator in the Japanese-held Gilberts. The objective was to trick the Japanese into diverting men and supplies from the Solomons, 1,200 miles to the southwest, where a major U.S. invasion of Guadalcanal had begun the day before.

The eight-day trip to Makin was almost unbearable, not only for the Marines, but for the boats' 201 crewmen. Everyone was cooped up below most of the time, and when the boats were submerged the temperatures rose into the 90s.

At last, before dawn on August 17, the Raiders launched their rubber boats into the rough waters off Makin and struggled to shore. By 5 a.m., all the Marines were on the beach and moving inland. The first

shot alerted the garrison troops, who hurried out to fight riding on bicycles and trucks. The Marines drove them back in several sharp skirmishes, helped by a rain of shells from the *Nautilus'* deck guns. The submarine gunners also sank two small ships moving into the lagoon.

The fighting went on for 10 hours, and the submarines had to dive repeatedly and run offshore to escape enemy bombers from other bases. But the boats always returned, and at 5 p.m. the Marines began coming off the beaches, paddling their rubber boats through churning surf that spilled them into the sea. That first night only four boats and 53 men made it out to the submarines. But the following day 139 Raiders returned, the last few riding in an island outrigger. Thirty Marines were missing and presumed dead. (Actually, nine had survived, but they were later captured and executed.)

The raid was a clear tactical success. The Marines had wiped out the entire 83-man garrison and had destroyed all of Makin's facilities. But while the U.S. could not know it at the time, the operation was a strategic failure. The Japanese apparently recognized it for what it was—and dispatched no reinforcements to the Gilberts from the Solomons.

High-ranking officers, an honor guard and a Navy photographer crowd the dock at Pearl Harbor to welcome the Marines upon their return from the raid on Makin Island.

Standing on the deck of the Nautilus, Admiral Chester W. Nimitz (center) presents a ceremonial sword to the commanding officer of the Makin raid, Colonel Evans F. Carlson.

ations, performed by many boats that the Navy could easily spare from combat duty.

Typical of the first phase, during the dark days of Japanese conquest, was the February 1942 mission of the *Seadragon;* she removed from Corregidor the personnel of a code-breaking unit whose capture might have compromised a major U.S. secret—that American cryptanalysts had broken one of the Japanese Naval codes. Similarly, the *Swordfish* evacuated Philippine President Manuel Quezon, along with his family and several aides, and then went back to pick up U.S. High Commissioner Francis B. Sayre. During the retreat of General MacArthur's command to Australia, the *Trout* transported some 20 tons of Philippine gold and silver from Manila banks to Pearl Harbor.

Such makeshift missions continued well into 1942. But with the landing of the Marines on Guadalcanal that August, the United States took a tentative first step toward seizing the initiative in the Pacific. Thereafter, submarines were used with increasing aggressiveness to poke and probe into places where no surface ship had yet ventured.

In carrying the war to the enemy, U.S. submarines transported small troop units to assault landings. They made close-in reconnaissance of hostile beaches, which were sometimes a considerable distance from the locations given on old charts. They developed a new art of periscope photography, bringing back detailed pictures of the terrain and defenses of future invasion targets. One of their most hazardous jobs was charting minefields before the arrival of the massed surface invasion fleets. And in their most satisfying special mission, the submariners reversed roles and became saviors instead of killers, rescuing hundreds of Army, Navy and Marine fliers who had been shot down or forced to ditch during attacks on Japanese strongholds.

After Guadalcanal and the Solomons campaign came the

invasion of Tarawa and other islands of the Gilbert group in the autumn of 1943. For that operation, Rear Admiral Richmond Kelly Turner, commanding the amphibious assault, wanted detailed photographic coverage of the invasion beaches. The job was given to the *Nautilus*, skippered by Commander William Irvin.

At that point, a few submarine skippers had made dramatic pictures of sinkings through their periscopes. But reconnaissance photos of a beach, arranged in precise, panoramic succession and showing such inconspicuous features as machine-gun nests, called for a much more exacting technique. Moreover, the task was complicated by the periscope's tendency to vibrate and its inability to admit more than 35 per cent of the ambient light.

Camera brackets were built for the *Nautilus'* periscope. The lower sonar room was converted into a darkroom. A Navy photographer was assigned and equipped with the three available cameras: a large view camera, a camera using medium-sized roll film and a miniature camera using 35mm film. So armed, the big submarine set out from Pearl Harbor and headed for the Gilberts. But each of the cameras left a good deal to be desired. In the roll-film camera, the range finder and the lens were separate; the camera could not, therefore, be accurately aimed through the periscope. The large size of the view camera made for awkward handling. The miniature's 35mm negatives turned out to be too small to be enlarged to the desired size without sacrificing the clarity of the image.

The *Nautilus'* executive officer, Lieut. Commander Richard Lynch, had a better alternative. An enthusiastic amateur photographer, Lynch owned a single-lens reflex camera called a Primaflex, which took 2¼ x 2¼ pictures. Because it was a single-lens reflex, the photographer, aiming through the periscope, could see what the lens was looking at. Its size was convenient and its negatives were larger than those of the miniature.

As the *Nautilus* maneuvered from point to point along the Tarawa coast, the Navy photographer overlapped his shots by 50 per cent. Each roll of 12 exposures was carefully coordinated with a chart of the island, giving the submarine's position and distance from the beach. The combined result was a detailed panorama of Tarawa's low-lying foreshore.

Admiral Turner was delighted, and the Navy immediately

A quartermaster uses a cotton swab dipped in alcohol to clean sea salt from a surface-search radar antenna mounted just below the optical head of a submarine's forward periscope. The radar's directional impulses determined a target's range and bearing in the darkest night, and permitted a submarine skipper to plan his attack while still submerged.

launched a search for more Primaflex cameras. But the Primaflex was German-made and hard to come by. Eventually, advertisements in photographic trade magazines rounded up 10 secondhand duplicates of Lynch's camera, and thereafter every Japanese target island was painstakingly presurveyed by a German lens looking through the eye of an American submarine.

On November 19, 1943, almost two months after that run to the Gilberts, the *Nautilus* was back off Tarawa on a special mission of a different sort. She was ordered to reconnoiter and report tide and surf conditions in advance of the Marine assault the next morning. After that, she was to off-load some passengers she had been carrying since leaving on patrol. They were 78 Marines of the Amphibious Reconnaissance Company of the V Amphibious Corps, and they were to be put ashore secretly to scout the small, lightly garrisoned island of Abemama, which was to be invaded after the fall of Tarawa and Makin.

By about 10 p.m. on November 19, the *Nautilus* had completed her tidal survey and was heading out with her Marines for Abemama. She was maneuvering through shallow water to clear a reef when, with no warning except a radar contact that she had taken to be from friendly vessels, a salvo of shells came down on her. One of them hit under the bridge, pierced the main air induction, slammed into the conning tower and came to rest in the superstructure—all, providentially, without exploding. The dud was a five-inch shell and had an American identification number on it.

Skipper Irvin shot aloft a green recognition flare and, despite the fangs of coral in the water nearby, dived for the shallow bottom. A barrage of shells followed the *Nautilus* down. One shellburst ruptured a waterline and started leaks in the bilges. With water also gushing through the hatch of the damaged conning tower, the submarine hung for hours at an awkward nose-down angle while damage-control parties struggled to stanch her wounds.

"We felt time was running out fast," Irvin later wrote in his patrol report. "The 78 Marines we had aboard were stoic but they were unanimous in the attitude that they would much prefer a rubber boat on a very hostile beach to their present predicament."

By early morning on November 20, the *Nautilus* was back on the surface and running for Abemama, where she landed the Marines that night. The island was as lightly defended as advertised, and on the following day the little party of leathernecks took it handily with the assistance of the *Nautilus'* 6-inch guns.

And which U.S. ships had nearly done the *Nautilus* to death? The U.S. destroyer *Ringgold* reported that she had sunk a Japanese patrol boat in the area where the *Nautilus* had been sailing. The light cruiser *Santa Fe* claimed to have helped the destroyer. These allegations held up until the *Nautilus* reached Pearl Harbor and displayed the dud shell. It was subsequently mounted in the officers' club at the submarine base as a reminder to the submariners that not even friendly warships could be entirely trusted.

Late in the summer of 1943, shortly before the Tarawa invasion, there came into being the so-called Lifeguard League, which would become the largest of the special submarine operations. It was conceived when Rear Admiral Charles A. Pownall, planning carrier strikes on Marcus Island, the Gilberts and Wake, called in Rear Admiral Charles Lockwood to ask that submarines wait offshore from the targets as potential rescuers. Lockwood hesitated. He wanted to save fliers, of course, and he realized that the possibility of rescue would give the airmen a great boost in morale. But each rescue effort would expose a submarine and her whole crew to protracted risk.

Submarines were as vulnerable as they were deadly. A boat's best protection against her enemies was to remain underwater. But rescue work meant staying on the surface in daylight, often within range of land-based enemy planes and sometimes under the guns of shore batteries. And then, as the *Nautilus* could attest, there was also the risk of accidental attack by friendly ships and planes.

For all his qualms, Lockwood finally agreed to do lifeguarding duty provided that Admiral Nimitz would bless the project. Nimitz did, and Lockwood assigned his operations officer, Captain Richard G. Voge, to work out the details.

It was at once apparent that no rescue submarine was likely to do anybody much good unless the aviator in trouble knew where to look for it. The first step, therefore, was to assign a base position for the lifeguard on a certain bearing and distance from a recognizable landmark. At first, communications presented serious difficulties. In the air the

135

fliers chattered among themselves and to their carrier by two-way voice radio. But the submarines lacked such radios and spoke only in Morse code. Relaying all information through the carriers would cause delay and numberless possibilities for foul-ups, unacceptable in an emergency.

The radiomen of the submarine fleet solved that problem. They pointed out that the ordinary commercial VHF receivers, mounted in the wardroom and crews' mess for entertainment, could be tuned to pick up the "zoomies," as they called the fliers. Thus a flier who was about to ditch —or his squadron mates—could directly notify the lifeguard where to look.

Each lifeguarding submarine was assigned a code name for the pilots to use that contained at least one letter *L*—on the decidedly shaky thesis that the Japanese could not pronounce the letter and could therefore be detected if they tried to contact a submarine using the code. The submarines on lifeguard duty had to accept such undignified *noms de guerre* as Lollypop, Lonesome Luke and Lillian Russell.

The first two lifeguard assignments, which stationed the *Snook* at Marcus and the *Steelhead* at Tarawa in the Gilberts, were abortive: Nobody got shot down. But at Wake Island on October 6 and 7, Commander Eugene McKinney's *Skate* had a wildly exciting time.

The *Skate* was waiting on the surface at her assigned position when the first waves of the carrier strikes came in before dawn. She was in a perfect position to enjoy a close-up view of one of the great shows of the Pacific war. Flares lighted the target in an eerie glow. The bombs began dropping and exploding in lurid bursts of fire. Flames boiled up from the target, reaching hundreds of feet in the air. Japanese antiaircraft speckled the sky with fireworks. For submariners, accustomed to operating in darkness and isolation, it was an eye-filling spectacle.

And its appeal led to trouble. There were a dozen men on the bridge and afterdeck when, rushing toward her first reported ditched flier, the submarine was strafed by a low-flying Japanese Zero. McKinney yelled, "Clear the bridge!" and followed 11 men through the hatch, and then slammed it behind him. The *Skate* went under with bullets rattling off the conning tower.

But as the boat dived deep, Lieutenant (jg.) Willis E. Max-

son III, the junior officer of the deck, collapsed in a heap. He had taken a bullet in the back and was unconscious.

The *Skate* rescued no fliers that day. Instead, she was repeatedly driven under by Japanese planes. After reporting Maxson's condition to Pearl, McKinney received orders to rendezvous with a destroyer and transfer his wounded officer. The *Skate* ran through the night to the rendezvous point, but no destroyer appeared. Maxson by now had regained consciousness, and though he was in agonizing pain, the young officer asked McKinney to keep the submarine on the job. Another message from Lockwood ordered the *Skate* to remain at Wake until nightfall on October 7 and then to take Maxson toward Midway at flank speed.

Shortly after dawn of the second day, four U.S. dive bombers dropped down over the *Skate*, signaling that they were lost and unable to find Wake. The boat signaled back a bearing and the bombers went on their way. Around 9 a.m. the *Skate* received a bearing on a plane that had gone down with two fliers about two miles from the beach. The submarine headed for the spot, but six miles out she was driven under by heavy fire from big guns onshore. Submerged, McKinney pressed on slowly for 45 minutes; then he surfaced again, holding the boat just barely awash with only the point of the bow and the bridge above water. He called for volunteers and sent three men wading up to the prow, ready to grab the two fliers as soon as they appeared. The Japanese shore battery was still firing, the shells hitting nearby, but strafing planes from the carriers kept working on the guns and finally silenced them.

Moments later the *Skate* made the Lifeguard League's first rescue: Lieutenant Harold J. Kicker was plucked out of a rubber raft. The second flier, Ensign Murray H. Tyler, was afloat in a Mae West life jacket and was so exhausted that he could not swim to the submarine. So Torpedoman Arthur G. Smith jumped over the bow with a life ring and brought in the flier. Before the War ended, Tyler would be rescued by submarines on three different occasions.

That night, with Maxson in urgent need of medical attention, McKinney drove the *Skate* as hard as she could go toward Midway. But while the submarine was on the way, Lockwood received a report from the retiring task force: Nine more fliers were down somewhere around Wake. From Pearl, Lockwood made the agonizing decision to send the *Skate* back for the fliers. As it happened, the decision made no difference. Maxson died around dawn on October 8, hours before he could have received skilled medical care. McKinney later ordered the engines stopped. In a brief funeral service, Maxson's body was committed to the sea.

The next morning, volunteer pickup men were on the bow again as the *Skate,* awash and barely surfaced, crept through the seas near Wake. At one point, when an unidentified plane came in on the boat, the pickup men had to struggle back through deepening sea water to get inside before the *Skate* dived.

That day the *Skate* rescued one flier. On October 10 she picked up three more. The last, Lieut. Commander Mark A. Grant, an air-group commander from the light carrier *Cowpens,* was found asleep in a rubber raft. He had been adrift for four days, since the start of the battle, and in a vain attempt to secure a meal he had fired off nearly all of his pistol ammunition at circling gooney birds. He brought back the single bullet he had saved for himself.

From the carrier *Lexington,* some of whose fliers were among those saved, came a grateful signal: "Anything on the *Lexington* is yours for the asking. If it's too big to carry away we will cut it up into small parts."

No matter what precautions were taken to protect the lifeguards from friendly attacks—lectures, briefings, stern admonitions, precisely prescribed safety zones—there was always, as they said in the Navy, "some sonofabitch who didn't get the word."

The *Tunny* was one of seven submarines sent to plug the entrances and exits from the Palaus, eastward from the Philippines, ahead of a series of carrier strikes at the end of March 1944. She had an exceptionally rewarding patrol before the carrier force arrived. She sank a Japanese submarine, the *I-42,* and even managed to get a fish into the 68,000-ton battlewagon *Musashi.* With a little more luck, the *Tunny* might have sunk or at least stopped the *Musashi,* but lookouts aboard a destroyer escorting the battleship saw the spread of six torpedoes coming in time to give warning. The *Musashi* zigged and took the blow forward, where she was least vulnerable.

With that, skipper John Scott turned the *Tunny* toward her lifeguard station 30 miles west of the Palaus to wait on the surface for calls to retrieve distressed aviators. She was there when a flight of nine Grumman Avenger torpedo bombers passed to westward on their way to the target. Two suddenly peeled off and began a run on the submarine. The first pilot realized in the middle of his run that he was making a mistake; he pulled up and flew away. But the second came on and dropped a 2,000-pound bomb that exploded only 30 feet to starboard of the submarine.

The *Tunny* survived, but the explosion sprang leaks so serious that she was forced to abandon the lifeguard mission and go to Brisbane for repair—and recrimination. As it turned out, more than a few submarines assigned to lifeguard duty would be the victims of misidentification, although not one was sunk.

In spite of the ill treatment some submarines received from trigger-happy airborne compatriots, the crewmen repeatedly went to extraordinary lengths to save fliers. The *Harder,* Samuel Dealey's submarine, broke off her combat patrol to start lifeguard duty at the Woleai atoll when Admiral Marc Mitscher's carriers struck there on April 1.

At 8:40 a.m. a Hellcat fighter came low and by voice radio reported a flier down and swimming toward the islet of Tagaulap to the west of Woleai. With fighters circling and zooming around the *Harder* to lead the way, Dealey ran west at full speed, all four diesels pounding furiously. Shortly before noon a lookout spotted the pilot lying on the white-sand beach inside the lagoon and 1,500 yards beyond the surf-sprayed barrier reef. The pilot saw the submarine. He struggled to his feet with the aid of a stick and waved feebly. He was obviously far-gone and in no condition to help himself.

Dealey eased his boat shoreward. Before long she was in the shallows; the water was shoaling and the Fathometer quit recording. A plane overhead reported what looked like an easier approach and Dealey backed off.

As Dealey watched, the stranded aviator fell and again lay stretched on the beach. "His collapse," said Dealey's report, "was undoubtedly due mainly to physical exhaustion but also to the disappointment in seeing his chances of rescue apparently fade away."

The alternative approach proved impractical, and Dealey returned to his original route. To hold the *Harder* in place against the surf during the rescue operation, Dealey pushed the boat gently forward until her prow was grounded on the coral reef, and he gave orders to hold her there by keeping the engines running. It was daring seamanship; even though the waters were relatively calm, Dealey ran the risk that some contrary current would swing the boat to port or starboard, to crash broadside onto the reef.

Meanwhile, a plane had dropped a rubber raft on the beach in response to a plea that the flier had managed to trace in the sand with his stick. He launched the raft and tried to paddle out toward the boat. But the tide was running against him, carrying him off in the opposite direction. At the same time, snipers hidden in the palms behind the beach began firing at both submarine and pilot. Overhead, the Hellcats began diving in to strafe the beach and keep the snipers down.

Dealey called for volunteers, and got more than he could conceivably use; his crew was by now committed to getting that man out, no matter what. Dealey picked three men and ordered a rubber boat launched. The volunteers went over the side and began swimming and pushing the boat across the lagoon, paying out a coil of light, strong line back to the submarine. It was slow, hard going. When they got far enough into the shallows to stand upright, they left one man to hold the boat while the other two went in pursuit of the drifting flier.

Gingerly picking their way over the sharp coral, they finally reached the pilot in his rubber boat. But then came a foul-up. Just as they started hauling themselves rapidly back to the Harder, a well-intentioned U.S. pilot in a floatplane from a cruiser appeared overhead and landed in the lagoon to see if there was anything he could do to help. In the process he taxied across the life line and cut it. The three volunteers started laboriously swimming and pushing the rubber boat with the injured pilot back across the lagoon—still under occasional Japanese fire.

Aboard the Harder, a fourth volunteer went over the side and swam toward the struggling rescuers, paying out another coil of line as he went. He reached them, and the line was lashed to the rubber boat. Amid gunfire from Japanese snipers, the line to the rubber boat was pulled to the submarine hand over hand.

After everybody was safely on board, Dealey carefully backed the Harder down off her rocky perch and returned to his routine of sinking ships. His passenger, Ensign John R. Galvin, from the Bunker Hill, remained aboard the Harder while Dealey sank a destroyer and a 7,000-ton freighter. As a consequence aviator Galvin was awarded a treasured war decoration, the submarine combat medal. Taking a proprietary interest in the life they had saved, the crewmen of the Harder kept close track of Galvin's career. When they learned he had shot down seven Japanese planes, they figured that they shared in the victories.

In its early days, lifeguarding was usually a piecemeal operation, seldom involving more than a single aviator or flight crew in need of help. But at Truk at the end of April 1944, the Tang went into business on a wholesale basis during massive strikes by land-based bombers and carrier planes.

The submarine's assigned station was at a point 40 miles due south of Moen, one of the three largest islands in the huge lagoon of the Truk atoll. This position left her 23 miles from the nearest point on the reef—and that was a matter of some distress to the Tang's skipper, Richard O'Kane, formerly the executive officer on Mush Morton's famed Wahoo. In order to rescue downed aviators, O'Kane thought, "we belonged up front, as close as we could get."

The Tang was on station before dawn. Carrier flights began arriving at daybreak, and the Tang was sent after a raft with a downed crew just off the southern face of the reef.

"The sight ahead would have brought a lump of pride to anyone's throat," O'Kane recalled later. "Our bombers were peeling off through a hole in the clouds above Tol Island, a hole filled with flak, and diving straight through. If they had that courage, we could at least get this survivor, two miles off the beach."

Guided to the raft by circling fighters, O'Kane took off three men with no great trouble. He sent them below for "a shot of depth-charge medicine, Lejon Brandy," and gave them a job helping the submarine's aviation information center. There they would be useful because they understood flier's jargon—a language all its own—and knew many of the pilots by name and even by voice.

The Tang had two more calls that day. One was for two men in a raft on the south side of Truk. But they were still inside the reef, inaccessible to the Tang. O'Kane reluctantly abandoned that effort, hoping the two could paddle across

Two American fliers, stranded when their PBY amphibian broke down in waters off Japan, wait to be taken aboard the submarine Tigrone. The PBY, which had a crew of seven, lost a propeller while attempting to take off after a rescue of its own; it carried aviators from a downed B-29. Soon both air crews, 16 men in all, were whisked away in the Tigrone.

the reef during the night and be picked up the next day. The other summons was on behalf of a raft so far south of the atoll that the submarine did not reach the area before nightfall. The Tang spent the night zigzagging, firing green flares in hopes the fliers would respond. They did not; the aviators had seen the flares but dared not respond for fear of attracting Japanese attention.

So far it had been a disappointing mission. O'Kane had responded to three distress calls, with only one rescue. What is more, the Japanese at this point were well aware of the American boat's presence; O'Kane had already engaged in a brief gun duel with a Japanese position at the fringe of the reef while on his way to the second raft.

Before dawn on May 1, O'Kane and the Tang made contact with a Japanese RO-class submarine. O'Kane dived and tried to get into position for a torpedo shot. But the enemy submarine also dived, and she disappeared before O'Kane could engage. O'Kane sent a contact report to the U.S. flagship and then went back to lifeguarding—making sure to lash his boat's American flags on the deck fore and aft so no flier would mistake him for the enemy.

Around 8:30 a.m. the day's first call came in: Two airmen were in a raft near the rescue point of the day before, perilously near the gun position on the reef. The Tang moved in—and came upon an astonishingly crowded scene. The pilot of a Kingfisher floatplane from the battleship North Carolina had landed to help the castaway fliers but had wrecked his plane in the process. A second Kingfisher had landed successfully and now began towing the raft, with its two occupants and the other Kingfisher pilot, toward the submarine. The two downed fliers were the same men whom the Tang had been unable to reach the day before because they were inside the reef.

The Tang took the three men aboard, and the successful Kingfisher took off. It was flown by Lieutenant J. A. Burns— whom the Tang would soon meet again.

Shortly thereafter the submarine lookouts saw a torpedo plane trailing smoke and coming down. The Tang headed for it at flank speed, again passing the Japanese gun emplacement; once more O'Kane called up the crewmen of his deck-mounted 4-inch gun, and they started blasting away to keep the Japanese quiet. The Tang took aboard three more guests, making nine.

Another call sent the Tang racing toward the reef, where three rafts were now reported. Once again Lieutenant Burns and his Kingfisher were there first. This time the audacious

pilot had collected seven fliers, including the two who had been afraid to respond to the *Tang's* flares the night before. Now, with some of the men loaded onto his float and wings and with others in tow on their rafts, Burns was trying to taxi toward the submarine through a choppy sea. But before the *Tang* could make the pickup, a call came for still another flier, this one downed in a narrow passage between the Truk reef and that of a nearby island, Kuop. Japanese troops were dangerously close at hand there, and O'Kane, deciding that Burns and his seven guests were relatively safe, turned away and headed for the new contact. O'Kane expected to be driven under by nearby enemy gunfire, so on the way he ordered a towing bridle lashed to the radar mast; if necessary, he would try to tow the flier's raft from the submerged boat. It was a technique the submariners had often discussed, but nobody knew if it would work.

That contingency would have to wait another mission. By this time the carrier task force had become gratefully aware of the perils faced by the *Tang* on behalf of the fliers. Now, wherever the submarine went, her private combat air patrol went along, strafing and bombing to keep the Japanese gunners from interfering. Said O'Kane later, "Never was a submarine better escorted."

The *Tang* got her man. And he was no sooner aboard than O'Kane headed for a swimmer just off the eastern reef of Kuop. The submarine arrived just in time. A plane had dropped a rubber boat to the swimmer, but the man had been too exhausted to clamber into it. With him aboard, O'Kane turned back to relieve Lieutenant Burns of his passengers on the Kingfisher. The aircraft was still afloat, but it was so battered by its day in the surf that it could no longer be flown. O'Kane loaded all hands—nine men including Burns and his crewman—and sadly ordered the submarine's aftergun to destroy the little seaplane to keep it from falling into Japanese hands.

The *Tang* was now crowded with 20 fliers—and more were to come. Another raft was soon reported south of the reef. Night was coming on and O'Kane, mindful of the futile search the night before, was afraid he would miss the downed pilots in the gathering dusk. He called the task force and asked for help. In response, Admiral Mitscher sent aloft three night fighters, equipped with radar.

Richard O'Kane later reported: "*Tang* slowed and we commenced a combing search downwind, the fighters now looking like black albatross as they flew their search patterns ahead and on our beams. Our chances of locating the raft seemed slim. Suddenly, one of our fighters dived, firing red stars. The result was a shower of red Very stars coming up from the sea, well ahead on our starboard bow. The fighters guided us in and were dismissed with thanks and Godspeed."

The *Tang* found two more airmen in the raft. And so, at last, she headed home to Pearl Harbor carrying 22 fliers.

After the exploits of the *Tang* and her sisters, it was amply evident to the Navy top command that lifeguarding was a godsend to carrier operations in enemy waters. But it was also obvious from the catch-as-catch-can early rescues that the techniques needed refinement. Starting in May 1944 a formal Submarine Combat Air Patrol—SCAP—was written into the operation orders for all carrier strikes. The SCAP pilots had definite chores to perform: protecting the submarine by strafing and bombing coastal-defense guns, shooting down enemy aircraft, warning off impetuous friendly pilots, finding downed fliers and leading the lifeguard to them. The submariners took kindly to this help and commonly referred to their SCAP colleagues as "our chickens."

The *Stingray* had reason to be grateful for the prompt arrival of her SCAP on the morning of June 12, 1944, outside Apra Harbor at Guam. She was on the surface when a twin-

On the deck of the Tang, 22 U.S. Navy airmen cluster around Richard O'Kane, the skipper who rescued them. The fliers had been shot down on scattered reefs during an April 1944 attack on Truk, and O'Kane had brought his boat into the shallows, defying enemy gunfire, to save them.

engined Japanese bomber came out of nowhere and made a strafing run on the bridge. As machine-gun bullets ricocheted off her hull, the Stingray dived, and the skipper, Sam Loomis Jr., waited for the bombs that were certain to come. When none did, Loomis raised the periscope—and saw three SCAP planes drive the bomber into the sea. Not long thereafter, the submarine repaid the favor: She picked up one of the SCAP pilots who had been forced to ditch after his engine stopped while he was chasing the bomber.

That afternoon the Stingray picked up the two-man crew of a Curtiss SB2C Helldiver that had crashed in Apra Harbor, within a quarter mile of anchored Japanese ships. A favoring wind and tide enabled the pair to put up their raft's sail and make their way from the harbor to the submarine.

The next day the Stingray herself boldly penetrated a shallow bay at Guam and performed the first rescue with a periscope tow—much the same technique O'Kane had prepared to use but had found unnecessary. The call came from waiting SCAP fighters at 10:15 a.m. A pilot was down in the harbor, about 500 yards from shore, at a point where cliffs rose steeply from the beach to a plateau topped by a Japanese airstrip and a ring of antiaircraft guns. Many of these had been destroyed in the first day's bombing, but at least one heavy gun was still firing. It now turned its attention to the Stingray as she raced into the harbor, and a shell splashed into the sea 400 yards to starboard.

Loomis eased his boat down to periscope depth. He now made up his mind that if the rescue attempt was to work at all, it would have to be accomplished with a periscope tow. He could only hope the pilot had been briefed on the technique. If not, the poor fellow was likely to have a terrifying experience, seeing that upthrust eye swimming straight at him like some sea monster.

The flier was in a rubber boat dropped to him by SCAP. The antiaircraft gunners were throwing an occasional shell at him; Loomis could see him ducking in his frail craft as though the air-filled doughnut could afford protection.

Shells were still splashing near the Stingray, some within 200 yards. Loomis stayed at his periscope as the submarine made a dead-slow approach. The flier waved, and Loomis was close enough to see that he had suffered a deep cut across the palm of his left hand.

For a moment, at 1:03 p.m. as Loomis later noted in the log, he thought that the Stingray had connected with her man. The pilot was so close that Loomis suddenly lost him in the scope's visual field. But then the pilot reappeared, and Loomis saw that they had missed.

Loomis dared not reverse his engines; the Stingray had a tendency to broach when backing while submerged, and showing the hull could be fatal. It took Loomis 49 minutes to get into position for another try. After a last slow turn, he moved in on the pilot. But for some reason, the flier was frantically paddling away from the oncoming periscope.

One hour later Loomis tried again. This time the pilot seemed to make a grab for the periscope, but missed again.

"I am getting damned disgusted, plus a stiff neck and a blind eye," Loomis wrote in the log. Nevertheless, he decided to make one more attempt. At 3:16 the Stingray ran directly into the rubber boat, and this time the pilot got a rope around the periscope and held on.

The submarine moved seaward at two knots. Even at that speed Loomis could see through the periscope that his client was having an agonizing ride through the choppy harbor waters. The pilot was yelling—pleading to be taken aboard. But Loomis had no intention of surfacing within range of the gun, which was still planting shellbursts dangerously close. He ran for an hour and then lowered the periscope, breaking the pilot's towline and cutting the rubber boat adrift. The man's face first showed alarm at being abandoned—and then beaming relief as the Stingray heaved up out of the sea.

"Picked up Ens. Donald Carol Brandt," Loomis wrote in the log. To explain his strange behavior during the approaches, Brandt said that he was afraid the periscopes were going to hit him and he tried to get out of the way. It turned out that while the pilot had been briefed on a rescue like this, he had been pretty well shaken up while bailing out and had been in something of a daze for a while; he had somehow tangled himself up in his parachute harness and had fallen upside down from 12,000 feet. "We're on speaking terms now," wrote Loomis. "But after the third approach I was ready to make him captain of the head."

Late in 1944, when Army B-29s began flying out of Saipan and Tinian in the Marianas to bomb Tokyo and other Japanese cities, lifeguarding became even more complicated.

One of the difficulties was psychological. By and large, Navy pilots knew enough about submarines and the sea to be able to ditch promptly and effectively and to cooperate in their own rescues. But to many Army airmen it was ridiculous to think of setting a plane down on the trackless waters, then clambering aboard a "tin cigar" and perhaps submerging in it—assuming it could ever find them. The Army fliers' every instinct was to stick with their damaged planes to the last, trying to nurse them back to dry land.

"The results of early arrangements were not highly successful, chiefly because of the aviators' desire to bring their ships home," Lockwood said. "They always seemed to believe that they could pull through on a wing and a prayer unless, of course, the aircraft was shot all to pieces."

To overcome this reluctance to ditch, and teach the airmen rescue techniques, Lockwood and the bomber command's boss, Major General Curtis E. LeMay, held a series of indoctrination sessions on Guam. Fliers who had been rescued by submarines assured their fellow B-29 crewmen that the boats were indeed capable of getting them home in one piece. Some aviators accepted invitations to go out on training cruises in the boats. A few submariners even flew in the big bombers.

To upgrade air-sea communication, all lifeguard submarines were now equipped with two-way VHF voice radio, so that the submariners could talk directly to pilots aloft. More precise aerial navigation was emphasized to improve the accuracy of the fliers' position reports to the submarines in case they were forced to ditch.

New tools were also added to increase the versatility of the air-sea rescue operation. The Navy assigned a number of PBM Mariners and PBY Catalinas to conduct search and rescue operations. These went under the code name of Dumbos, and until the U.S. Marines won their fierce battle for Iwo Jima in March of 1945, these slow, poorly armed planes operated only to the south of that island. To fly search missions over the more dangerous waters closer to Japan, the Air Force contributed Super Dumbos, B-17s and B-29s powerful enough to take care of themselves in a fight and long-legged enough to stay aloft for nine and 14 hours respectively. The Dumbos and Super Dumbos carried cargoes of emergency equipment—life rafts equipped with aluminum targets that would register on a submarine's radar and hand-cranked Gibson-girl radio transmitters. The Super Dumbos even carried motorboats that could be dropped from the air. But the main job, that of retrieving airmen from the sea, still fell to the submarines—and they became marvelously expert at the job. In February 1945, submarines rescued nearly 50 per cent of all the men who went down at sea in B-29s.

By then there were few places where American submarines dared not go, and in that same February the Pomfret, under John B. Hess, crept to within 25 miles of Tokyo itself to pluck airmen from the sea.

The Pomfret's feat was a by-product of a carrier raid on Japan launched in support of the Iwo Jima invasion. Having already taken part in an eight-submarine sweep to clear the seas ahead of the striking force, the Pomfret on February 16 took lifeguard station off a lighthouse at the entrance to the Sagami Sea, the waters leading into Tokyo Bay. The weather was brutal: snow, freezing rain and a sea that kept the surfaced submarine pitching and rolling so violently that it was almost impossible to maintain footing on the bridge.

Ironically, the Pomfret's first rescue of the day was a Japanese pilot picked up from a wildly tossing life raft. At first the flier took off his life jacket and tried to drown himself; finally he allowed himself to be hauled aboard. Given a potion of brandy, he downed it through chattering teeth and spoke one word in English: "More!"

Just before dark the weather cleared enough for SCAP planes to lead the Pomfret to an American flier, Lieutenant (jg.) Joseph P. Farrell. That rescue concluded the first day's business.

The summons to higher adventure came just after noon on the second day. A flier was reported in the drink far up the Sagami Sea, an area close to the Yokosuka naval base and framed on three sides by Japanese air bases and shore gun installations. The Pomfret's lookouts could not see the land; a thick surface haze blotted out the view. But they saw waves of U.S. fighter-bombers passing only a few hundred feet overhead, and they heard the crump of bombs falling on Yokosuka.

Navigating by radar and radioed directions from friendly fighters, John Hess drove his boat closer and closer to the unseen land. His plight grew palpably worse when the SCAP pilots told him they were nearly out of fuel and would soon have to retire. One by one they turned back, until Hess was left with only one tenacious escort, which stayed in the vicinity until the *Pomfret* picked up Ensign R. L. Buchanan, a fighter pilot.

Hess later recalled: "The moment Buchanan was aboard, the lone pilot overhead dipped his wings, said, 'Congratulations on a wonderful job well done,' and left in haste since he was not sure he had enough gas left to get back himself. I hope he had not miscalculated."

The *Pomfret* ran out as fast as the turbulent sea would permit. On the way, her lookouts spotted one more castaway, a pudgy Japanese clinging to a swamped boat. He came aboard with alacrity, was assigned as a cook's helper and was nicknamed Butterball. By the time the *Pomfret* reached base, Butterball had learned to sing a fair rendition of "God Bless America."

The submarine rescue rate continued to climb. For the month of May 1945, the boats saved an amazing 80 per cent of all ditched bomber crews. And that month saw the start of perhaps the most fruitful sea-rescue mission by a single submarine.

In the early afternoon of May 26, off the east coast of Honshu, the *Tigrone* picked up a distress call from a Navy twin-engined bomber. The pilot reported that he had lost an engine and also his own whereabouts. The *Tigrone's* skipper, Hiram Cassedy, asked if the pilot could see land. The reply was no. Cassedy told the pilot to fly straight west until he saw the coast of Japan and then describe what he saw. Cassedy went to his own charts and identified the lost plane's location. He gave the pilot a course to the *Tigrone*. Nearly an hour later, the crippled aircraft ditched just to starboard of the submarine's bow. Within minutes, the five-man crew was safe aboard.

Four days later another call took the *Tigrone* to a crippled PBY Catalina, itself on air-sea rescue duty. The seaplane had landed and picked up nine men from a ditched B-29, but while the plane was trying to take off, the prop on the left engine had broken and ripped through the pilot's compartment, gravely injuring Lieutenant Royal Stratton. Cassedy maneuvered alongside and took off everybody before sinking the cripple with gunfire. With the seven-man crew of the PBY and the nine from the B-29, the *Tigrone's* guest list was now up to 21. Cassedy sent an emergency call for a destroyer to take off the injured pilot, but before the *Tigrone* could make the rendezvous, Stratton died.

That night the weather turned nasty, the sea marching past in waves reaching 30 feet from trough to crest. To make the *Tigrone* manageable, Cassedy took her down to 100 feet. At dawn, despite a still-turbulent ocean, he surfaced and consigned to the sea the body of Lieutenant Stratton.

Toward sunset that evening, a PBY Dumbo reported that it was circling a raft carrying part of the crew of a ditched B-29. When the *Tigrone* reached the scene, the wind had abated but the seas were still high, making it difficult to put the submarine alongside the raft. To make matters worse, the castaways, who had been adrift throughout the storm of the night before and had repeatedly been washed overboard, were by now too exhausted to assist in their own rescue. Finally the submarine passed close to the raft, and one of the *Tigrone's* officers, Lieutenant H. D. Ragge, jumped aboard. He succeeded in securing the raft to the submarine. The seven new arrivals brought the number of those rescued by the *Tigrone* to 28. Before the submarine reached Guam on July 3, she had rescued two more fliers for a final total of 30—the highest total run up by any submarine on a single sea-rescue patrol.

All told, the American submarines saved 504 fliers, including a few British and Australians. Of course, lifeguarding on this grand a scale would not have been possible in the face of strong Japanese opposition. To the strategic planners, it was quite obvious as early as February of 1944 that Japan was weakening rapidly. And for this deterioration in enemy strength the United States owed much to the destructive work of the submarines.

READY FOR ANY JOB ANY TIME

Moving dangerously close to shore, the Harder teams up with a floatplane to rescue a downed airman in the face of Japanese gunfire from the trees.

RUNNING A GANTLET OF EXTRA RISKS

An hour out of Fremantle on May 26, 1944, skipper Samuel D. Dealey of the *Harder* broke the seal on his orders and briefed his men on their special mission. They were to creep in to shore on Borneo and, with a pair of collapsible kayaks, evacuate six Australian intelligence agents who had been sabotaging oil refineries and inciting local resistance to Japanese occupation. Said Dealey, "I suggest we make the first try a success. I don't like hanging around in shallow water."

Shallow water—too shallow to hide a submarine from the eyes and bombs of enemy pilots—was only one of the dangers that U.S. submarines faced in their remarkable assortment of special missions. There were Japanese patrol boats, some of which almost sank the *Trout* as she probed into Illana Bay to deliver supplies to Philippine guerrillas. There were coastal batteries: The *Redfin* ran a gantlet of them to rescue ambushed crewmen who had gone to fetch some spies. Enemy depth charges were a particular horror in confined waters near land, as the *Narwhal* found out in the Philippines while fleeing two destroyers that had caught her smuggling underground leaders ashore. Enemy snipers and gunfire from trigger-happy friendly aircraft also imperiled many submarines as they rescued downed airmen and civilian refugees behind enemy lines.

Yet time and again, the submarines ran their risks and survived. Among their many accomplishments in the course of the War, they delivered 1,300 tons of supplies to the Philippine guerrillas and ran 14 photographic reconnaissance patrols to find paths of least resistance for future invasions.

The skippers who excelled in these missions owed their success to steady nerves, sound judgment and plain luck—all of which Dealey had in ample measure on his trip to Borneo. He picked up the six agents without a hitch on June 8—but then ran into trouble. Before the *Harder* reached Fremantle, Dealey brought her through two depth-charge attacks, a heavy bombing and the tremendous explosion—only 80 feet overhead—of a destroyer he had just torpedoed. Such was the buffeting that a rescued Australian said glumly: "I'd rather be back in Borneo."

American refugees, picked up in the Philippines by the submarine Crevalle, assemble on deck while en route to safety in Darwin, Australia.

An Australian intelligence agent and four New Guinean allies mark time in the Dace while waiting to be smuggled ashore on enemy-held New Guinea.

PHOTO RECON: A DEADLY GAME OF HIDE AND SEEK

It was a nerve-racking task to photograph an enemy-held shoreline for U.S. invasion planners. Virtually every submarine that undertook a photoreconnaissance mission was harried by coastal patrol boats or sent diving by enemy aircraft.

The *Spearfish* was chased by a submarine near Iwo Jima. The *Greenling* spent anxious days off Guam before she finally shook a motorized sampan whose captain was both a clever and a determined man. "It is apparent that he has no sound gear," reported the skipper of the *Greenling*. "He must follow the birds which are always hovering over us."

Yet for all the danger, only one submarine failed to return from a photographing mission. She was the *Swordfish*, sent on December 22, 1944, to reconnoiter the shore defenses at Okinawa. Though the Navy never pinpointed the cause of her loss, officials concluded that she was sunk by depth charges or a coastal mine.

To reduce the risky picturetaking time, the periscope photographers and the submarine crews worked hard to refine their techniques. Cyrus C. Cole, the skipper of the *Spearfish*, drilled his seven-man photographic team so thoroughly on the way to Iwo Jima that they could raise the periscope the necessary four feet above the water, shoot a 12-exposure panorama and lower the scope in less than 40 seconds. Each submarine carried at least two cameras so that one could be reloaded while the other was in use.

Unfortunately, the cameras the Americans used for periscope photography were subject to breakdowns, and on-the-spot repairs had to be improvised. T. W. Miller, the engineer on the *Greenling*, solved one problem during a recon mission off Saipan. Miller carefully took apart a balky camera and discovered that the function of the shutter was impaired by the high humidity of the submarine's interior. He cleaned and oiled the shutter parts, then he dried them in an improvised oven at low heat. Thereafter, the cameras worked without fail—and were stored in the oven until they were needed.

A lighthouse on Honshu stands out in this reconnaissance photograph taken by the Pickerel in 1943.

This photo of a refinery on Tinian sent Marine invaders to another beach less likely to be defended.

Rugged Pagan Island, near Tinian in the Marianas, was shot by the Flying Fish on February 14, 1943, while she was searching for enemy garrisons.

A *Trout* crewman reaches out to heft a paper-wrapped gold ingot, one of 583 destined for safekeeping in the United States.

THE GOLDEN VOYAGE OF THE "TROUT"

As the *Trout* headed home to Pearl Harbor after a special mission in February 1942, her unlikely cargo rivaled that of a Spanish treasure galleon. Below her spartan deck was stowed part of the national treasury of the Philippines, some 20 tons of gold and silver worth more than $25 million.

The *Trout* had not made the trip to collect treasure; she had been dispatched to deliver 3,500 antiaircraft shells to Corregidor for General Douglas MacArthur's beleaguered garrison. But with that task completed, someone suggested that she take back the Philippine treasure, which had just recently been transferred from Manila.

Loading all of the gold and silver took the whole night. Working furiously against time—at daylight the submarine would have to submerge to hide from enemy bombers—the crewmen passed the gold bars and bags of silver coins into the boat. Some of the bags, rotted by years of storage in Manila bank vaults, burst open and sent coins clattering over the dock and plinking into the water.

At sunrise, with shells exploding over nearby Bataan, the *Trout* submerged; she waited until dusk, then slipped out to sea. And, wholly undeterred by the enormous value of her cargo, she attacked and sank two Japanese ships before arriving safely at Pearl Harbor.

On the deck of the Trout, crew members forming a bucket brigade transfer the submarine's precious cargo of gold and silver to a launch at Pearl Harbor.

THE TRICKY BUSINESS OF LANDING COMMANDOS

Except for the advantage of underwater stealth, a submarine was ill-suited to her special role as troop transport in amphibious landings on Japanese territory. The cramped interior of a boat could accommodate at most 120 troops and no landing craft more substantial than inflatable dinghies. The submarine's hatches were so tight—25 inches in diameter—that big men wearing their battle gear could not fit through them, and the narrow deck made it difficult to mass the landing party for quick disembarkation. Nevertheless, submarines landed several assault forces for successful attacks.

One of the trickiest was a diversionary raid on Attu in the Aleutian Islands in May 1943. The *Nautilus* and the *Narwhal* arrived offshore with 215 soldiers of the Provisional Scout Battalion, formed for this operation. Their job was to draw Japanese troops away from a main invasion beach seven miles distant and to prevent them from escaping into the mountains.

Three times the assault had been postponed by blustery snowstorms and hazardous surf, and even on the night of the landing a blanket of fog made it difficult for the submarines to maneuver. As the raiders began to leave the *Narwhal*, skipper Frank D. Latta warned them that if enemy ships appeared the boat would dive instantly, no matter how many of them had taken to the dinghies.

But the men had rehearsed their disembarkation many times, and now the practice paid off. No Japanese ship appeared, and all the dinghies were loaded smoothly. Then the assault leader signaled the submarine, and she slipped underwater.

The raid itself was successful, but costly. The assault troops, including 165 more Scouts who were landed by destroyer to back up those landed by the submarines, lost 11 men dead and 20 wounded, not counting some 300 frostbite cases. But they did manage to distract the Japanese long enough for the main invasion force to gain the beachhead. In fact, the raiders caused such a commotion that one of the defenders insisted that "enemy strength must be a division."

In the daylight tranquillity of American-held Dutch Harbor, Alaska, U.S. Army Scout troops practice disembarkation from the Nautilus for the invasion of Attu.

REFIT BETWEEN PATROLS

Returning from patrol for maintenance and resupply, the crews of five submarines muster on deck to turn over their boats to the refit teams at Pearl Harbor.

SWIFT SERVICE FOR BATTLE-SCARRED BOATS

Battered by Japanese depth charges, the U.S. submarine *Crevalle* limped into her base at Fremantle, Australia, on May 28, 1944. Her skipper, Lieut. Commander Frank D. Walker Jr., reported more than 50 items in need of repair, among them a malfunctioning diesel engine, two smashed periscopes, ruined radar gear, a broken compass and assorted leaks that had flooded the bilges. Walker's squadron commander noted on his status report, "*Crevalle* will require longer than the normal refit period," and put her in the care of the submarine tender *Orion*.

Such were the challenges that faced refit teams when the boats returned from patrol. As soon as a combat-weary crew came ashore, bound for hotels, beaches and beer halls, technicians swarmed over the boat, repairing the items on the "weeplist." If necessary, the submarine was popped into a floating dry dock, where maintenance crews replaced chipped propellers, overhauled torpedo tubes and scraped the hull clean of barnacles and seaweed. Repair work ceased and resupply work began only after the skipper had inspected the whole boat and pronounced himself satisfied.

As the undersea war crept closer to Japan, the submarines' journey for refit at their original bases became inconveniently long. Tenders solved the problem by serving as advance bases at western Pacific islands. Each of the 400-foot mother ships bulged with machine shops, spare-parts stockrooms, optical shops for periscope work, foundries, living quarters for more than 500 men, and stores of food, diesel oil, ammunition and medical supplies for the squadron of 12 to 18 boats assigned to it. The high quality of the tenders' work prompted the commander of the southwest Pacific submarine fleet, Rear Admiral Charles Lockwood, to call them "the heart and soul of all submarine squadrons."

Certainly the *Orion* merited that kind of praise. Exceeding all expectation, the tendermen completed repairs on the battered *Crevalle* in two weeks—the usual refit time for a boat that had suffered much less damage. The *Crevalle*, almost as good as new, thereupon cleared the Fremantle harbor and headed for the South China Sea to fight again.

A submarine settles into a floating dry dock for hull repairs. As the water was pumped from the dry dock, the boat sank gently onto keel blocks.

Clustered around a torpedo, sailors assigned to stockroom detail take a break from their work of supplying and servicing weapons for the submarines.

At the submarine base in Brisbane, officers of the Growler join repairmen in discussing just where to slice away the boat's bow, bent when she rammed a Japanese provision ship by accident in February 1943. By May, the refit crew had welded a new 18-foot bow section onto the boat.

Bobbing in a rowboat, two seamen apply a badly needed coat of paint to the side of a submarine. The subs, buffeted by gale-driven spray and churning seas, were repainted from the waterline up during every refit.

A submarine crew's mattresses and pillows, reeking of diesel-oil fumes when the boat reached port, are aired out on a line. The crewmen's clothes not only smelled bad; they were so grimy at the end of a long war patrol that many submariners discarded them and acquired new outfits.

Technicians in the optical shop of a submarine tender use a micrometer to check a periscope tube for damage. The most sensitive equipment on a submarine, periscopes required precise alignment of their components.

Members of a submarine crew browse through the books and records they will take to sea. To entertain the men, most boats carried a small film library and projector.

Unloading a supply truck parked on the dock, crewmen carry boxed provisions aboard their boat for the upcoming patrol. The ship's cook was permitted to choose his mates' favorite foods from commissary stocks.

Cradling a flexible metal hose, crewmen put 140,000 gallons of diesel oil into a boat's seven fuel tanks. Whenever it was possible, submarines stopped briefly at advance bases to top off with fuel en route to their patrol areas.

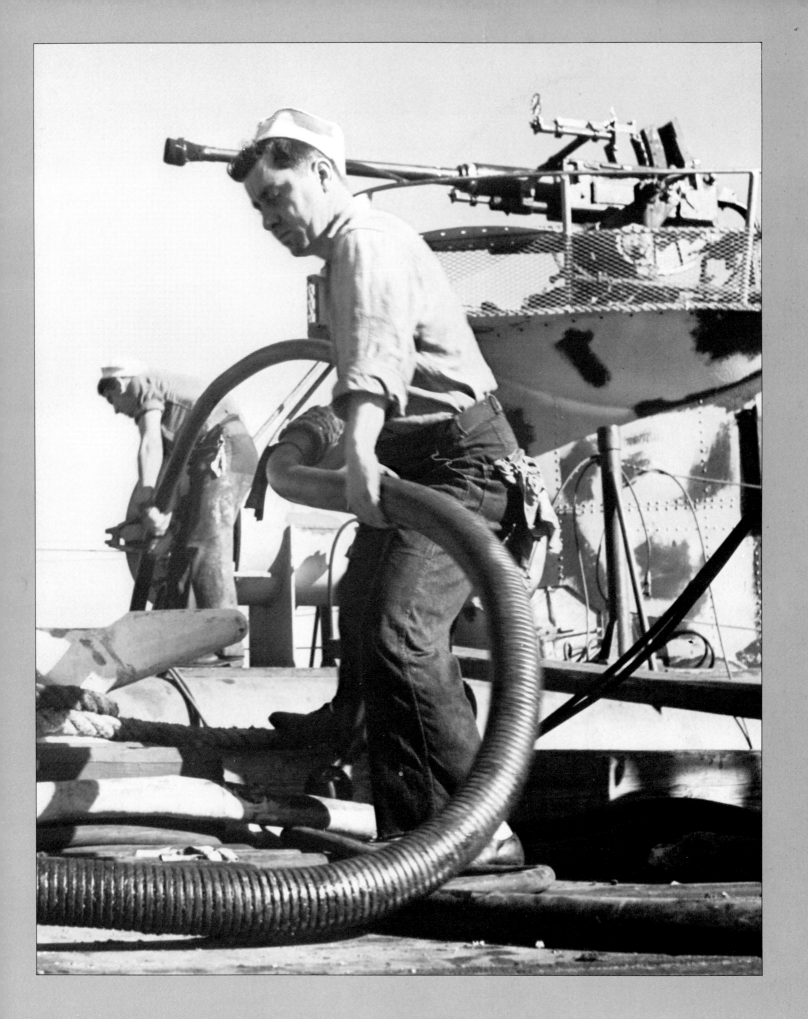

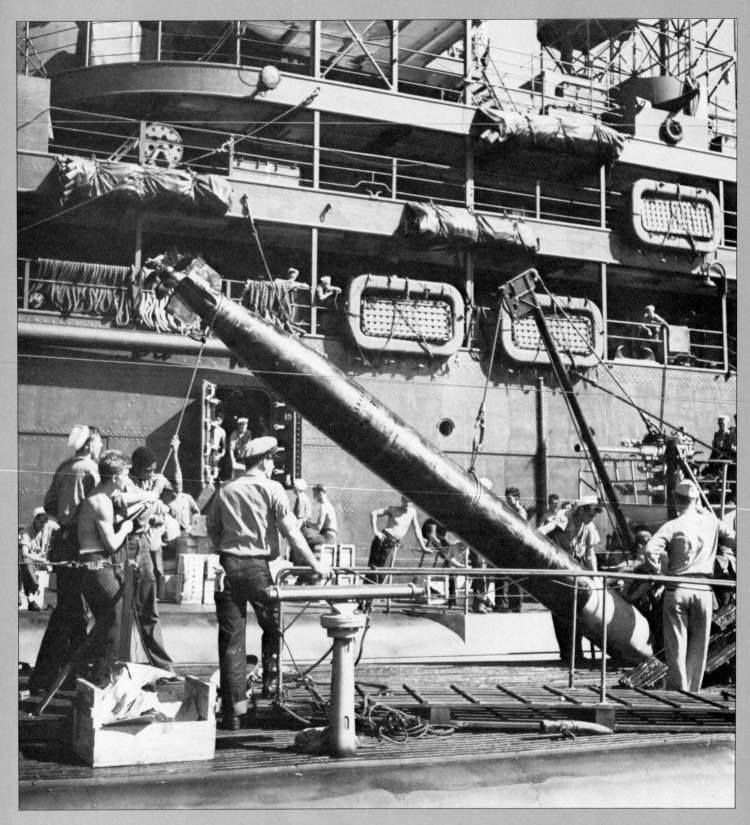

Submarine crewmen use a crane to lower a torpedo into the forward torpedo hatch of their boat. Belowdecks, each weapon was strapped to a skid with rollers and moved along a track to racks or torpedo tubes.

Carried in cylindrical storage cans, cartridges for a submarine's 5-inch gun are eased down a ramp and piled on deck. Most of the ammunition went to a magazine in the after battery. For quick access, a few rounds were kept in pressure-proof lockers in the conning tower's steel bulkhead.

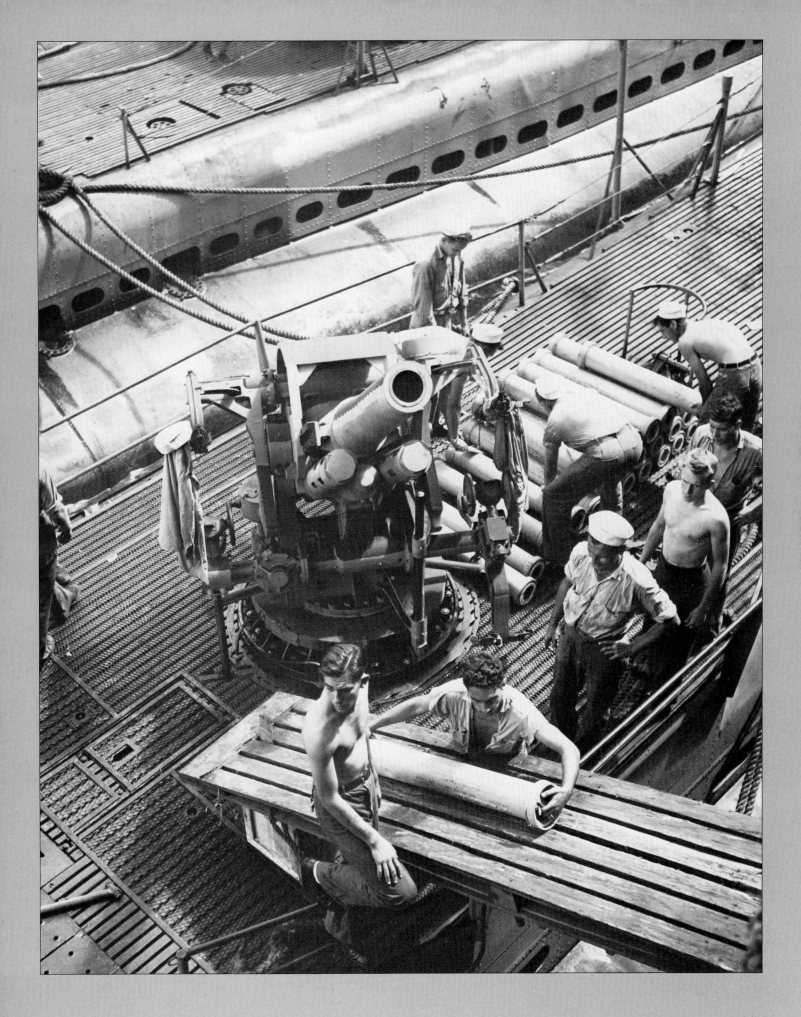

Restored to fighting trim, a submarine stands out to sea from the base at Midway. Other boats are undergoing refits at finger piers (top left), tenders (top center)

and a floating dry dock (top right). Though the submariners compared Midway unfavorably with luxurious Pearl Harbor, it was 1,200 miles closer to the action.

submarine. Tracers reached out for her and shellbursts splashed around her. Ramage stayed on the bridge with a volunteer, but sent everyone else below. He kept the boat speeding along and swerving wildly. "I called on the engine house," he said later, "to pour in all the oil they had." He fired five torpedoes one after another; some hit, but in all the confusion Ramage had no idea how much damage they had caused.

Now a small freighter aimed herself at the *Parche* and came rushing in to ram. Ramage swung the boat hard right, passed down the enemy's beam a bare 50 feet away and found himself boxed in on three sides by furiously firing escorts, with a big ship dead ahead. Ramage fired three forward tubes. One missed but the next two caught the big ship—it was a passenger-cargo vessel—near the bow. The vessel came to a halt. Ramage ran past her, swung to port and fired one stern fish; it hit amidships. As Ramage maneuvered for a finishing blow, the ship sank by the bow and went under.

Suddenly it was all over. "There were still several small craft and escorts around," Ramage recalled, "but no worthwhile targets that we could see. I decided to put some distance between us and this hornet's nest."

In 46 minutes Ramage had fired 19 torpedoes. Postwar accounting gave the *Parche* credit for a 10,200-ton tanker, a 4,400-ton passenger-cargo vessel and a half share with the *Steelhead* for an 8,990-ton transport. The *Steelhead* sank a 7,100-ton freighter and an 8,200-ton transport.

Ramage was awarded the Medal of Honor—less for what he had done than for the way he had done it. He was the first living submariner to receive the decoration. When he was asked what had inspired his furious rush at the convoy, Ramage shrugged and said, "I got mad."

The Whelchel-Ramage shoot-out in Luzon Strait dramatized the fact that there were rich pickings to be had in this ocean bottleneck, where Japanese convoy routes converged. As the summer of 1944 wore on, Admiral Lockwood sent his wolf packs there in increasing numbers. The result was calamitous for Japan. In mid-August two small packs were patrolling in or near the strait. One pack, led by Glynn Donaho in the *Picuda*, included Gordon Underwood in the *Spadefish* and Louis D. McGregor in the *Redfish*. Another pack, consisting of Henry Munson's *Rasher* and Charles Henderson's *Bluefish*, was hunting nearby.

For a while the boats had no luck. But around 5 a.m. on August 18, in rainy weather, the *Redfish* made contact with a large convoy. McGregor fired at three and missed them all. But on receiving his report the other four boats raced to join the *Redfish*.

Munson in the *Rasher* made a radar contact with the convoy on the night of the 18th. It was a huge convoy of 20 cargo ships and 15 escorts, lumbering along 15,000 yards away. Munson closed in through the heavy rain, which he considered "absolutely ideal for night attack."

At a range of 2,800 yards, Munson fired two torpedoes at what seemed to be a big tanker. Both fish hit and, recalled Munson, "the entire sky was a bright red momentarily and

THE SKIPPERS WHO LED ALL THE REST

Courage and luck—rather than length of service—distinguished the War's five top-scoring U.S. submarine skippers. Three of the five—O'Kane, Cutter and Morton—scored all their kills in one year or less; none led more than six war patrols.

The rankings were based on the number of enemy ships sunk, not total tonnage, and skippers received fractional credit for shared sinkings. A skipper's claims, hastily made in the confusion of combat, were often altered by the Joint Army-Navy Assessment Committee (JANAC) after a careful postwar review of Japanese records. One dramatic change overtook William S. Post Jr., who ranked fifth with 19 ships to his credit until JANAC reduced his kills to 8½; Post came in 34th.

Richard H. O'Kane, 24 ships   Slade D. Cutter, 19 ships

the target and the whole convoy was seen for an instant. Part of the ship blew off and landed about 500 yards from the remainder of the tanker and both parts burned fiercely for about 20 minutes and then disappeared from sight in one grand final explosion."

Munson had been wrong about one thing: His victim, far from being a tanker, was a 20,000-ton aircraft carrier.

Munson had every reason to expect an energetic counterattack, but none materialized. He later wrote: "The rear escort decided something was wrong, he fired his guns at all points of the compass, reversed course and fiercely depth-charged something or other two miles astern of us. Pandemonium reigned in the convoy, lights flashed on and off, depth charges fell in every direction, gunfire broke out all over. Two ships appeared to indulge in a spirited gun duel for a few moments. We proceeded up the starboard side of the convoy about 4,000 yards off, reloading and enjoying the spectacle."

He now had 16 torpedoes remaining, and at 3,300 yards he fired 10 of them at two cargo ships. He got both of them. Two fish missed their targets but slammed into two other ships beyond. Then he moved off to reload and, with only six torpedoes left, he radioed for help.

The *Rasher* closed in again, and Munson saw that the convoy had split into small groups. He chased two large ships flanked by a pair of smaller vessels. Slanting across the group's course, he fired all six of his torpedoes at the large ships. Five hit, sinking one vessel and damaging the other.

Fresh out of fish, Munson ended his chase before dawn.

But his rainy night's work had sunk four enemy ships totaling 47,928 tons—one of the most fruitful one-day ship performances of the War.

Munson's attack had sent the big convoy scattering in confusion. And now other members of the wolf packs circled in for their kills. Henderson in the *Bluefish* sank a 6,500-ton tanker. Around 3 a.m. on August 19, Underwood in the *Spadefish* came upon more stragglers, fired at a 9,500-ton transport and hit her. "Loud explosion from target," he reported. "Radar pip died down and disappeared. No doubt about this fellow."

On August 22, Underwood came upon another convoy—two large tankers with escorts. He fired a total of six torpedoes, three at each tanker. The first one sank, adding another 10,000 tons to Underwood's score. The second ship, although badly damaged, escaped into Pasaleng Bay on the coast of Luzon. Underwood pursued the stricken tanker into the bay, but was driven off by a patrolling destroyer. At this point Underwood was running out of torpedoes, and upon orders from Donaho, he set out for Saipan to get a new load.

Donaho and McGregor had so far gone empty-handed. But near the Luzon coast on the 25th of August, Donaho in the *Picuda* came upon a 10-ship convoy and sank a 2,000-ton transport. Then, when a destroyer charged him, he sank her too, with a down-the-throat shot, to chalk up another 1,200 tons. Alerted by the explosions, McGregor maneuvered his *Redfish* into position and atoned for his earlier misses, sinking a 6,000-ton freighter with three torpedoes.

Dudley W. Morton, 19 ships   Eugene B. Fluckey, 16⅓ ships   Samuel D. Dealey, 16 ships

KEEPING SCORE
ON GAUDY BATTLE FLAGS

By 1944, the U.S. submarine crews were busily engaged in a double competition: to outdo one another in sinking enemy ships—and in bragging about their victories. For the bragging contest the men spent their spare time on patrol creating flashy battle flags with symbols representing their successes. Each crew ran its banner up the periscope as the boat returned in triumph to home base.

The battle flags were easy enough to fashion; every submarine was equipped with a sewing machine and bolts of colored cloth for making signal flags. First, the crew agreed on the main design feature, usually a caricature of the fish after which the boat was named. The design was cut out and sewed onto a long cloth of contrasting color.

For a while, the crews were satisfied to display a small, standard set of symbols (below) for types of ships sunk and kinds of special missions. But this visual vocabulary was quickly expanded in the heat of friendly competition. Many crews added a star to their flags for each war patrol. One submarine, the Ray, sported triangular pennants for sampans, junks and other small merchant vessels sunk by deck guns. The crewmen of the Hammerhead sewed on symbols representing the four mines they had destroyed.

The imaginative crewmen of the Barb assembled one of the busiest battle flags. It displayed unit citations, a swastika for a German cruiser sunk during their shakedown cruise in the Atlantic in 1943, cannon representing Japanese towns shelled by the deck guns, even a train destroyed on a commando raid by eight of the Barb's crew. In fact, the Barb flag was so crowded with symbols that the crew almost ran out of room for more sinkings.

●	JAPANESE MERCHANT SHIP SUNK
○	JAPANESE MERCHANT SHIP DAMAGED
※	JAPANESE WARSHIP SUNK
※	JAPANESE WARSHIP DAMAGED
⛉	AVIATOR RESCUE MISSION

U.S.S. SEGUNDO

U.S.S. HAMMERHEAD

BARB

U.S.S. SPEARFISH

U.S.S. SPADEFISH

night. Radar reports battleship pip getting smaller—that it has disappeared. Battleship sunk—the sun set."

The *Sealion II* had sunk the *Kongo*, veteran of the Pearl Harbor attack and many an action since. Her companion, the *Haruna*, got away.

Another, even larger capital ship was sent down eight days later by the *Archerfish*, commanded by Joseph F. Enright. This submarine was originally assigned to patrol southward from the entrance to Tokyo Bay as lifeguard for a B-29 strike at Tokyo. But she had been excused from that duty when the strike was called off.

Skipper Enright was a second-timer in command. Earlier in the War he had taken the *Dace* on her first patrol but had then asked to be relieved because he doubted his own ability. However, he had regained his confidence, and would soon prove his abilities even to his own satisfaction.

Around 9 p.m. on November 28, the *Archerfish* picked up a radar contact more than 14 miles away. Enright ordered a chase at flank speed, and within an hour he was able to identify his target as a carrier, headed south at a speed of 20 knots.

"From here on," Enright wrote later, "it was a mad race for a possible firing position. His speed was about one knot in excess of our best, but his zig plan allowed us to pull ahead very slowly."

All the same, Enright despaired of getting in an effective shot until, at 3 a.m. on November 29, the carrier took another zag—which put her directly in the submarine's sights. Enright submerged, and 16 minutes later, at the ideal range of 1,500 yards, he fired four forward tubes. Then, as the carrier zigged, he fired two more from the stern.

The first torpedo run was 47 seconds, with the others following at close intervals. At the periscope Enright saw his first fish hit astern. Ten seconds later another hit farther forward. "Large ball of fire climbed his side," Enright noted. The *Archerfish* headed down to evade an oncoming destroyer. On the way, Enright heard four more hits. He stayed down until 6:10 a.m. and then rose to periscope depth for a look. The sea was empty.

Enright believed that he had sunk a 28,000-ton *Hayatake*-class carrier. After the War he learned that he had actually sunk the *Shinano*, 59,000 tons and by far the biggest flattop ever built to that time. She had, in fact, originally been laid

Flying her victory pennants, the Tautog glides home from her 13th and final war patrol early in 1945. In terms of the total number of enemy ships sunk, the Tautog was the most successful submarine in the Silent Service: Under the leadership of three skippers, she sent to the bottom 26 Japanese vessels—two more than her nearest rival, the Tang.

184

down as a battlewagon and was intended to be a sister ship to the *Musashi* and the *Yamato*. But she had been converted to a carrier during her construction. Enright had got her on her first voyage.

By the end of 1944, a number of submarine captains shared Enright's qualms about their ability to handle the responsibilities thrust upon them. It was natural enough; the new skippers were younger, on the average, than those who had started the War. But most of them, like Enright, more than met the challenge.

George Grider was no exception, though he was a veteran submariner when he received his first command. His boat was the *Flasher,* already a famous submarine. Under her only previous captain, Reuben Whitaker, she had sunk 60,846 tons of enemy shipping and was among the top scorers in the service. "I had become conditioned to the idea of calling the captain in any emergency," Grider recalled. "Now, suddenly, there was no one to call but me. A lonely feeling, and a disquieting one."

But Grider need not have worried: He had learned his business well in the old *Wahoo,* under Morton and O'Kane.

Grider made his first patrol as a skipper in company with the *Hawkbill* and the *Becuna*. Their hunting grounds were west of Mindoro in the Philippines. On the morning of December 4, following several days of storm and poor visibility, the *Flasher* was 200 miles to the west of Mindoro and approximately 15 miles out of position when she received from the *Hawkbill* a contact report on a Japanese convoy that was heading west. The *Flasher* was lucky: Her navigational error had put her directly on the convoy's track. She submerged and prepared to attack.

"I stood in the quiet conning tower," wrote Grider, "feeling the rush of blood to my skin, knowing that the test I had dreamed and wondered and worried about was upon me at last."

Then the *Flasher* ran into a series of squalls. The boat was groping through a cloudburst, her periscope useless, when Grider's executive officer, Lieut. Commander Philip T. Glennon, reported the sound of rapid screws approaching. Straining at the periscope, Grider suddenly made out a gray silhouette in the curtain of rain.

"It's a destroyer," he shouted, and he called out the firing data for the torpedo officer.

Grider fired four fish and heard two hits. Long after, he would still remember the moment: "Even as I swung the scope to look, a feeling of exaltation like nothing I had ever experienced swept over me. By Heaven, I had paid my way as a skipper."

He continued to pay it. He made out a big tanker beyond the sinking destroyer, and fired two torpedoes. Then, seeing a second escort vessel charging at the *Flasher,* he went deep, and on the way down both torpedoes were heard to explode. Glennon breathed, "My God. We hit him!"

Then came the depth-charge punishment, and an hour and a half passed before it seemed safe to come up to periscope depth. Grider found the tanker burning and settling aft. Another destroyer, mysteriously stopped, lay between the *Flasher* and the tanker. Grider fired four tubes, two set shallow for the destroyer, two set deep for the tanker. Then he was forced deep again.

That afternoon he surfaced. Both destroyers had sunk. The tanker was still burning and, upon examination, proved to be abandoned. Grider fired one more killer shot at the tanker. The explosion blew out the fire—causing some distress to Grider, who had hoped to photograph a burning victim. Then the tanker went down.

Grider's first attacks had sunk one 10,000-ton tanker and two destroyers of 2,100 tons each—a fair bag for any normal 24-torpedo patrol. But the *Flasher* still had 15 fish in the tubes and on the racks, and to use them up George Grider turned his submarine westward toward the Indochina coast and Camranh Bay.

On December 21 in heavy weather, the submarine spotted a convoy of four big tankers and their escorts. With the sea too turbulent for accurate shooting, Grider let them go by and then pursued, waiting for the weather to abate. By the time the seas calmed, the *Flasher* had lost contact, and Grider cursed himself for poor judgment.

"As the afternoon wore away, I went bitterly to the wardroom for a glum dinner at which no one spoke to me and I spoke to no one," he wrote later. The radar screen remained empty until 1 a.m. on December 22, when the scope showed what appeared to be a small island moving on a steady course. It was, in fact, the tightly clustered convoy, hugging the coast 12 miles from land in very shallow water.

"The relief that swept over me was tremendous," Grider recalled. "I felt like a prisoner who has been reprieved on his way to the death chamber."

When it proved impossible to get past the tankers' escorts from the seaward side, Grider took the *Flasher* ahead and around the convoy to hit from the dangerous shallows on the land side. In one slashing attack the *Flasher* sent three more tankers to the ocean bottom for a total of 28,638 tons. With the tanker sunk earlier, the *Flasher* had accounted for the highest tonnage of tankers sunk by any submarine on a single patrol.

On a later patrol the *Flasher* managed to sink an insignificant 850-ton freighter. But when all the numbers were added up, that last minor sinking had raised the *Flasher's* total tonnage destroyed under her two captains to 100,231. That was the highest score in the War, followed closely by the *Rasher* with 99,901. However, skippers were ranked by the number of ships they sank, not by total tonnage.

By the end of 1944, the U.S. submarines had virtually worked themselves out of a job—at least so far as their primary mission of sinking enemy ships was concerned. Their enormous year-long toll of steel-hulled ships had finished off Japan's merchant fleet. What shipping remained was either out of reach in the Yellow Sea and the Sea of Japan or hugging the coasts by day and scuttling into harbors at night during the submarines' preferred hunting hours.

Lifeguard duty for downed carrier pilots and B-29 fliers continued as a useful activity, but otherwise the boats had a slow and disappointing time. Some frustrated skippers took to shooting up sampans and fishing junks until that pastime began to seem unsporting.

Running out of patience, a few skippers decided that if the Japanese ships refused to come out to be sunk, the submarines would go in and get them. The *Barb's* Eugene Fluckey dodged mines and rocks to sink at least one cargo ship in Namkwan Harbor on the China coast. Still unsatisfied, Fluckey carried his private war to the land, shelling Sakhalin Island north of Japan's home islands with his deck gun and a deck-mounted rocket launcher. He even sent a nighttime commando party ashore in rubber boats to sabotage a railway. They had planted their 55-pound demolition charges and were going back to the boat when a train came down the track. Reported Fluckey: "Wreckage flew two hundred feet in the air. Cars piled up and rolled off the tracks in a writhing, twisting mass of wreckage. Cheers!"

The year 1945 saw the Silent Service involved in only three noteworthy events. In June, Admiral Lockwood sent nine submarines on a make-work patrol into the Sea of Japan. In 15 days the pack managed to sink 28 ships of various types for a total of 54,784 tons. One submarine, the *Bonefish,* was lost to a depth-charge attack somewhere in the shallow Toyama Bay.

The second event was the sinking of the last U.S. submarine to be lost in the War, bringing the service's casualties in the Pacific to 49 boats. On August 6, the day the first atomic bomb was dropped on Hiroshima, a Japanese Army plane depth-charged an American submarine off the coast of Bali near the northern end of Lombok Strait. The *Bullhead,* on patrol in that area, never came home.

The final event of the war under the Pacific occurred on August 14, 1945. Commander Bafford Lewellen's *Torsk,* patrolling off the southwest coast of Honshu in the Sea of Japan, torpedoed and sank a small Japanese frigate. The victim, designated Coastal Defense Vessel No. 47, was the last Japanese ship to be sunk during World War II.

That night, at 11:04, Admiral Nimitz ordered all naval units to cease hostile operations. Later, writing in praise of the submariners, Nimitz did not hesitate to compare them and their record to the best: "As British airmen are credited with saving Britain in those critical days after Dunkirk, so our gallant submarine personnel filled the breach after Pearl Harbor, and can claim credit, not only for holding the line, but also for carrying the war to the enemy."

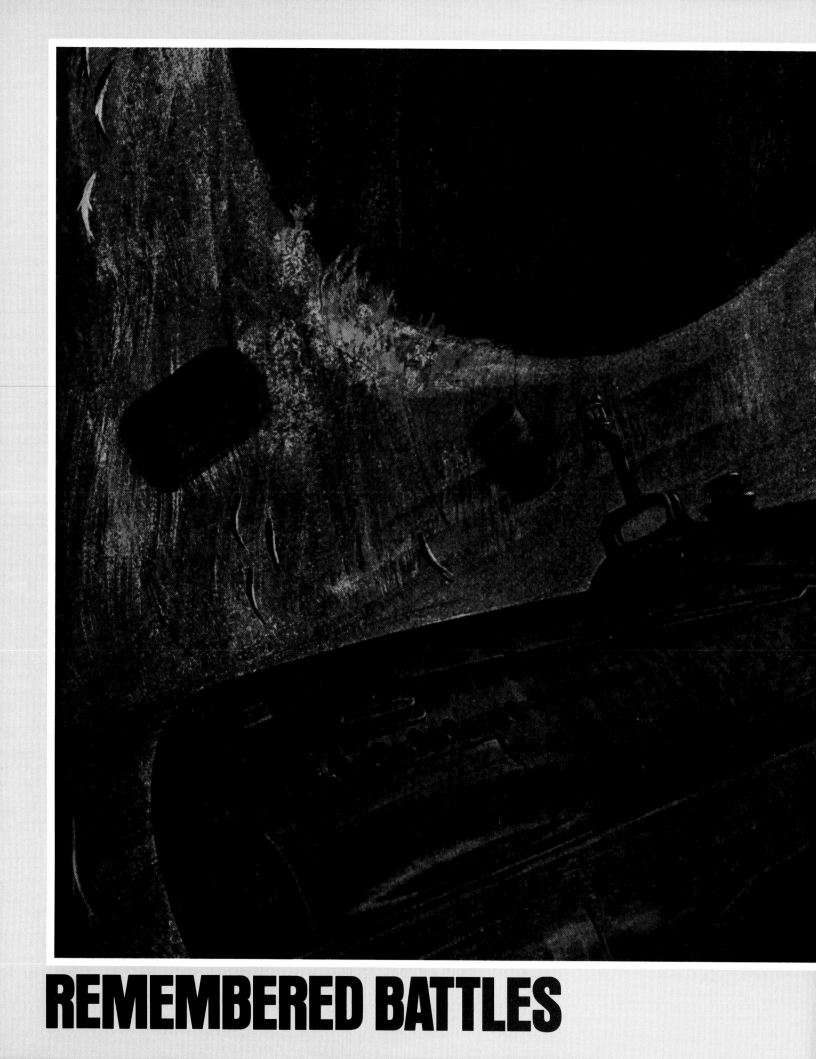

REMEMBERED BATTLES

The Guardfish, after sinking two freighters in August 1942, barely survived a fierce depth-charging. One charge exploded so close (right) that it heeled her over.

THE CORSAIRS OF THE MODERN WORLD

What made the Silent Service a unique and overpowering success? Many of the men who scoured the Pacific in submarines knew the answer as well as they knew their own jobs, and some expressed it with uncommon eloquence.

"We were corsairs in a world that had almost forgotten the word," wrote Captain George Grider, a veteran of nine war patrols. In each patrol area, a submarine searched for prey with the freedom of a pirate ship—although with an efficiency undreamed of by the buccaneers.

The crew, wrote veteran skipper Edward L. Beach, "operates with the unity of purpose of an ant colony. It acts under a single directive force—a single brain—the captain's." Nothing less than instantaneous execution of orders would suffice during the violent moments of attack or counterattack. "In submarines perhaps more than in any other fighting unit," said skipper Richard O'Kane, "the survival of all could depend on the performance of any individual."

As the U.S. submarine fleet grew, the teamwork that unified each crew was applied to wolf packs, which patrolled the same area and sometimes attacked in unison. Yet even at peak strength of 182 boats, the Silent Service was so small that nearly everyone knew someone on dozens of other boats. The web of friendships gave the fleet added strength —an unsurpassed *esprit de corps*. The loss or the triumph of any boat was felt personally by admiral and messboy alike.

There were heroes aplenty to celebrate. The feats of Lawson P. Ramage and the ordeal of the *Puffer (page 73)* were almost mythic throughout the fleet. Every submariner paid proud and sorrowful tribute to men like Howard Gilmore, who saved his boat at the cost of his own life *(page 63)*.

Praise for the Silent Service came from many outsiders, among them Air Force generals whose downed crews were rescued by the submariners. Tribute of another sort came from writers and artists who knew the work of the undersea fleet. One of the latter was painter Fred Freeman, who served as a Naval officer in the Pacific. Working from the submariners' reports, Freeman depicted some of their best-known exploits in the action pictures shown on these pages.

The Sealion, the first U.S. submarine lost in the War, was sunk in the Japanese air raid on Manila's Cavite Naval Station on December 10, 1941.

The S-39's crew invaded a jungle island to rescue British refugees from Singapore in February of 1942. Veteran S-boats were often given such tasks.

Despite heavy enemy fire, skipper Lawson Ramage kept the Parche on the surface throughout a daring night attack on a convoy off Formosa in July 1944.

Spying a torpedo from the Gudgeon, the I-173's crew abandoned ship off Midway in January 1942. The I-173 was the first warship sunk by U.S. submarines.

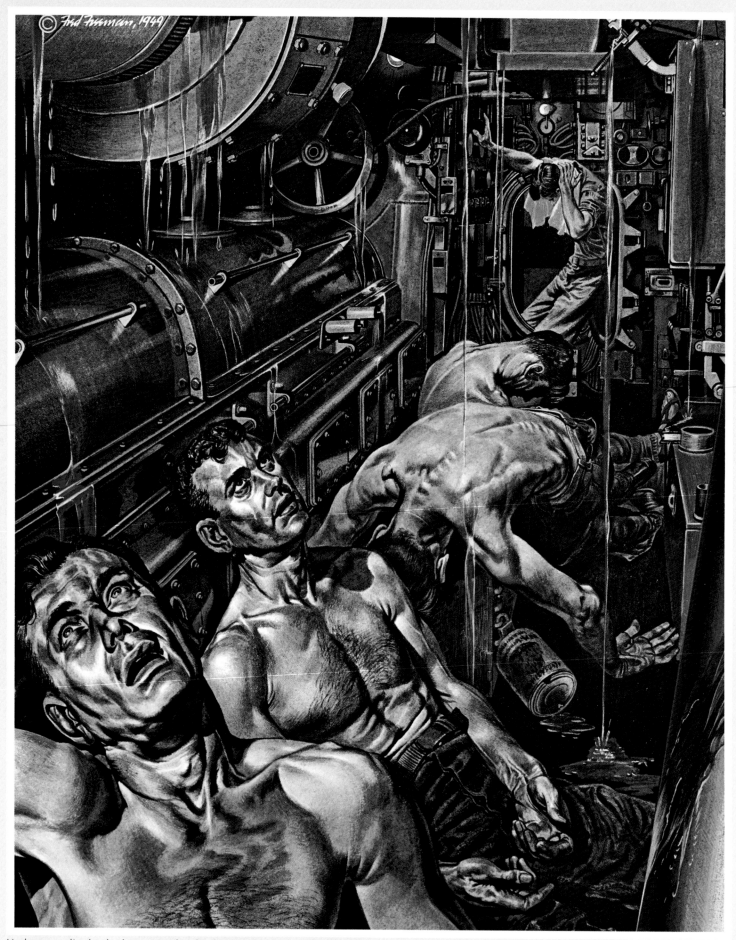

Under sporadic depth-charge attacks, the men of the Puffer endured nearly 38 sweltering hours at the extreme depth of 500 feet, in October of 1943.

194

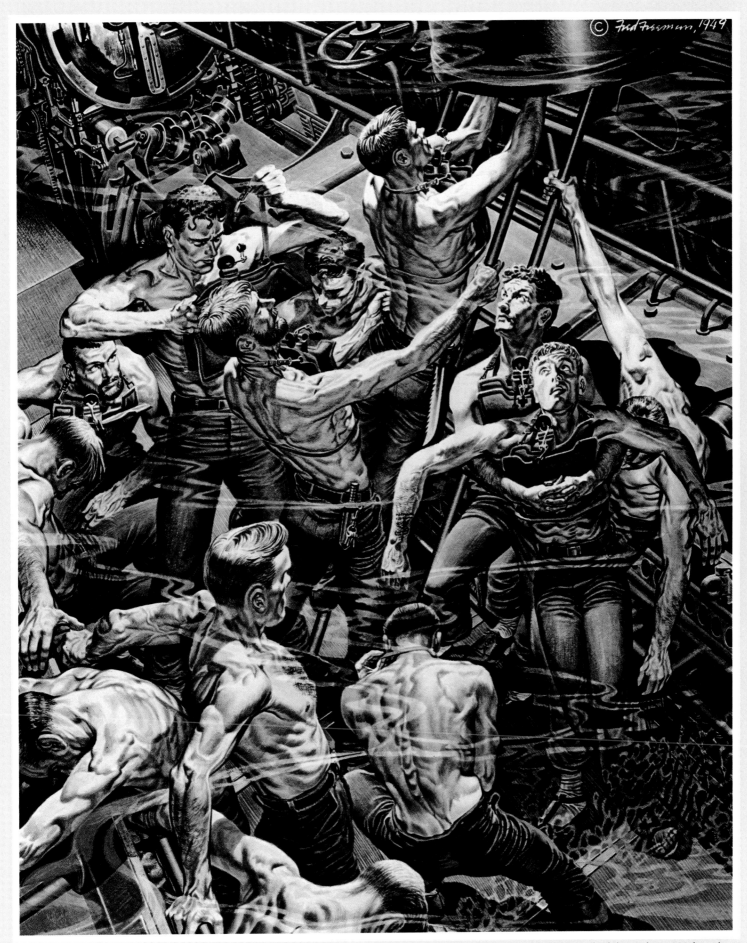

The Tang's crew donned Momsen Lungs to escape from the mortally damaged boat in October 1944. Only eight men reached the surface, 180 feet above.

Howard Gilmore, injured in a collision that killed two crewmen, ordered the Growler to dive—sacrificing his life to save his submarine in February 1943.

Captain John Cromwell, entrusted with military secrets, went down with the *Sculpin* in November 1943, rather than run the risk of capture and torture.

Diving to escape a pursuing Japanese destroyer in September 1944, the Barb left behind two flaming victims, an oil tanker and a light carrier. The boat belonged to a high-scoring wolf pack, one of several such groups that were formed late in the War to patrol and attack in concert.

The S-44, depicted at the critical moment in a submarine attack, stood by at periscope depth so that her skipper could watch a torpedo speeding toward its target—the 8,800-ton cruiser Kako. The Kako went to the bottom in August 1942—the largest Japanese warship sunk to that time.

BIBLIOGRAPHY

Alden, John D., *The Fleet Submarine in the U.S. Navy: A Design and Construction History*. U.S. Naval Institute, 1979.

Bagnasco, Erminio, *Submarines of World War Two*. London: Arms and Armour Press, 1977.

Barnes, Robert Hatfield, *United States Submarines*. H. F. Morse Assoc., 1944.

Barrows, Nat A., *Blow All Ballast! The Story of the Squalus*. Dodd, Mead, 1940.

Beach, Edward L., *Submarine!* Henry Holt, 1946.

Blair, Clay, Jr., *Silent Victory: The U.S. Submarine War against Japan*. J. B. Lippincott, 1975.

Brown, Ernest W., "The Human Mechanism and the Submarine." *Proceedings*, U.S. Naval Institute, November 1940.

"Bureau of Naval Personnel Training Bulletin." U.S. Navy, August 15, 1945.

Carmer, Carl, *The Jesse James of the Java Sea*. Farrar & Rinehart, 1945.

Casey, Robert J., *Battle Below: The War of the Submarines*. Bobbs-Merrill, 1945.

Cohen, Jerome B., *Japan's Economy in War and Reconstruction*. Univ. of Minnesota Press, 1949.

Cope, Harley, and Walter Karig, *Battle Submerged: Submarine Fighters of World War II*. W. W. Norton, 1951.

Cross, Wilbur, *Challengers of the Deep: The Story of Submarines*. William Sloane Assoc., 1959.

D'Albas, Andrieu, *Death of a Navy*. Transl. by Anthony Rippon. Devin-Adair, 1957.

Davis, H. F. D., "Building U.S. Submarines in World War II." *Proceedings*, U.S. Naval Institute, July 1946.

Dull, Paul S., *A Battle History of the Imperial Japanese Navy (1941-1945)*. U.S. Naval Institute, 1978.

Frank, Gerold, and James D. Horan with J. M. Eckberg, *U.S.S. Seawolf: Submarine Raider of the Pacific*. G. P. Putnam's Sons, 1945.

Fuchida, Mitsuo, and Masatake Okumiya, *Midway*. U.S. Naval Institute, 1955.

Fujita, Nobuo, "I Bombed the U.S.A." *Proceedings*, U.S. Naval Institute, June 1961.

Fukaya, Hajime, "Three Japanese Submarine Developments." *Proceedings*, U.S. Naval Institute, August 1952.

Fyfe, Herbert C., *Submarine Warfare: Past and Present*. London: E. Grant Richards, 1907.

Garrett, Richard, *Submarines*. London: Weidenfeld and Nicolson, 1977.

Grider, George, with Lydel Sims, *War Fish*. Little, Brown, 1958.

Gunston, Bill, *Submarines in Color*. Arco Publishing, 1977.

Hashimoto, Mochitsura, *Sunk: The Story of the Japanese Submarine Fleet, 1941-1945*. Transl. by E. H. M. Colegrave. Henry Holt, 1954.

Hawkins, Maxwell, *Torpedoes Away, Sir!* Henry Holt, 1946.

Holmes, W. J., *Undersea Victory*. Doubleday, 1966.

Horie, Y., "The Failure of the Japanese Convoy Escort." *Proceedings*, U.S. Naval Institute, October 1956.

Howard, Warren S., "The Dragon Puts to Sea." *Proceedings*, U.S. Naval Institute, August 1951.

Hoyt, Edwin P.:
The Lonely Ships. David McKay, 1976.
War in the Deep: Pacific Submarine Action in World War II. G. P. Putnam's Sons, 1978.

The Imperial Japanese Navy in World War II: A Graphic Presentation of the Japanese Naval Organization and List of Combatant and Noncombatant Vessels Lost or Damaged in the War. U.S. Army, Military History Section, Special Staff, General Headquarters, Far East Command, February 1952.

Ingham, Travis, *Rendezvous by Submarine: The Story of Charles Parsons and the Guerrilla-Soldiers in the Philippines*. Doubleday, Doran, 1945.

Ito, Masanori, *The End of the Imperial Japanese Navy*. Transl. by Andrew Y. Kuroda and Roger Pineau. W. W. Norton, 1962.

Japanese Naval Vessels at the End of War. Compiled by Shizuo Fukui. U.S. Army, Administrative Division, Second Demobilization Bureau, April 1947.

The Japanese Navy in World War II: An Anthology of Articles Originally Published in Proceedings. U.S. Naval Institute, 1969.

Jentschura, Hansgeorg, Dieter Jung and Peter Mickel, *Warships of the Imperial Japanese Navy, 1869-1945*. Transl. by Antony Preston and J. D. Brown. U.S. Naval Institute, 1975.

Joint Army-Navy Assessment Committee, *Japanese Naval and Merchant Shipping Losses during World War II by All Causes*. U.S. Navy Department, 1947.

Knott, Richard C., *The American Flying Boat: An Illustrated History*. U.S. Naval Institute, 1979.

Kroese, A., *The Dutch Navy at War*. London: George Allen and Unwin, 1945.

Lenton, H. T.:
American Submarines. Doubleday, 1973.
British Submarines. London: Macdonald, 1972.

Lipscomb, F. W., *The British Submarine*. London: Conway Maritime Press, 1975.

Lockwood, Charles A.:
Down to the Sea in Subs. W. W. Norton, 1967.
Sink 'Em All: Submarine Warfare in the Pacific. E. P. Dutton, 1951.

Lockwood, Charles A., and Hans Christian Adamson:
Hell at 50 Fathoms. Chilton, 1962.
Hellcats of the Sea. Greenberg, 1955.
Through Hell and Deep Water: The Stirring Story of the Navy's Deadly Submarine, the U.S.S. Harder. Greenberg, 1956.
Zoomies, Subs and Zeros. Greenberg, 1956.

Long, E. John, "Japan's 'Undersea Carriers.'" *Proceedings*, U.S. Naval Institute, June 1950.

Lord, Walter, *Incredible Victory*. Harper & Row, 1967.

Mars, Alastair, *British Submarines at War: 1939-1945*. U.S. Naval Institute, 1971.

Masland, John W., "Japanese-German Naval Collaboration in World War II." *Proceedings*, U.S. Naval Institute, June 1952.

Meskill, Johanna Menzel, *Hitler & Japan: The Hollow Alliance*. Atherton Press, 1966.

Middleton, Drew, *Submarine: The Ultimate Naval Weapon*. Playboy Press, 1976.

Millis, Walter, *This Is Pearl!* William Morrow, 1947.

Moore, John E., ed., *Jane's Pocket Book of Submarine Development*. Collier Books (Macmillan), 1976.

Morison, Samuel Eliot:
History of United States Naval Operations in World War II, Little, Brown.
Vol. 4, *Coral Sea, Midway and Submarine Actions*, 1949.
Vol. 8, *New Guinea and the Marianas*, 1953.
Vol. 14, *Victory in the Pacific*, 1960.
The Two-Ocean War: A Short History of the United States Navy in the Second World War. Little, Brown, 1963.

Newcomb, Richard F., *Abandon Ship! Death of the U.S.S. Indianapolis*. Indiana Univ. Press, 1958.

Oi, Atsushi, "Why Japan's Antisubmarine Warfare Failed." *Proceedings*, U.S. Naval Institute, June 1952.

O'Kane, Richard H., *Clear the Bridge! The War Patrols of the U.S.S. Tang*. Rand McNally, 1977.

Okumiya, Masatake, and Jiro Horikoshi with Martin Caidin, *Zero!* E. P. Dutton, 1956.

ONI-222J: The Japanese Navy. U.S. Navy, Division of Naval Intelligence, June 1945.

Orita, Zenji, and Joseph D. Harrington, *I-Boat Captain*. Major Books, 1976.

Paine, T. O., *Submarining: Three Thousand Books and Articles*. Center for Advanced Studies, General Electric Company—TEMPO, 1971.

Potter, E. B.:
Illustrated History of the United States Navy. Galahad Books, 1971.
Nimitz. U.S. Naval Institute, 1976.

Potter, E. B., and Chester W. Nimitz, eds.:
The Great Sea War: The Story of Naval Action in World War II. Prentice-Hall, 1960.
Sea Power—A Naval History. Prentice-Hall, 1960.

Potter, John Deane, *Yamamoto: The Man Who Menaced America*. Viking, 1965.

Preston, Antony, *Submarines: The History and Evolution of Underwater Fighting Vessels*. London: Octopus Books, 1975.

Preston, Antony, and John Batchelor, *The Submarine Since 1919*. Leeds: BPC Publishing, 1974.

Reynolds, Clark G., *Famous American Admirals*. Van Nostrand Reinhold, 1978.

Roscoe, Theodore:
Pigboats: The True Story of the Fighting Submariners of World War II. Bantam Books, 1949.
United States Submarine Operations in World War II. U.S. Naval Institute, 1949.

Roskill, S. W., *The War at Sea: 1939-1945*:
Vol. 3, *The Offensive, Part I: 1st June 1943—31st May 1944*. London: Her Majesty's Stationery Office, 1960.
Vol. 3, *The Offensive, Part II: 1st June 1944—14th August 1945*. London: Her Majesty's Stationery Office, 1961.

Rush, C. W., and W. C. Chambliss and H. J. Gimpel, *The Complete Book of Submarines*. World Publishing, 1958.

Russell of Liverpool, Lord, *The Knights of Bushido*. E. P. Dutton, 1958.

Saville, Allison W., "German Submarines in the Far East." *Proceedings*, U.S. Naval Institute, August 1961.

Sheridan, Martin, *Overdue and Presumed Lost: The Story of the U.S.S. Bullhead*. Marshall Jones, 1947.

Shrader, Grahame F., *The Phantom War in the Northwest*. Grahame F. Shrader, 1969.

Spencer, Louise Reid, *Guerrilla Wife*. Thomas Y. Crowell, 1945.

Sterling, Forest J., *Wake of the Wahoo*. Chilton, 1960.

Stewart, Allen J., *The Use of Japanese Midget Submarines at Pearl Harbor*. Unpublished, 1974.

Submarine Operations: December 1941—April 1942. U.S. Army, Military History Section, Headquarters, Army Forces Far East, no date.

"Submarine School." *Life*, March 30, 1942.

The Submarine in the United States Navy. U.S. Navy, Naval History Division, 1969.

Submarines in Combat. Compiled by Joseph B. Icenhower. Franklin Watts, 1964.

Tanabe, Yahachi, "I Sank the *Yorktown* at Midway." *Proceedings*, U.S. Naval Institute, May 1963.

Torisu, Kennosuke, "Japanese Submarine Tactics." *Proceedings*, U.S. Naval Institute, February 1961.

Trumbull, Robert, *Silversides*. Henry Holt, 1945.

United States Naval Administration in World War II: Submarine Commands, Vols. 1 and 2. U.S. Navy, Office of Naval History, February 1946.

United States Strategic Bombing Survey:
The Campaigns of the Pacific War. Government Printing Office, 1946.
The Effects of Air Attack on Japanese Urban Economy. Government Printing Office, March 1947.
Interrogations of Japanese Officials, Vols. 1 and 2. Government Printing Office, 1946.
Japanese Merchant Shipbuilding. Government Printing Office, January 1947.
Japanese Naval Shipbuilding. Government Printing Office, November 1946.
The War against Japanese Transportation: 1941-1945. Government Printing Office, May 1947.

United States Submarine Data Book. Submarine Force Library & Museum Assoc., 1976.

United States Submarine Losses: World War II. U.S. Navy, Naval History Division, Office of the Chief of Naval Operations, 1963.

Van Der Rhoer, Edward, *Deadly Magic: A Personal Account of Communications Intelligence in World War II in the Pacific.* Charles Scribner's Sons, 1978.

Warren, C. E. T., and James Benson, *Above Us the Waves: The Story of Midget Submarines and Human Torpedoes.* London: George G. Harrap, 1953.

Warshofsky, Fred, *War under the Waves.* Pyramid Books, 1962.

Watts, Anthony J.:
  A Source Book of Submarines and Submersibles. London: Ward Lock, 1976.
  World War 2 Fact Files: Allied Submarines. Arco Publishing, 1977.
  World War 2 Fact Files: Axis Submarines. Arco Publishing, 1977.

Watts, Anthony J., and Brian G. Gordon, *The Imperial Japanese Navy.* Doubleday, 1971.

Weller, George, *The Story of Submarines.* Random House, 1962.

Wheeler, Harold F. B., *War in the Underseas.* London: George G. Harrap, 1919.

Wheeler, Keith, *The Pacific Is My Beat.* E. P. Dutton, 1943.

Yokota, Yutaka:
  Kamikaze Submarine (formerly *The Kaiten Weapon* and *Suicide Submarine*). Tower Publications, 1980.
  "Kaiten—Japan's Human Torpedoes." *Proceedings,* U.S. Naval Institute, January 1962.

Zim, Herbert S., *Submarines: The Story of Undersea Boats.* Harcourt, Brace, 1942.

Zimmerman, Sherwood R., "Operation Forager." *Proceedings,* U.S. Naval Institute, August 1964.

PICTURE CREDITS

Credits from left to right are separated by semicolons, from top to bottom by dashes.

DUST JACKET, COVER, and page 1: U.S. Navy, National Archives Neg. No. 80-G-468544.

EVOLUTION OF A WEAPON—6, 7: U.S. Naval Historical Center. 8: U.S. Navy, National Archives. 9-12: U.S. Naval Historical Center. 13: U.S. Navy, National Archives—The Mariners Museum; courtesy Newport News Shipbuilding—courtesy Newport News Shipbuilding. 14: U.S. Naval Historical Center. 15: U.S. Navy, National Archives. 16, 17: U.S. Naval Historical Center. 18, 19: U.S. Navy, National Archives. 20, 21: U.S. Submarine Force Library and Museum.

A FORCE UNREADY FOR WAR—25, 26: U.S. Navy, National Archives. 28, 29: Map by Tarijy Elsab. 33: U.S. Naval Historical Center. 36-39: Illustrations by John Batchelor, London. 41: U.S. Submarine Force Library and Museum. 45: Henry Groskinsky, courtesy U.S. Submarine Force Library and Museum.

BUILDING THE UNDERSEA NAVY—48-53: U.S. Navy, National Archives. 54, 55: U.S. Navy, National Archives; Bernard Hoffman for *Life.* 56: U.S. Navy, National Archives, courtesy Fred Freeman. 57: U.S. Navy, National Archives. 58, 59: U.S. Navy, National Archives, except top left, U.S. Submarine Force Library and Museum. 60, 61: U.S. Navy, National Archives.

THE YEAR THAT TURNED THE TIDE—65: U.S. Navy, courtesy Fred Freeman. 67: U.S. Navy, National Archives. 68: Bottom, U.S. Office of Naval Intelligence. 69: U.S. Office of Naval Intelligence, except top left. 71: Courtesy U.S. Naval Historical Center, collection of Rear Admiral C. C. Burlingame. 74, 75: U.S. Navy, National Archives, except center, U.S. Navy, courtesy Fred Freeman. 77: U.S. Navy, National Archives. 78, 79: National Archives.

FIND 'EM, CHASE 'EM, SINK 'EM—82-84: U.S. Navy, courtesy Fred Freeman. 85-89: U.S. Navy, National Archives; U.S. Navy, courtesy Fred Freeman. 90, 91: U.S. Navy, National Archives. 92-94: U.S. Navy, courtesy Fred Freeman. 95: U.S. Navy, courtesy Fred Freeman; U.S. Navy, National Archives—U.S. Navy, National Archives (2); U.S. Navy, courtesy Fred Freeman (2).

THE ENEMY BELOW—98: *Mainichi Shimbun,* Tokyo. 100: Bert Webber, from *Retaliation: Japanese Attacks and Allied Countermeasures on the Pacific Coast in World War II,* published by Oregon State University Press, 1975. 102, 103: Bundesarchiv, Koblenz, except bottom right, courtesy Karl-Wilhelm Grützemacher, Deisenhofen. 105: *Mainichi Shimbun,* Tokyo. 107: Süddeutscher Verlag, Bilderdienst, Munich. 109: Courtesy Yutaka Yokota, from *I-Boat Captain,* by Zenji Orita and Joseph Harrington, published by Major Books, Canoga Park, Calif., 1976; U.S. Navy, National Archives. 110, 111: U.S. Navy, National Archives, except bottom left, U.S. Naval Historical Center. 113: U.S. Navy, National Archives. 115: U.S. Navy, National Archives, inset, *Mainichi Shimbun,* Tokyo.

ALL THE EMPEROR'S BOATS—118, 119: *Mainichi Shimbun,* Tokyo. 120: Courtesy Kennosuke Torisu, Tokyo. 121-123: U.S. Navy, National Archives. 124, 125: Shizuo Fukui, courtesy U.S. Submarine Force Library and Museum—*Mainichi Shimbun,* Tokyo. 126: Shizuo Fukui, courtesy U.S. Submarine Force Library and Museum—Karl-Wilhelm Grützemacher, Deisenhofen. 127: Shizuo Fukui, courtesy U.S. Submarine Force Library and Museum. 128, 129: Courtesy Kennosuke Torisu, Tokyo.

ON SPECIAL ASSIGNMENT—132-140: U.S. Navy, National Archives.

READY FOR ANY JOB ANY TIME—144, 145: U.S. Navy, National Archives. 146: From *U.S. Submarine Operations in World War II,* by Theodore Roscoe, published by U.S. Naval Institute, 1958. 147-153: U.S. Navy, National Archives.

REFIT BETWEEN PATROLS—154, 155: U.S. Navy, courtesy Fred Freeman. 156, 157: U.S. Navy, National Archives. 158: U.S. Navy, courtesy Fred Freeman—U.S. Navy, National Archives. 159-163: U.S. Navy, National Archives. 164, 165: U.S. Navy, courtesy Fred Freeman.

A TIME OF SLAUGHTER—169: U.S. Navy, National Archives (2)—U.S. Navy, courtesy Fred Freeman (2). 170: U.S. Navy, courtesy Fred Freeman. 172, 173: U.S. Navy, National Archives. 175: U.S. Naval Institute Reference Library. 176-179: U.S. Navy, National Archives. 180, 181: Henry Groskinsky, courtesy U.S. Submarine Force Library and Museum, except bottom left. 184, 185: U.S. Navy, National Archives.

REMEMBERED BATTLES—188-199: Paintings by Fred Freeman, photographed by Henry Groskinsky.

ACKNOWLEDGMENTS

For help in the preparation of this book, the editors wish to thank Thomas Banks-Bey, Baltimore, Md.; Carole Boutté, Senior Researcher, U.S. Army Audio-Visual Activity, Pentagon, Arlington, Va.; Captain Henry J. Cappello, USN (Ret.), Alexandria, Va.; V. M. Destefano, Chief of Reference Branch, U.S. Army Audio-Visual Activity, Pentagon, Arlington, Va.; Joseph Farrell, Washington, D.C.; Commander Fred Freeman, USN (Ret.), Essex, Conn.; Shizuo Fukui, Yokohama, Japan; Elmer Griffin, Baltimore, Md.; Karl-Wilhelm Grützemacher, Deisenhofen, Germany; Charles R. Haberlein Jr., Photographic Section, Curator Branch, Naval History Division, Department of the Navy, Washington, D.C.; Chief Karl Hochstetler, USN, Submarine Force Library and Museum, Naval Submarine Base New London, Groton, Conn.; Richard G. Hutchinson, Timonium, Md.; Captain Richard C. Knott, USN, Fairfax, Va.; Admiral Francis B. McCorkle, USN (Ret.), Providence, R.I.; Carol Forsyth Mickey, Washington, D.C.; Chief Gary Morrison, USN, Submarine Force Library and Museum, Naval Submarine Base New London, Groton, Conn.; James O'Connor, Baltimore, Md.; Rear Admiral Richard Hetherington O'Kane, USN (Ret.), Sebastopol, Calif.; Operational Archives, U.S. Naval History Division, Washington Navy Yard, Washington, D.C.; Rear Admiral Roger Warde Paine Jr., USN (Ret.), El Cajon, Calif.; Commander Anthony David Ellis Pender-Cudlip, RN, British Navy Staff, Washington, D.C.; Captain Arthur Rawson, USN (Ret.), Bethesda, Md.; John H. Reichart, Joppa, Md.; John C. Reilly, Ships' Histories Branch, U.S. Naval History Division, Washington Navy Yard, Washington, D.C.; Tyrone Rogers, Baltimore, Md.; Captain William Scarborough, USN (Ret.), Hilton Head Island, S.C.; The Honorable William Donald Schaefer, Mayor, Baltimore, Md.; Greg Schaler, Alexandria, Va.; Basil Simms, Rockville, Md.; Robert Simms, Operating Supervisor, U.S.S. *Torsk,* Baltimore, Md.; Lawrence Slotkoff, M.D., Ph.D., Department of Physiology, Georgetown University Medical Center, Washington, D.C.; Edward Sodosky, Baltimore, Md.; John Steele, Washington, D.C.; Phyllis Stephenson, Newport News Shipbuilding & Dry Dock Co., Newport News, Va.; Kenichi Takeuchi, Tokyo; Douglas S. Tawney, Director of Recreation and Parks, Baltimore, Md.; Kennosuke Torisu, Tokyo; James H. Trimble, Archivist, National Archives, Still Photo Branch, Washington, D.C.; Bunzo Tsujiguchi, *Mainichi Shimbun,* Tokyo; Eric Turner, Baltimore, Md.; Clarke van Vleet, Historian, Naval Aviation History Office, Washington Navy Yard, Washington, D.C.; Jan W. van Waning, Embassy of the Netherlands, Washington, D.C.; Mike Walker, Archivist, Naval Aviation History Office, Washington Navy Yard, Washington, D.C.; Leroy Webb, Submarine Force Library and Museum, Naval Submarine Base New London, Groton, Conn.; Tommy Yost, Gaithersburg, Md.; Ray Young, Manitowoc, Wis. Certain quotations from Clay Blair Jr.'s *Silent Victory* reprinted by permission of the author, Harper & Row, Publishers, Inc., and the author's agents, Scott Meredith Literary Agency, Inc., 845 Third Avenue, New York, N.Y. 10022.

The index for this book was prepared by Nicholas J. Anthony.

APPENDIX: A ROLL CALL OF U.S. SUBMARINES IN THE PACIFIC WAR

In the course of World War II, 250 U.S. submarines saw duty in the Pacific. Their names are listed in alphabetical order below, along with a brief summary of their service life, including commanding officers who went on war patrol. There were 190 boats that sank at least one major Japanese vessel (that is, steel-hulled and of more than 100 tons; small wooden sampans and fishing trawlers were not counted). The entry for each submarine includes the number of ships sunk and the total tonnage, as finally established in postwar reviews by the U.S. Joint Army-Navy Assessment Committee; a dash indicates no sinking credited to the submarine.

SUBMARINE	COMMANDERS	DATE OF COMMISSION	VESSELS SUNK	TOTAL TONNAGE	DISPOSITION
Albacore	R. C. Lake, O. E. Hagberg, J. W. Blanchard, H. R. Rimmer	June 1, 1942	10	49,861	Sunk November 7, 1944, off Hokkaido, Japan
Amberjack	J. A. Bole	June 19, 1942	2	5,225	Sunk February 16, 1943, off Rabaul, New Guinea
Angler	R. I. Olsen, F. G. Hess, H. Bisell Jr.	October 1, 1943	3	5,401	Decommissioned February 2, 1947
Apogon	W. P. Schoeni, A. C. House Jr.	July 16, 1943	3	7,575	Decommissioned February 25, 1947
Archerfish	G. W. Kehl, W. H. Wright, J. F. Enright	September 4, 1943	2	59,800	Decommissioned June 12, 1946
Argonaut	S. G. Barchett, J. R. Pierce	April 2, 1928	—	—	Sunk January 10, 1943, between Lau and Rabaul
Argonaut II	J. S. Schmidt	January 15, 1945	—	—	Decommissioned December 2, 1968
Aspro	H. C. Stevenson, W. A. Stevenson, J. H. Ashley Jr.	July 31, 1943	5	21,854	Decommissioned January 30, 1946
Atule	J. H. Maurer	June 21, 1944	6	33,379	Decommissioned September 8, 1947
Balao	R. H. Crane, C. C. Cole, M. F. DeRamirez, R. K. Worthington	February 4, 1943	6	31,920	Decommissioned August 20, 1946
Bang	A. R. Gallagher, O. W. Bagby	December 4, 1943	8	20,181	Decommissioned February 12, 1947
Barb	E. B. Fluckey, J. R. Waterman, N. Lucker Jr.	July 8, 1942	17	96,628	Decommissioned February 12, 1947
Barbel	R. A. Keating, C. L. Raguet	April 3, 1944	6	15,263	Sunk February 4, 1945, off Palawan Island, the Philippines
Barbero	I. S. Hartman	April 29, 1944	3	9,126	Decommissioned June 30, 1950
Bashaw	R. E. Nichols, H. S. Simpson	October 25, 1943	3	19,269	Decommissioned June 20, 1949
Batfish	W. R. Merrill, J. K. Fyfe, W. L. Small	August 21, 1943	6	10,230	Decommissioned April 6, 1946
Baya	A. H. Holtz, B. C. Jarvis	May 20, 1944	4	8,855	Decommissioned May 14, 1946
Becuna	H. D. Sturr, W. J. Bush, J. M. Hyde, J. T. Hardin,	May 27, 1944	1	1,945	Decommissioned November 7, 1969
Bergall	J. M. Hyde	June 12, 1944	4	15,684	Decommissioned October 18, 1958
Besugo	T. L. Wogan, H. E. Miller	June 19, 1944	4	12,450	Decommissioned March 21, 1958
Billfish	F. C. Lucas Jr., V. C. Turner, L. C. Farley Jr.	April 20, 1943	3	4,302	Decommissioned November 1, 1946
Blackfin	G. H. Laird Jr., W. L. Kitch	July 4, 1944	2	4,325	Decommissioned November 19, 1948
Blackfish	J. F. Davidson, E. Olsen, G. E. Laird, R. F. Sellars, R. C. Gilette	July 22, 1942	1	2,087	Decommissioned May 11, 1946
Blenny	W. H. Hazzard	July 27, 1944	7	18,087	Decommissioned November 7, 1969
Blower	J. H. Campbell, N. P. Watkins	August 10, 1944	—	—	Decommissioned November 16, 1950
Blueback	M. K. Clementson	August 28, 1944	1	300	Decommissioned May 23, 1948
Bluefish	G. E. Porter, C. M. Henderson, G. W. Forbes Jr.	May 24, 1943	12	50,839	Decommissioned February 12, 1947
Bluegill	E. L. Barr Jr.	November 11, 1943	10	46,212	Decommissioned March 1, 1946
Boarfish	R. L. Gross, E. C. Blonts	September 23, 1944	1	6,968	Decommissioned May 23, 1948
Bonefish	T. W. Hogan Jr., J. H. Corbus, L. L. Edge	May 31, 1943	12	61,345	Sunk June 18, 1945, off Honshu, Japan
Bowfin	J. H. Willingham Jr., W. T. Griffith, J. H. Corbus, A. K. Tyree	May 1, 1943	16	67,882	Decommissioned February 12, 1947
Bream	W. G. Chapple, J. L. McCallum	January 24, 1944	2	6,934	Decommissioned January 31, 1946
Brill	H. B. Dodge	October 26, 1944	—	—	Decommissioned May 23, 1948
Bugara	A. F. Schade	November 15, 1944	—	—	Decommissioned October 1, 1970
Bullhead	W. T. Griffith, E. R. Holt Jr.	December 4, 1944	—	—	Sunk August 6, 1945, off Bali, Indonesia
Bumper	J. W. Williams	December 9, 1944	1	1,189	Decommissioned November 16, 1950
Burrfish	W. B. Perkins, M. M. Lytle	September 13, 1943	1	5,894	Decommissioned October 10, 1946
Cabezon	G. W. Lautrup Jr.	December 30, 1944	1	2,631	Decommissioned October 24, 1953
Cabrilla	D. T. Hammond, W. C. Thompson Jr., H. C. Lauerman	May 24, 1943	7	38,767	Decommissioned August 7, 1946
Cachalot	W. N. Christensen, G. A. Lewis, H. C. Stevenson	December 1, 1933	—	—	Decommissioned October 17, 1945
Caiman	J. B. Azer, W. L. Fey Jr., F. C. Lucas Jr.	July 17, 1944	—	—	Decommissioned June 30, 1972
Capelin	E. E. Marshall	June 4, 1943	1	3,127	Sunk December 2, 1943, off Celebes, Indonesia
Capitaine	E. S. Friedrick	January 26, 1945	—	—	Decommissioned February 10, 1950
Carbonero	C. L. Murphy Jr.	February 7, 1945	—	—	Decommissioned December 1, 1970
Carp	J. L. Hunnicutt	February 28, 1945	—	—	Decommissioned March 18, 1968
Catfish	W. A. Overton	March 19, 1945	—	—	Decommissioned July 1, 1971
Cavalla	H. J. Kossler	February 29, 1944	4	34,180	Decommissioned March 16, 1946
Cero	D. C. White, E. F. Dissette, R. Berthrong	July 4, 1943	5	18,159	Decommissioned June 8, 1946
Charr	F. D. Boyle	September 23, 1944	—	—	Decommissioned June 28, 1969
Chub	C. D. Rhymes Jr.	October 21, 1944	1	492	Decommissioned May 23, 1948
Cisco	J. W. Coe	May 10, 1943	—	—	Sunk September 28, 1943, off Mindanao, the Philippines
Cobia	A. L. Becker, F. N. Russell	March 29, 1944	6	16,835	Decommissioned May 22, 1946
Cod	J. C. Dempsey, J. A. Adkins, E. M. Westbrook	June 21, 1943	8	26,985	Decommissioned June 22, 1946
Corvina	R. S. Rooney	August 6, 1943	—	—	Sunk November 16, 1943, off Truk, in the Carolines
Crevalle	H. G. Munson, F. D. Walker Jr., E. H. Steinmetz	June 24, 1943	9	51,814	Decommissioned July 20, 1946
Croaker	J. E. Lee, W. B. Thomas	April 21, 1944	6	19,710	Decommissioned June 15, 1946
Cutlass	H. C. Jukes	March 17, 1945	—	—	Decommissioned April 12, 1973
Cuttlefish	M. P. Hottel, E. E. Marshall	June 8, 1934	—	—	Decommissioned October 24, 1945
Dace	J. F. Enright, B. D. Claggett, O. R. Cole Jr.	July 23, 1943	6	28,689	Decommissioned February 12, 1947

SUBMARINE	COMMANDERS	DATE OF COMMISSION	VESSELS SUNK	TOTAL TONNAGE	DISPOSITION
Darter	W. S. Stovall Jr., D. L. McLintock	September 7, 1943	3	19,429	Sunk October 24, 1944, by U. S. forces after grounding off Palawan
Dentuda	J. S. McCain Jr.	December 30, 1944	—	—	Decommissioned December 11, 1946
Devilfish	E. C. Stephan	September 1, 1944	—	—	Decommissioned September 30, 1946
Dolphin	J. B. Griggs Jr., G. B. Rainer	June 1, 1932	—	—	Decommissioned October 2, 1945
Dragonet	J. H. Lewis	March 6, 1944	—	—	Decommissioned April 16, 1946
Drum	R. H. Rice, B. F. McMahon, D. F. Williamson	November 1, 1941	15	80,580	Decommissioned February 16, 1946
Entemedor	W. R. Smith Jr.	April 6, 1945	—	—	Decommissioned December 10, 1948
Escolar	W. J. Millican	June 2, 1944	—	—	Sunk October 17, 1944, in the Yellow Sea
Finback	J. L. Hull, J. A. Tyree Jr., J. L. Jordan, R. R. Williams	January 31, 1942	13	59,383	Decommissioned April 21, 1950
Flasher	R. T. Whitaker, G. W. Grider	September 25, 1943	21	100,231	Decommissioned March 16, 1946
Flier	J. D. Crowley	October 18, 1943	1	10,380	Sunk August 13, 1944, in Balabac Strait, off North Borneo
Flounder	C. A. Johnson, J. E. Stevens	November 29, 1943	1	2,681	Decommissioned February 12, 1947
Flying Fish	G. R. Donaho, F. T. Watkins, R. D. Risser	December 10, 1941	15	58,306	Decommissioned May 28, 1954
Gabilan	K. R. Wheland, W. B. Parham	December 28, 1943	3	1,354	Decommissioned February 23, 1946
Gar	D. McGregor, P. D. Quirk, G. W. Lautrup Jr., M. Ferrarra	April 14, 1941	8	20,392	Decommissioned December 11, 1945
Gato	R. J. Foley, R. M. Farrell, R. Holden, W. G. Myers	December 31, 1941	9	26,085	Decommissioned March 16, 1946
Golet	J. M. Clement, P. H. Ross, J. S. Clark	November 30, 1943	—	—	Sunk June 14, 1944, north of Honshu
Grampus	E. S. Hutchinson, J. R. Craig	May 23, 1941	1	8,636	Sunk March 5-6, 1943, Solomon Islands
Grayback	W. A. Saunders, E. C. Stephan, J. A. Moore	June 30, 1941	14	63,835	Sunk February 27, 1944, off Okinawa
Grayling	E. Olsen, J. E. Lee, R. M. Brinker	March 1, 1941	5	20,575	Sunk September 9-12, 1943, off Manila, the Philippines
Greenling	H. C. Bruton, J. D. Grant, J. D. Gerwick	January 21, 1942	15	59,234	Decommissioned October 16, 1946
Grenadier	A. R. Joyce, W. A. Lent, B. L. Carr, J. A. Fitzgerald	May 1, 1941	1	14,457	Scuttled April 21, 1943, after damage by Japanese aircraft off Penang, Malaya
Grouper	R. R. McGregor, M. P. Hottel, F. H. Wahlig, C. E. Duke	February 12, 1942	4	17,983	Decommissioned December 2, 1968
Growler	H. W. Gilmore, A. F. Schade, T. B. Oakley Jr.	March 20, 1942	10	32,607	Sunk November 8, 1944, in South China Sea
Grunion	M. L. Abele	April 11, 1942	2	600	Sunk July 30, 1942, off Kiska, Alaska
Guardfish	T. B. Klakring, N. G. Ward, D. T. Hammond	May 8, 1942	19	72,424	Decommissioned May 25, 1946
Guavina	C. Teideman, R. H. Lockwood	December 23, 1943	6	24,366	Decommissioned March 27, 1959
Gudgeon	E. W. Grenfell, H. B. Lyon, W. S. Stovall Jr., W. S. Post Jr., R. A. Bonin	April 21, 1941	12	71,047	Sunk April 18, 1944, off the Mariana Islands
Guitarro	E. D. Haskins, T. B. Dabney	January 26, 1944	8	23,132	Decommissioned December 6, 1945
Gunnel	J. S. McCain Jr., G. E. O'Neil Jr.	August 20, 1942	6	24,265	Decommissioned May 18, 1946
Gurnard	C. H. Andrews, N. D. Gage, G. S. Simmons III	September 18, 1942	10	57,866	Decommissioned November 7, 1945
Hackleback	F. E. Janney	November 7, 1944	—	—	Decommissioned March 20, 1946
Haddo	W. A. Lent, J. Corbus, C. W. Nimitz Jr., F. C. Lynch	October 9, 1942	9	21,618	Decommissioned February 16, 1946
Haddock	A. H. Taylor, R. M. Davenport, A. R. Strow, W. H. Brockman Jr., J. P. Roach	March 14, 1942	8	33,585	Decommissioned February 12, 1947
Hake	J. C. Broach, F. E. Hayler	October 30, 1942	7	37,923	Decommissioned July 13, 1946
Halibut	P. H. Ross, I. J. Galantin	April 10, 1942	12	45,257	Decommissioned July 18, 1945
Hammerhead	J. C. Martin, G. H. Laird Jr., F. M. Smith	March 1, 1944	11	35,635	Decommissioned February 9, 1946
Harder	S. D. Dealey	December 2, 1942	16	54,002	Sunk August 24, 1944, off Luzon, the Philippines
Hardhead	F. McMasters, F. A. Greenup, J. L. Haines	April 18, 1944	9	20,146	Decommissioned May 10, 1946
Hawkbill	F. W. Scanland Jr.	May 17, 1944	5	7,856	Decommissioned September 20, 1946
Herring	R. W. Johnson, J. Corbus, D. Zabriskie Jr.	May 4, 1942	6	19,959	Sunk June 1, 1944, off the Kurile Islands, Japan
Hoe	V. B. McCrea, M. P. Refo III	December 16, 1942	3	13,999	Decommissioned August 7, 1946
Icefish	R. W. Peterson	June 10, 1944	2	8,404	Decommissioned June 21, 1946
Jack	T. M. Dykers, A. E. Krapf, A. S. Fuhrman	January 6, 1943	15	76,687	Decommissioned June 8, 1946
Jallao	J. B. Icenhower	July 8, 1944	1	5,795	Decommissioned September 30, 1946
Kete	R. L. Rutter, E. Ackerman	July 31, 1944	3	6,881	Sunk March 1945, between Okinawa and Midway
Kingfish	V. L. Lowrance, H. L. Jukes, T. E. Harper, T. D. Keegan	May 20, 1942	14	48,866	Decommissioned March 9, 1946
Kraken	T. H. Henry	September 8, 1944	—	—	Decommissioned May 9, 1946
Lagarto	F. D. Latta	October 14, 1944	3	7,664	Sunk May 4, 1945, in the Gulf of Siam
Lamprey	W. T. Nelson, L. B. McDonald	November 17, 1944	—	—	Decommissioned June 3, 1946
Lapon	O. G. Kirk, L. T. Stone, D. G. Baer	January 23, 1943	11	53,443	Decommissioned July 25, 1946
Lionfish	B. M. Ganyard, E. D. Spruance	November 1, 1944	—	—	Decommissioned January 16, 1946
Lizardfish	O. M. Butler	December 30, 1944	1	100	Decommissioned June 24, 1946
Loggerhead	R. M. Metcalf	February 9, 1945	—	—	Decommissioned September 22, 1945
Macabi	A. H. Dropp	March 29, 1945	—	—	Decommissioned June 16, 1946
Manta	E. P. Madley	December 18, 1944	—	—	Decommissioned June 10, 1946
Mingo	R. C. Lynch Jr., J. J. Staley, J. R. Madison	February 12, 1943	2	11,586	Decommissioned January 27, 1947
Moray	F. L. Barrows	January 26, 1945	—	—	Decommissioned April 12, 1946
Muskallunge	W. A. Saunders, M. P. Rusillo, L. A. LaJaunie Jr., W. H. Lawrence	March 15, 1943	1	7,163	Decommissioned January 29, 1947
Narwhal	C. W. Wilkins, F. D. Latta, J. C. Titus, W. G. Holman	May 15, 1930	7	13,829	Decommissioned April 23, 1945
Nautilus	W. H. Brockman Jr., W. D. Irvin, G. A. Sharp, W. Michael	July 1, 1930	6	21,149	Decommissioned June 30, 1945
Paddle	R. H. Rice, B. H. Nowell, J. P. Fitzpatrick	March 29, 1943	5	18,798	Decommissioned February 1, 1946
Pampanito	P. E. Summers, F. W. Fenno	November 6, 1943	5	27,332	Decommissioned December 15, 1945
Parche	L. P. Ramage, W. W. McCrory	November 20, 1943	8	31,696	Decommissioned December 11, 1945
Pargo	I. C. Eddy, D. B. Bell	April 26, 1943	9	27,983	Decommissioned June 12, 1946
Perch	D. A. Hurt	November 19, 1936	—	—	Scuttled March 3, 1942, after Japanese depth-charging between Java and Borneo
Perch II	B. C. Hills, C. D. McCall	January 1, 1944	—	—	Decommissioned January, 1947
Permit	A. M. Hurst, W. G. Chapple, C. L. Bennet, D. A. Scherer	March 17, 1937	3	5,741	Decommissioned November 15, 1945
Peto	W. T. Nelson, P. Van Leunen, R. H. Caldwell	November 21, 1942	7	29,139	Decommissioned June 25, 1946
Picuda	A. L. Raborn, G. R. Donaho, E. T. Shepard	October 16, 1943	12	49,539	Decommissioned September 25, 1946
Pickerel	B. E. Bacon, A. H. Alston Jr.	January 26, 1937	4	6,472	Sunk April 3, 1943, off Honshu

SUBMARINE	COMMANDERS	DATE OF COMMISSION	VESSELS SUNK	TOTAL TONNAGE	DISPOSITION
Pike	L. D. McGregor Jr., W. A. New, W. A. Parham	December 2, 1935	1	2,022	Decommissioned November 15, 1945
Pilotfish	R. H. Close	December 16, 1943	—	—	Decommissioned August 29, 1946
Pintado	B. A. Clarey	January 1, 1944	8	42,956	Decommissioned March 6, 1946
Pipefish	W. N. Deragon	January 22, 1944	2	1,818	Decommissioned March 19, 1946
Piper	B. F. McMahon	August 23, 1944	—	—	Decommissioned June 16, 1967
Piranha	H. E. Ruble	February 5, 1944	2	12,277	Decommissioned May 31, 1946
Plaice	C. B. Stevens Jr., R. S. Andrews	February 12, 1944	4	2,943	Decommissioned April 30, 1948
Plunger	D. C. White, R. H. Bass, E. J. Fahy	November 19, 1936	12	48,328	Decommissioned November 15, 1945
Pogy	G. H. Wales, R. M. Metcalf, P. E. Molteni Jr., J. M. Bowers	January 10, 1943	16	63,633	Decommissioned July 20, 1946
Pollack	S. P. Moseley, R. E. Palmer, B. E. Lewellen, E. H. Steinmetz	January 15, 1937	11	30,278	Decommissioned September 21, 1945
Pomfret	F. C. Acker, J. B. Hess	February 19, 1944	4	20,936	Decommissioned April 30, 1952
Pompano	L. S. Parks, W. M. Thomas	June 12, 1937	5	21,443	Sunk September, 1943, off Honshu
Pompon	E. C. Hawk, S. H. Gimber, J. A. Bogley	March 17, 1943	3	8,772	Decommissioned May 11, 1946
Porpoise	J. A. Callaghan, J. R. McKnight Jr., C. L. Bennet	August 15, 1935	3	9,741	Decommissioned November 15, 1945
Puffer	M. J. Jensen, F. G. Selby, C. R. Dwyer	April 27, 1943	8	36,392	Decommissioned June 28, 1946
Queenfish	C. E. Loughlin, F. N. Shamer	March 11, 1944	8	40,767	Decommissioned March 1, 1963
Quillback	R. P. Nicholson	December 29, 1944	—	—	Decommissioned May 8, 1952
Rasher	E. S. Hutchinson, W. R. Laughon, H. G. Munson, B. E. Adams Jr., G. D. Nace	June 8, 1943	18	99,901	Decommissioned June 22, 1946
Raton	J. W. Davis, M. W. Shea, G. F. Gugliotta	July 13, 1943	13	44,178	Decommissioned March 11, 1949
Ray	B. J. Harral, W. T. Kinsella	July 27, 1943	12	49,185	Decommissioned February 12, 1947
Razorback	R. S. Benson, C. D. Brown	April 3, 1944	1	820	Decommissioned August, 1952
Redfin	R. D. King, M. H. Austin, C. K. Miller	August 31, 1943	6	23,724	Decommissioned November 1, 1946
Redfish	L. D. McGregor Jr.	April 12, 1944	5	42,615	Decommissioned June 27, 1968
Robalo	S. H. Ambruster, M. M. Kimmel	September 28, 1943	—	—	Sunk July 26, 1944, off Palawan
Rock	J. J. Flachsenhar	October 26, 1943	1	834	Decommissioned May 1, 1946
Ronquil	H. S. Monroe, R. B. Lander	April 22, 1944	2	10,615	Decommissioned May 29, 1952
Runner	F. W. Fenno, J. H. Bourland	July 30, 1942	2	6,274	Sunk June or July 1943, between Midway and Japan
Runner II	R. H. Bass	February 6, 1945	1	630	Decommissioned June 29, 1970
S-18	W. J. Millican, G. H. Browne, J. H. Newsome	April 3, 1924	—	—	Decommissioned October 20, 1945
S-23	J. P. Pierce, H. E. Duryea, H. E. Ruble	October 30, 1923	—	—	Decommissioned November 2, 1945
S-27	H. L. Jukes	January 22, 1924	—	—	Grounded and destroyed June 19, 1942, Amchitka Island
S-28	J. D. Crowley, V. A. Sisler, J. G. Campbell	December 13, 1923	1	1,368	Foundered July 4, 1944, off Pearl Harbor
S-30	F. W. Laing, W. A. Stevenson	October 29, 1920	1	5,228	Decommissioned October 9, 1945
S-31	T. F. Williamson, R. F. Sellars	March 8, 1923	1	2,864	Decommissioned October 19, 1945
S-32	M. G. Schmidt, F. J. Harlfinger	February 21, 1923	—	—	Decommissioned October 19, 1945
S-33	W. P. Schoeni, C. B. Stevens Jr.	December 21, 1922	—	—	Decommissioned October 23, 1945
S-34	T. L. Wogan, R. A. Keating	April 23, 1923	—	—	Decommissioned October 23, 1945
S-35	H. S. Monroe, J. E. Stevens, R. B. Byrnes	May 7, 1923	1	5,430	Decommissioned March 17, 1945
S-36	J. R. McKnight Jr.	April 4, 1923	—	—	Destroyed January 20, 1942, after grounding on reef in Makassar Strait, Indonesia
S-37	J. C. Dempsey, J. R. Reynolds, T. S. Baskett	July 16, 1923	2	4,676	Decommissioned February 6, 1945
S-38	W. G. Chapple, H. G. Munson, C. D. Rhymes Jr.	May 11, 1923	2	11,073	Decommissioned December 14, 1944
S-39	J. W. Coe, F. E. Brown	September 14, 1923	1	6,500	Destroyed August 14, 1942, after grounding off Rossel Island, in the Louisiade Archipelago
S-40	N. Lucker Jr., F. M. Gambacorta	November 20, 1923	—	—	Decommissioned October 27, 1945
S-41	I. S. Hartman, G. M. Holley	January 15, 1924	1	1,036	Decommissioned February 13, 1945
S-42	O. G. Kirk, P. E. Glenn, H. K. Nauman	November 20, 1924	1	4,400	Decommissioned October 25, 1945
S-43	F. E. Brown, E. R. Hannan	December 31, 1924	—	—	Decommissioned October 10, 1945
S-44	J. R. Moore, R. T. Whitaker, F. E. Brown	February 16, 1925	3	17,070	Sunk October 7, 1943, off the Kuriles
S-45	I. C. Eddy, R. H. Caldwell Jr.	March 31, 1925	—	—	Decommissioned October 30, 1945
S-46	R. C. Lynch Jr., G. Campbell, E. R. Crawford	June 5, 1925	—	—	Decommissioned November 2, 1945
S-47	J. W. Davis, F. E. Hayler, L. V. Young	September 16, 1925	—	—	Decommissioned October 25, 1945
Sailfish	M. C. Mumma Jr., R. G. Voge, J. R. Moore, R. E. M. Ward	May 15, 1940	7	45,029	Decommissioned October 27, 1945
Salmon	E. B. McKinney, N. J. Nicholas, H. K. Nauman	March 15, 1938	4	24,107	Decommissioned September 24, 1945
Sandlance	M. E. Garrison, J. G. Glaes	October 9, 1943	10	37,368	Decommissioned February 14, 1946
Sargo	R. V. Gregory, E. S. Carmick, T. D. Jacobs, P. W. Garnett	February 7, 1939	7	32,777	Decommissioned June 22, 1946
Saury	J. L. Burnside Jr., L. S. Mewhinney, A. H. Dropp, R. A. Waugh	April 3, 1939	5	28,542	Decommissioned June 22, 1946
Sawfish	E. T. Sands, A. B. Banister, D. H. Pugh	August 26, 1942	6	22,504	Decommissioned June 20, 1946
Scabbardfish	F. A. Gunn	April 29, 1944	2	2,345	Decommissioned January 5, 1948
Scamp	W. G. Ebert, J. C. Hollingsworth	September 18, 1942	5	34,108	Sunk November 16, 1944, east of Tokyo Bay
Scorpion	W. N. Wylie, M. G. Schmidt	October 1, 1942	4	18,316	Sunk January 5, 1944, in the Yellow Sea
Sculpin	L. H. Chappell, F. Connaway	January 16, 1939	3	9,835	Sunk November 19, 1943, off Truk
Sea Cat	R. R. McGregor, R. H. Bowers	May 16, 1944	—	—	Decommissioned December 2, 1968
Sea Devil	R. H. Styles, C. F. McGivern	May 24, 1944	7	29,519	Decommissioned September 9, 1948
Sea Dog	V. L. Lowrance, E. T. Hydeman	June 3, 1944	9	21,469	Decommissioned June 27, 1956
Sea Fox	R. C. Klinker	June 13, 1944	—	—	Decommissioned October 15, 1952
Sea Owl	C. L. Bennet, W. C. Hall Jr.	July 17, 1944	2	1,689	Decommissioned November 15, 1969
Sea Poacher	F. H. Gambacorta, C. F. Leigh	July 31, 1944	—	—	Decommissioned November 15, 1969
Sea Robin	P. C. Stimson	August 7, 1944	6	13,472	Decommissioned October 1, 1970
Seadragon	W. E. Ferrall, J. H. Ashley Jr., R. L. Rutter	October 23, 1939	10	43,450	Decommissioned November 15, 1945
Seahorse	D. McGregor, S. D. Cutter, C. W. Wilkins, H. H. Greer Jr.	March 31, 1943	20	72,529	Decommissioned March 2, 1946
Seal	K. C. Hurd, H. B. Dodge, J. H. Turner	April 30, 1938	7	27,765	Decommissioned November 15, 1945
Sealion I	R. G. Voge	November 27, 1939	—	—	Scuttled December 25, 1941, at Cavite, the Philippines, after being damaged by Japanese aircraft
Sealion II	E. T. Reich, C. F. Putnam	March 8, 1944	11	68,297	Decommissioned February 16, 1946
Searaven	T. C. Aylward, H. Cassedy, M. H. Dry, R. Berthrong	October 2, 1939	3	20,492	Decommissioned December 11, 1946

SUBMARINE	COMMANDERS	DATE OF COMMISSION	VESSELS SUNK	TOTAL TONNAGE	DISPOSITION
Seawolf	F. B. Warder, R. L. Gross, A. M. Bontier, R. B. Lynch	December 1, 1939	18	71,609	Sunk October 30, 1944, in error by the U.S.S. *Rowell*, off Morotai Island, Indonesia
Segundo	J. D. Fulp Jr., S. L. Johnson	May 9, 1944	2	4,665	Decommissioned August 1, 1970
Sennet	G. E. Porter, C. R. Clark	August 22, 1944	7	17,726	Decommissioned December 2, 1968
Shad	E. J. MacGregor, L. V. Julihn, R. F. Pryce, D. L. Mehlhop	June 12, 1942	3	6,209	Decommissioned 1947
Shark I	C. J. Cater, L. Shane Jr.	January 25, 1936	—	—	Sunk February 11, 1942, off Celebes
Shark II	E. N. Blakely	February 14, 1944	4	21,672	Sunk October 24, 1944, off Formosa
Silversides	C. R. Burlingame, J. S. Coye Jr., J. C. Nichols	December 15, 1941	23	90,080	Decommissioned April 17, 1946
Skate	E. B. McKinney, W. P. Gruner Jr., R. B. Lynch	April 15, 1943	10	27,924	Decommissioned December 11, 1946
Skipjack	C. L. Freeman, J. W. Coe, G. G. Molumphy, H. F. Stoner, R. S. Andrews	June 30, 1938	6	27,876	Decommissioned August 28, 1946
Snapper	H. L. Stone, H. E. Baker, A. R. St. Angelo, M. K. Clementson, W. W. Walker	December 15, 1937	4	8,145	Decommissioned November 15, 1945
Snook	C. O. Triebel, G. H. Browne, J. F. Walling	October 24, 1942	17	75,473	Sunk April 8, 1945, off Sakishima-gunto, east of Formosa
Spadefish	G. W. Underwood, W. J. Germershausen	March 9, 1944	21	88,091	Decommissioned May 3, 1946
Spearfish	C. C. Cole, R. F. Pryce, G. A. Sharp, J. C. Dempsey, J. W. Williams	July 19, 1939	4	17,065	Decommissioned June 22, 1946
Spikefish	R. R. Managhan, N. J. Nicholas	June 30, 1944	1	1,660	Decommissioned April 2, 1963
Spot	W. S. Post Jr., J. M. Seymour	August 3, 1944	1	3,005	Decommissioned June 19, 1946
Springer	R. E. Kefauver, J. F. Bauer	October 18, 1944	4	3,940	Decommissioned April 25, 1946
Steelhead	D. L. Whelchel, R. B. Byrnes	December 7, 1942	3	22,159	Decommissioned June 29, 1946
Sterlet	O. S. Robbins, H. H. Lewis	March 4, 1944	4	15,803	Decommissioned September 18, 1948
Stickleback	H. K. Nauman	March 29, 1945	—	—	Decommissioned June 26, 1946
Stingray	R. S. Lamb, R. J. Moore, O. J. Earle, S. C. Loomis Jr., H. F. Stoner	March 15, 1938	4	18,558	Decommissioned October 17, 1945
Sturgeon	W. L. Wright, H. A. Pieczentkowski, C. L. Murphy Jr.	June 25, 1938	9	41,350	Decommissioned November 15, 1945
Sunfish	R. W. Peterson, E. E. Shelby, J. W. Reed	July 15, 1942	16	59,815	Decommissioned December 26, 1945
Swordfish	C. C. Smith, A. C. Burrows, J. H. Lewis, F. M. Parker, K. G. Hensel, F. L. Barrows, K. E. Montross	July 22, 1939	12	47,928	Sunk January 12, 1945, off Okinawa
Tambor	S. H. Ambruster, R. E. Kefauver, W. J. Germershausen, J. W. Murphy Jr.	June 3, 1940	11	33,479	Decommissioned December 10, 1945
Tang	R. H. O'Kane	October 15, 1943	24	93,824	Sunk October 24, 1944, by own torpedo off Formosa
Tarpon	L. C. Wallace, T. L. Wogan, T. B. Oakley Jr., S. Filippone	March 12, 1936	2	27,910	Decommissioned November 15, 1945
Tautog	J. H. Willingham Jr., W. B. Sieglaff, T. S. Baskett	July 3, 1940	26	72,606	Decommissioned December 8, 1945
Tench	W. B. Sieglaff, T. S. Baskett	October 6, 1944	4	5,069	Decommissioned June 15, 1946
Thornback	E. B. Abrahamson	October 13, 1944	—	—	Decommissioned April 6, 1946
Threadfin	J. J. Foote	August 30, 1944	3	3,394	Decommissioned December 10, 1952
Thresher	W. L. Anderson, W. J. Millican, H. Hull, D. C. MacMillan, J. R. Middleton	August 27, 1940	17	66,172	Decommissioned December 13, 1945
Tigrone	H. Cassedy, V. E. Schumaker	October 25, 1944	—	—	Decommissioned March 30, 1946
Tilefish	R. M. Keithley, W. F. Schlech	December 15, 1943	2	1,019	Decommissioned October 12, 1959
Tinosa	L. R. Daspit, D. F. Weiss, R. C. Latham	January 15, 1943	16	64,655	Decommissioned June 23, 1949
Tirante	G. L. Street III	November 6, 1944	8	15,886	Decommissioned July 20, 1946
Toro	J. D. Grant	December 8, 1944	—	—	Decommissioned February 2, 1946
Torsk	B. E. Lewellen	December 16, 1944	3	2,473	Decommissioned March 4, 1968
Trepang	R. M. Davenport, A. R. Faust	May 22, 1944	11	23,850	Decommissioned June 27, 1946
Trigger	J. H. Lewis, R. S. Benson, R. E. Dornin, F. Harlfinger, D. R. Connole	January 31, 1942	18	86,552	Sunk March 28, 1945, in East China Sea
Triton	W. A. Lent, C. C. Kirkpatrick, G. K. MacKensie	August 15, 1940	11	31,788	Sunk March 15, 1943, north of the Admiralty Islands, in the Bismarck Archipelago
Trout	F. W. Fenno, L. P. Ramage, A. H. Clark	November 15, 1940	12	37,144	Sunk February 29, 1944, northwest of the Philippines
Trutta	A. C. Smith, F. P. Hoskins	November 16, 1944	—	—	Decommissioned 1947
Tullibee	C. F. Brindupke	February 15, 1943	3	10,579	Sunk March 26, 1944, by own torpedo off the Palau Islands
Tuna	J. L. Detar, A. H. Holtz, J. T. Hardin, E. F. Steffanides	January 2, 1941	4	14,986	Decommissioned December 11, 1946
Tunny	J. A. Scott, G. E. Pierce	September 1, 1942	6	26,837	Decommissioned February 12, 1946
Wahoo	M. G. Kennedy, D. W. Morton	May 15, 1942	20	60,038	Sunk October 11, 1943, in La Pérouse Strait, Japan
Whale	J. B. Azer, A. C. Burrows, J. B. Grady, F. H. Carde Jr.	June 1, 1942	9	57,716	Decommissioned June 1, 1946

INDEX

Numerals in italics indicate an illustration of the subject mentioned.